THE TRUTH ABOUT
RUDOLF HESS

JAMES DOUGLAS-HAMILTON

Foreword by Lord Bullock

MAINSTREAM
PUBLISHING
EDINBURGH AND LONDON

To
Squadron Leader Lord David Douglas-Hamilton
Killed on operations 2 August 1944

'A lie can be halfway around the world before truth has got his boots on'
Prime Minister Jim Callaghan, 11 November 1976

Copyright © Lord James Douglas-Hamilton, 1993

First published as *Motive for a Mission* by Macmillan in 1971
Second edition published under the same title by Mainstream in 1979
and by Corgi in 1981
This edition published in Great Britain in 1993 by
MAINSTREAM PUBLISHING COMPANY (EDINBURGH) LTD
7 Albany Street
Edinburgh EH1 3UG

This Edition, 2002

ISBN 1 84018 699 2

A catalogue record for this book is available from the British Library

Typeset in 10/11 Ehrhardt by Keyboard Services, Luton

The Random House Group Limited supports The Forest Stewardship
Council (FSC®), the leading international forest certification organisation.
Our books carrying the FSC label are printed on FSC® certified paper.
FSC is the only forest certification scheme endorsed by the leading
environmental organisations, including Greenpeace. Our
paper procurement policy can be found at
www.randomhouse.co.uk/environment

Printed and bound in Great Britain by Clays Ltd, St Ives PLC

THE TRUTH ABOUT RUDOLF HESS

Contents

Acknowledgments

The author and publishers wish to thank the following who have kindly given permission for the use of copyright material: George Allen and Unwin Limited and Houghton Mifflin Company, Boston, for extract from *The Memoirs of Dr Eduard Beneš* (1954) by Eduard Beneš; the Revd. Dr Eberhard Bethge for permission to quote from a personal letter and from *Dietrich Bonhoeffer, A Biography* (Collins 1970); the British Broadcasting Corporation and Mrs Temple for extract from *The Broadcast by the Revd. Dr William Temple, Archbishop of York, 2nd October 1939*; Cassell and Company Limited and McClelland and Stewart Limited, Canada for extract from *The War Speeches* Vol II of Sir Winston S. Churchill; Cassell and Company Limited and Houghton Mifflin, Boston for extracts from *The Reckoning: The Eden Memoirs* by the Earl of Avon, and extracts from *Their Finest Hour* and *The Gathering Storm* from the Second World War Vols II and III by Sir Winston S. Churchill; *Chicago Daily News* for extracts from *The Ciano Diaries* (1947); Collins Publishers and Curtis Brown Limited for extract from *Ambassador on a Special Mission* by Viscount Templewood; Sefton Delmer for extracts from *Black Boomerang*; Doubleday and Co. Inc., for extracts from *Total Power* by Edmund Walsh; Hamish Hamilton for extracts from *Black Record – Germans Past and Present* by Sir Robert Vansittart; Dr Karl-Heinz Harbeck for permission to quote from his unpublished thesis: *Die Zeitschrift für Geopolitik* (Kiel 1963); Professor Dr Heinz Haushofer for permission to quote from *The Hartschimmelhof Papers*, and to reproduce *Albrecht Haushofer's Peace Plan* (1941) and *The Sonnets of Moabit*; Sir Alan Herbert C.H. for poem 'Hess' from *Let Us Be Glum* by A. P. Herbert (Methuen 1941); Dr Rainer Hildebrandt for extracts from *Wir Sind Die Letzten* (1950); H.M.S.O. for extracts from *Hansard, Documents on German Foreign Policy 1918-45* Series D. Vols XI and XII, and also from *Trials of German Major War Criminals at Nuremberg*; Professor Rolf Italiaander for extracts from *Besiegeltes Leben* (1949), and from *Akzente eines Lebens* (Carl Schunemann Buchverlag Bremen); Dr Ursula Laack (neé Michel) for permission to quote from her unpublished theses: *Albrecht Haushofer und Nationalsozialismus* (Kiel 1964); E. P. S. Lewin for extracts from *Hitler – The Missing Years* (1957) by Ernst Hanfstaengl; Paul List Verlag, Munich for extracts from *Das Spiel Um Deutschland* (1953) by Fritz Hesse; The National Archives of U.S.A., Washington for extracts from *Speeches and Discussions in 1941*; Gerald Reitlinger and The Viking Press, Inc., for extracts from *The S.S. Alibi of a Nation* by Gerald Reitlinger; The Royal Institute of International Affairs, Chatham House for permission to quote from *Albrecht Haushofer's Lecture 29th April 1937*, which was given to a private off-the-record meeting; Martin Secker and Warburg Limited and Simon Schuster for extracts from *The Rise and Fall of the Third Reich* (1960) by William Shirer; David Higham Associates and

Butterworth for, *The Case of Rudolph Hess* by J. R. Rees; Deutsche Verlags Anstalt, Stuttgart, for, *'In Memoriam – Albrecht Haushofer'* by Walter Stubbe, in an article from *The Quarterly Bulletin for Contemporary History*, (Munich, July 1960); Atlantis Verlag for *'Memoirs'* by Ulrich Von Hassell (1948); Professor von Weizsaecker for *In Memoriam Albrecht Haushofer* by Carl F. von Weizsaecker; Weidenfeld and Nicolson for *Inside the Third Reich: Memoirs* by Albert Speer. The publishers have been unable to trace the copyright holders of some extracts but will be pleased to make the necessary arrangement at the first opportunity.

I also wish to thank Peter Janson-Smith, Harold Lind, Bill Campbell, Patrick Janson-Smith, Dr Ursula Laack, Peter Padfield, the late Mrs Johnson, Mrs Christa Wichmann, Ben Barkow and their colleagues at the Wiener Library, Mr Mellor and Wing Commander Lambert of the Public Record Office at Kew, John Campsie, the House of Commons Library and everyone who has given assistance.

In particular, I wish to record my gratitude to my uncle, the Earl of Selkirk, for his comments, and to my father, who, whilst he was alive, provided me with the information which gave him the key to the rest of the story; and to Mr Theodore Kay for his kind and invaluable help in translating and checking the authenticity of the original German documents including the Sonnets of Moabit.

I wish also to thank Dr Eugene Pugatch and Mr Daniel Knutson for their translations into verse of the Sonnets of Moabit, to Roy Nesbit for all his assistance with research into the technical details of Hess's flight, to Dudley Cowderoy, and to Sebastian Cox of the Ministry of Defence Air Historical Branch. I am also grateful to Dr Martin Haushofer, member of the Bavarian Landtag, for access to the Hartschimmelhof Papers, General Professor Karl Haushofer being his grandfather, Albrecht his uncle and Field Marshal Hindenburg his great-uncle by marriage to his wife, Renata.

Finally I would thank my Oxford tutor, Martin Gilbert, who wrote Sir Winston Churchill's official biography, for rousing in me a great interest in modern history, and in particular Lord Bullock who, with infinite patience, gave invaluable guidance at every stage of the researches of this book.

Foreword

by
Lord Bullock

When I wrote a foreword to the first edition of James Douglas-Hamilton's book in 1971, I described the flight by Rudolf Hess to Britain in May 1941 as one of the most bizarre episodes in the history of the two Great Wars and listed a few of the questions still unanswered. Since then, the Soviet refusal to release Hess from Spandau prison, where he remained the sole prisoner under a guard provided by the four occupying powers, and his suicide at the age of ninety-three, have added to this bizarre character. At the same time, controversy has been revived by two alternative conspiracy theories; the first that it was not Hess but an imposter who flew to Scotland and ended his life in Spandau, the second that Hess was able to make his flight successfully because he was expected and arrangements had been made for him to fly through the British defence, a theory first propounded by the Soviet K.G.B.

The quiet but effective way in which the author, with the help of Roy Nesbit, has shown that neither claim stands up to examination provides a satisfying and convincing example of historical detection work. In addition, James Douglas-Hamilton's persistence in following up new leads in a story which first aroused his interest as a boy, has again borne fruit, this time in further material from his father's (the Duke of Hamilton's) papers, in the final release of material dealing with the Hess episode in the Public Records Office, and in a surprising number of unpublished photographs. The result is finally to dispose of any suggestion that the Duke of Hamilton was in any way privy to or involved in Hess's project.

Unless some unsuspected new source comes to light – improbable, but never impossible – James Douglas-Hamilton has produced as near an authoritative account of the Hess episode as we are ever likely to have. Once the suspicions and myths that grew up around it have been removed, Hess's peace initiative proves to have been a non-event. What gives the account that follows, however, a lasting human interest is the contrast between Hess and the anti-hero of the story, Albrecht Haushofer, whose fate was closely involved with that of Hess, and is graphically described in the pages that follow.

While Hess never succeeded in freeing himself from the illusions which had carried him into the Nazi movement in the first place, Haushofer never had any about the character of the Nazi regime and its leaders. What proved fatal to him was the temptation to believe that he could do more good by remaining in office and working against it from within than by going into exile.

Both men, caught up in events that proved too big for them, sought unsuccessfully for a way out. In Hess's case this led to imprisonment for life in Spandau, in Haushofer's to summary execution by an S.S. firing squad in the very last days of the war.

Unlike Hess, however, Albrecht Haushofer left behind, in his letters to his mother and later in the poems he wrote in prison (the Sonnets of Moabit), a record of his thoughts without illusion or self-deception. James Douglas-Hamilton has now added to the passages he included in earlier editions new translations for some of the poems by Dr Eugene Pugatch with the help of Daniel Knutson. Haushofer's *Nachlass* remains one of the most illuminating human documents to survive from a period of history which in its conflict of loyalties searched men to their roots, and gives an enduring value to James Douglas-Hamilton's book.

St Catherine's College
Oxford

Introduction

by
Roy Conyers Nesbit

Rudolf Hess took off from the Messerschmitt Works at Augsburg at 17.45 hours British Double Summer Time on Saturday 10 May 1941[1] in a Messerschmitt Bf110, radio code VJ+0Q, works number 3869. His own description of the flight was contained in a long letter which he wrote to his young son 'Buz' (Wolf Rüdiger) between 10 and 15 June 1941.[2] He flew over Germany via Bonn and then to the Dutch coast near Harlingen, from where he turned north-east along the Dutch Frisian Islands and then north-west over the North Sea. Eventually he turned west towards England and his intended destination of Dungavel House, the home of the Duke of Hamilton, south of Glasgow. When approaching the English coast he could see that there was no cloud cover, contrary to his expectations, and he turned back east and flew to and fro in order to lose time until the sky darkened. Turning west once more, he arrived south of Holy Island on the coast of Northumberland soon after sunset.

His approaching track was picked up by British radar stations at about 15,000 feet and confirmed at 22.08 hours, being designated as a single aircraft 'Raid 42'. Hunted by two Spitfires already on patrol, Hess dived and crossed the coast at high speed, pursued by another Spitfire which took off to intercept the intruder but also failed to catch him. He continued at very low level and at over 300 m.p.h. above English fields, monitored at intervals by volunteers manning the posts of the Royal Observer Corps. Soon after he crossed the Scottish border, he was reported by one of these posts as having climbed to 5,000 feet. He flew very close to Dungavel House but failed to spot it and reached the west coast of Scotland at 22.54 hours, hunted by a Defiant nightfighter which had also taken off to intercept him. He turned back to the east, climbed to 6,000 feet and zigzagged, in a last attempt to find his destination in the blacked-out countryside. By this time he was running short of fuel and, unknown to him, the nightfighter was closing up. He baled out over Bonnyton Moor, about ten miles south of the centre of Glasgow. His machine, which carried machine-guns but no ammunition or air gunner, struck the ground and exploded at 23.09 hours. The parts of this Messerschmitt were gathered up by the R.A.F.'s No. 69 Maintenance Unit and taken to the dump at Carluke, near Glasgow, but some important remnants were rescued and are still available for public inspection at the Imperial War Museum in London.

This flight, which must be classed as one of the most extraordinary episodes of the Second World War, has given rise to several books. One which is considered the most authoritative is entitled *Motive for a Mission*, written by James Douglas-Hamilton and published in 1971. The facts in this book were not seriously challenged at first, either in Britain or abroad. It was several years before books containing conspiracy theories were put forward. These appeared after the second edition of *Motive for a Mission*, which drew on records of the Prime Minister and War Cabinet released under the Thirty Year Rule, was published in 1979.

One of these conspiracy theories was formed by a former officer in the R.A.M.C., Dr Hugh Thomas, and published in 1984 under the title *The Murder of Rudolf Hess*[3]. In this, Hugh Thomas asserted that the pilot of the German aircraft was not Rudolf Hess but an imposter with a very similar physical appearance. He based this theory on medical evidence, for he attended the prisoner at Spandau Prison during September 1973, when he served in the R.A.M.C. as a consultant in general surgery in Berlin. Hess's medical records showed that he had been shot in the left lung when serving in Romania in 1917, but Hugh Thomas could not find any scars on the prisoner's bare chest during a medical examination, and X-rays did not show up any trace of a bullet's passage.

Following these discoveries, Hugh Thomas carried out a detailed investigation into the circumstances of Hess's flight on 10 May 1941. He concluded that the Deputy Fuehrer took off from Augsburg in a Bf110, code NJ+C11, with the intention of flying to Stockholm in order to discuss peace terms with the British, but was shot down by a German fighter on the orders of Hermann Goering. At the same time, the imposter took off from Denmark in another Bf110D, with the code NJ+0Q, and was the person who parachuted over Scotland; the reasons for this flight are not made clear in the book, which was also serialised in the *Sunday Telegraph* and attracted much publicity.

I have to say that I do not believe this theory holds water, when examined in the light of official and other evidence. As the second edition of *Motive for a Mission* made clear when it was published in 1979, Hess was positively identified after his arrival in Britain by the Foreign Office expert on Germany, Ivone Kirkpatrick, who had no reservations about his findings. Since that time the Governments of Britain, France, Russia, the U.S.A. and Germany have never questioned that identification. Nor has Hess's family expressed any doubts.

As regards medical matters, I am a layman and can only quote the opinions of others who are far more qualified than myself. In the first place Professor Bernard Knight, the eminent Professor of Forensic Pathology at the University of Wales College of Medicine, sent me a letter which included the following comment: 'In forensic pathology there is a wise adage, "Never say never, never say always", and therefore I would hesitate to say that a bullet scar must always be visible or palpable, though I would say that it must always be detectable on a microscopic scale, assuming one knew where to look.' Secondly, the German historian Dr Ulrich Lappenküper examined Hess's medical record on behalf of B.B.C.2 *Timewatch* and read from it during the TV programme[4] that the exit wound from the bullet was merely 'the size of a cherry stone'; the entry wound could have been no larger than this. Thirdly, in a letter to the *Sunday Telegraph* sent soon after the serialisation of Hugh Thomas's book, the surgeon Mr S. Subsachs pointed out that the scars of bullet wounds in elderly patients were sometimes difficult to detect. Fourthly, according to the Protestant pastor who attended Hess in Spandau, Charles A. Gabel, the prisoner was examined by two doctors after publication of Hugh Thomas's book and the scars of the bullet wound were found.[5] Lastly, the German magazine *Der Spiegel* reported a remark which Hess made to his wife Ilse when she queried the presence of the bullet scars. He said, 'You see, the scar is still there, don't worry. It has grown smaller, but it is still there.'[6]

Whatever the medical facts, it can be clearly demonstrated that the Messerschmitt which took off from Augsburg is the same machine which crashed at Bonnyton Moor; thus it was Rudolf Hess who parachuted out over Scotland. With regard to the details of the flight, some of Hugh Thomas's statements are not borne out by other evidence. He begins by asserting that the machine took off from Augsburg without drop-tanks and could not have reached Scotland, since its maximum range with internal tanks was about 850 miles, whereas the distance it actually travelled was about 1,260 miles. He then goes on to say that, even if the Messerschmitt had carried two drop-tanks containing 396 extra gallons, the range would have increased to only 1,200 miles. This cannot be true. The internal tanks contained 294 gallons. The Messerschmitt did not consume a part of its fuel at 850 miles ÷ 294 = 2.89 miles per gallon, and another part at 350 miles ÷ 396 = 0.88 miles per gallon.

The true facts of the fuel carried by Hess's Messerschmitt were sent to me a few years ago by the person responsible for fitting up the machine at Augsburg and air testing it. This was *Flugkapitän a.D.* Helmut Kaden, who in 1941 was a test pilot at the Messerschmitt Works and also the assistant airfield manager; later in 1941 he became the chief test pilot for the Messerschmitt Works. Helmut Kaden, who has since died, verified that the machine *did* carry two drop-tanks containing a total of 396 gallons of fuel, and indeed he sent me a photograph of the machine itself with these tanks clearly visible.[7]

The accurate details of fuel consumption of the Messerschmitt Bf110 are those issued to the German crews by the Luftwaffe Headquarters in Rechlin, near Berlin. Copies were sent to me by a former navigator in these machines, Hanfried Schliephake.[8] These tables show that, when carrying drop-tanks containing 396 gallons and a normal war load, and flying at about 15,000 feet at a speed of 236 m.p.h. in 'still air' conditions, the aircraft could travel for a distance of 1,867 miles over the ground. Without the war load, the machine would have been able to achieve an even greater distance. Of course, this fuel consumption varied considerably at different altitudes and speeds. For instance, Hess must have burnt up fuel at a much higher rate when flying at maximum speed and at low level over the British countryside. But he carried ample fuel to reach Scotland from Augsburg.

Then there is the question of the aircraft letters. These were painted on the sides of the fuselage and underneath the wings of German military machines, and used as radio codes. According to Hugh Thomas, Hess took off in NJ+C11. But Helmut Kaden stated emphatically that the machine was VJ+0Q, and his pilot's log book clearly shows these letters, with Hess's name against them. Helmut Kaden flew the machine with Hess on five occasions, the last on 6 May, four days before Hess flew to Scotland. During three of those days, according to Professor Willi Messerschmitt, Hess received instruction in the use of the machine.[9] Helmut Kaden stated that his instructor was *Flugkapitän* Willi Stoer, who at the time was the chief test pilot at the Messerschmitt Works.

Hugh Thomas asserts that the fuselage of the machine, which is now on public display at the Imperial War Museum at Lambeth in London, bears the letters NJ+0Q. Anyone who believes this should examine the fuselage himself or herself. Nobody that I know could mistake the 'V' for an 'N'. The letters on the fuselage are VJ+0Q. They are the same as those which appear in Helmut Kaden's log book, and the fuselage is thus part of the machine which Hess flew from Augsburg to Scotland.

Finally, there is the matter of handwriting. When Hess was a prisoner in Britain, he sent many letters to his family and friends in Germany via the Red Cross. The originals of some of these letters are now available for scrutiny at the Public Record Office. His handwriting and his signature are identical with those of letters he sent before his flight, as can be seen in the example reproduced here.

Other conspiracy theories emerged during the late 1980s after the Russian Secret Service decided to publish most of its papers relating to Hess. Most of these papers were

The beginning of the letter written by Rudolf Hess on 10 to 15 May 1941 to his son 'Buz' (Wolf Rüdiger) describing his flight to Scotland, while in British hands (Public Record Office)

A note sent by Rudolf Hess on 5 August 1940 to Frau Gerda Bormann, congratulating her on the birth of her fourth child (Peter Padfield)

drafted a considerable time after Hess's flight to Britain. They alleged, firstly, that the Duke of Hamilton had met Hess at the Olympic Games in 1936; secondly, that the British Secret Service had invited Hess to Britain during the Second World War as part of a peace plot, in the name of the Duke of Hamilton but without his knowledge; and thirdly that the R.A.F. had been given orders to allow Hess's aircraft to pass unmolested through their defences.

The first and second parts of these allegations are answered fully by James Douglas-Hamilton in this book, partly drawing on the mass of British documents from the Hess files released for public scrutiny in May and July of 1992. These documents give no support whatsoever to the Russian suspicions, and indeed provide evidence which contradicts them. However, the true facts relating to the third allegation have been available at the Public Record Office for the past twenty years. An incorrect interpretation of these records was presented in *Ten Days that Saved the West* by John Costello.[10] In this book, the author implies that the Duke of Hamilton was aware of Hess's flight and made clandestine arrangements for the aircraft to pass safely through the British defences. However, an examination of the statements in this book reveals significant errors, apparently resulting from a failure to understand the R.A.F. command structure coupled with misinterpretations of R.A.F. and other records.

In the early part of his description of Hess's flight, John Costello states that a *Knickebein* transmitter from Stollberg 'in the heart of Germany' directed its beam to cross the Scottish border to pass directly over Dungavel, presumably with the connivance of the Luftwaffe. As the authority for this statement he quotes Volume 1 of Professor Hinsley's

14

British Intelligence in the Second World War. But in this official history there is no mention of the transmitter at Stollberg being used in this way, although the *Knickebein* system of navigation is accurately described; it was a system of transmitted dots and dashes on either side of a centre line, which merged into a continuous signal when the aircraft flew directly along the middle of the beam. In fact, the Stollberg transmitter was very close to the border with Denmark, near the island of Sylt.[11] Dungavel was over 500 miles from this transmitter, well outside its range. The effective range of *Knickebein* was about 250 miles when the aircraft was at 15,000 feet, and only 60 miles when the aircraft flew at 300 feet.[12] Hess flew at low level over Northumberland. Moreover, these beams were being jammed by the British in 1941.

The system of navigation used by Hess was described to me by Helmut Kaden, who fitted up the Messerschmitt at Augsburg. Hess took with him the frequency of a radio beacon at Kalundborg in Denmark, which is on almost the same latitude as Dungavel House. Flying up the middle of the North Sea, he was able to turn west to the English coast when Kalundborg bore due east on a radio-compass which had been installed in his aircraft. Thereafter, according to Hess, he flew solely by visual pilot-navigation, for he had spent many hours studying maps in advance.

However, the method of navigation is perhaps of little importance to John Costello's main argument, for he describes Turnhouse, the R.A.F. station west of Edinburgh where the Duke of Hamilton was the station commander, as the 'nerve-centre of 13 Group'. He then states that the Duke of Hamilton was the man on the spot responsible for responding to Raid 42, as Hess's approaching aircraft was designated by Fighter Command. This is not true. The command centre of 13 Group was at R.A.F. Ouston, near Newcastle-upon-Tyne.[13] In turn, 13 Group took its orders for intercepting enemy aircraft from the headquarters of Fighter Command at Bentley Priory in Middlesex. The outcomes then appeared on command, group and sector operations tables. The fighter sector at Turnhouse was solely responsible for giving orders to a Spitfire squadron based there and a Hurricane squadron at nearby R.A.F. Drem.[14] The Duke of Hamilton took no part whatsoever in the attempts to intercept Raid 42, for Turnhouse and Drem were too far from the scene of the action. However, he was able to watch the progress of the raid on his operations table at Turnhouse, when his W.A.A.F. plotters put down their counters.

John Costello refers to Corporal Felicity Ashbee of the W.A.A.F., who was on duty as a 'teller' in the filter room of HQ Fighter Command on 10 May. Her function was to watch the large gridded map of the eastern and southern coasts of Britain on which 'plotters' linked to the C.H. (Chain Home) radar stations put down coloured counters to indicate the positions of incoming aircraft. When a 'filter officer' decided on the true track from a trail of these counters, sometimes emanating from several radar stations, and put a small plastic arrow on it, the teller passed the information through the mouthpiece of her headphone to the operations room next door. The filter room was responsible for aircraft up to the points where they crossed the coastline, when they were taken over by the Royal Observer Corps. Orders to intercept were given by the operations room to the fighter groups of the R.A.F. *This* was the true nerve-centre of the air defences of Great Britain.

Felicity Ashbee (who ended the war as a Flight Officer) had been allotted the area which Hess was approaching, and 'told' the approaching aircraft to the shores of Northumberland. On several occasions in the past few years, she has discussed her recollections of that day with myself. The track was first picked up by the radar station at Ottercops Moss and then by other radar stations. It was unusual in that it appeared to be a single aircraft travelling fast and not part of a bomber stream, at a time of mass raids. But she confirms that there was nothing unusual about the procedure in the filter room, except that Ottercops Moss had a reputation for getting aircraft mixed up with thunderstorms and that at first the report was not taken seriously. However, other radar stations picked up the approaching aircraft, and Felicity Ashbee watched the track until it reached the coast, where it was taken over by the Royal Observer Corps.[15]

John Costello describes the area over which Hess flew as 'heavily defended'. The facts can be seen to be quite different, if one examines the locations of fighter squadrons. In contrast to the three fighter groups to the south, which controlled fifty-four squadrons altogether, 13 Group could muster only eight squadrons, spread over a very large area. Of these, four squadrons were in southern Scotland, one in Yorkshire and one in Northern Ireland. Those at Turnhouse and Drem did not fly operationally on that night.[16]

Only two squadrons of 13 Group were in a position to intercept Hess's aircraft when it approached the coast of Northumberland. These were 317 (Polish) Squadron, equipped with Hurricanes and based at Ouston, and 72 Squadron, equipped with Spitfires and based at Acklington in Northumberland. But the Polish squadron was not fully operational, for it had been formed only a few weeks before. The pilots were not sufficiently familiar with English radio-telegraphy procedure nor were they proficient at flying Hurricanes at night. John Costello points out that the Duke of Hamilton was in error when he reported on 11 May that a section of Hurricanes had been directed to intercept Raid 42, for he could find no trace of these aircraft in his researches, even though he had examined all the records of the fighter squadrons in 13 Group. Yet the references are there, in the Operations Record Book for 317 Squadron. Three Hurricane Is were in the air, having taken off at 21.50 hours for training at dusk.[17] The Duke of Hamilton must have seen the counters of these Hurricanes on his operations table and assumed that 13 Group would order them to intercept. They were not instructed to do so, for they were not considered capable of operating at night and were not in a good position to make an interception.

The Spitfires of 72 Squadron at Acklington were in the best geographical position to intercept Hess's Messerschmitt as it approached Northumberland. According to John Costello, there was an unusual delay between the confirmation of the raid, which the records show as 22.08 hours, and the time the first aircraft took off to tackle it, at 22.23 hours. This is not correct. Firstly, the aircraft to which John Costello refers is recorded as taking off at 22.20 hours, not 22.23 hours. Secondly, this was *not* the first aircraft to be ordered to intercept Raid 42. It is curious to read that some of the evidence of the earlier attempt is set out in the document which John Costello consulted and indeed quotes in his own annotated notes, the operations record book of R.A.F. Ouston: 'At 22.08 raid 42, one plus aircraft at below 9,000 feet approached from south-east. R.D.F. plotted raid as travelling towards Holy Island and turning east, fading. This may have arisen from plots 72 White who *were detailed to raid* (my italics) and were searching off Farne and Holy Island.'

Thus the correct facts are that two Spitfires of 72 Squadron were already in the air and were soon vectored on to the approaching 'bandit'. But then the radar plots of these two Spitfires were misinterpreted as those of the approaching raid, so that the pilots were being vectored by ground control on to themselves. Similar information is also contained in a report dated 18 May 1941 by Fighter Command's 'Operational Research Section', which stated 'the filtered track after Q4535 is not that of Raid 42 but fighter aircraft *despatched to intercept Raid 42* (my italics)'. This report also states that 'very little R.D.F. information was forthcoming on Raid 42 because of its height and position with respect to various stations'.[18] On this occasion, there was thus some confusion as to the approaching Raid 42. The technology was advanced for its time, but it was not perfect and such confusion could easily take place, in spite of the attentions of the filter officer and the fighter sector controllers.

Following this confusion, Sergeant Maurice H. Pocock of 72 Squadron was ordered to scramble from Acklington and hunt for the enemy aircraft.[19] Normally, Spitfire pilots patrolled in pairs during the daytime but operated only singly at dusk or night. Pocock took off at 22.20 hours, shortly before Hess crossed the English coast, and climbed to 15,000 feet. By then, however, Hess had dived into low-lying coastal haze and was travelling at over 300 m.p.h., a very fast speed for any expected enemy bomber. Pocock (who ended the war as a Flight Lieutenant) was an experienced and determined pilot who had flown in the Battle of Britain. He had one confirmed victory to his credit, as well as several 'probables' and 'possibles'. However, Spitfires were not fitted with airborne interception radar and depended on visual sightings after vectoring by ground control. Pocock was vectored on to the plotted track but was unable to see the Messerschmitt in a fading light against the dark hills of Northumberland. Hess escaped, although he stated in his letter of 10–15 June 1941 to his son that it seemed a Spitfire was only five kms behind him at this stage. However, as Maurice Pocock emphatically told B.B.C. T.V. during an interview, he would have attacked the Messerschmitt in the normal way if he had seen and caught it.[20]

John Costello states in his book that 'Pocock himself admits that he had been scrambled far too late to have any chance of giving chase to the incoming raid', and gives as his authority an interview in January 1990. But Maurice Pocock has assured me that he has never had any contact with John Costello, and firmly denies the allegation that he has ever stated he was scrambled far too late.[21]

Hess sped at low altitude across the countryside of Northumberland, accurately identified by the Royal Observer Corps as an Me 110 and tracked almost continuously.[22] The R.A.F. refused to believe these reports at first, for the arrival of a fighter such as an Me 110 seemed unlikely, even though the machine could carry a light bomb load; it was thought the aircraft must be a Do217 bomber.[23] Hess climbed to 5,000 feet after crossing the Scottish border and missed Dungavel House, although he flew very close to it.

Hess continued to the west coast of Scotland, near West Kilbride, and then turned east in a final attempt to identify his objective. Meanwhile, at 22.35 hours, Pilot Officer William A. Cuddie had been scrambled from Ayr in a Defiant nightfighter of 141 Squadron, the second of 13 Group's two fighter squadrons in the south-west of Scotland.[24] John Costello states that this aircraft came under the control of Turnhouse and the Duke of Hamilton; he is incorrect once more, for it was part of the Ayr fighter sector. He also dismisses the Defiant as 'a lumbering two-seater' but, in my opinion, this was one of the most dangerous periods for Hess in his flight. The Defiant had a respectable top speed of about 300 m.p.h. and, although outclassed by Messerschmitt Bf109 single-engined fighters on daylight operations, was proving successful as a nightfighter. This squadron was enjoying a particularly successful period, having shot down three Heinkel 111s on the previous Monday night, three more on the Tuesday night, and a Heinkel 111 and a Junkers 88 on the Wednesday night. Those enemy bombers which crashed over land had been confirmed.

Hess had slowed down and was zigzagging as well as climbing. Having watched the plots on his operations table, Hamilton reported the next day that 'a Defiant fighter in hot pursuit was approximately four miles away' when Hess baled out. William Cuddie, who later attained the rank of Squadron Leader, was killed on 3 October 1943 when leading an attack by Beaufighters of 46 Squadron against a German invasion fleet approaching the island of Cos in the Dodecanese. However, it seems probable that if Hess had remained in his aircraft for only a few minutes more, he would have been attacked by Cuddie's Defiant. The tactics of these nightfighter crews were to fly fairly low and to look upwards for enemy bombers silhouetted against the night sky, before climbing towards them. With two pairs of eyes on watch, each crew had a better chance of picking out an enemy than the Spitfire pilots. Cuddie's gunner, Sergeant Hodge, would then have fired the four Brownings in his

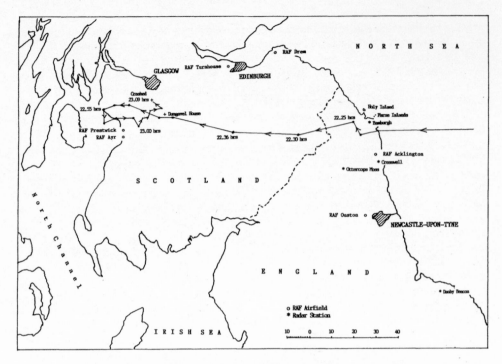

The track of Rudolf Hess's aircraft on 10 May 1941 (Roy Conyers Nesbit)

turret upwards into the belly of the German machine. Almost certainly, such an attack would have resulted in the sudden demise of the Deputy Fuehrer.

John Costello's opinion is that the effort made by the R.A.F. on that night was 'puny'. It is doubtful if anyone who has studied the above facts and also has had practical experience of night operations in those days would agree with him. As a navigator in light bombers, I flew on forty-nine operational sorties during 1941. Our aircraft was intercepted by single German nightfighters on only three of those occasions, and fortunately we were able to take evasive action or beat off the aggressors with gunfire. It would have been extremely alarming if as many as four fighters had pursued us on a single night, especially if we had been in an aircraft without ammunition or an air gunner. On the British side, R.A.F. nightfighters flew on 3,280 sorties during May 1941 and claimed the destruction of ninety-six German bombers, an average under three per cent of their attempts.[25] Of these nightfighter squadrons, 141 Squadron was one of the most successful, even though its Defiants were not fitted with airborne interception radar.

Of course, the chances of surviving a large number of sorties in either German or R.A.F. bombers were slim. But Hess flew on only a single occasion, on a one-way sortie over a lightly-defended territory, and took a calculated risk. His flight was well planned, skilfully executed, and met with success. However, as this book shows, he failed in the purpose of his mission.

NOTES

1. In Germany at this time, Central European Summer Time (two hours in advance of GMT) was the same as British Double Summer Time (also two hours in advance of GMT).
2. Public Record Office, *F01093/1*.
3. Thomas, H. *The Murder of Rudolf Hess*. London: Hodder & Stoughton, 1979.
4. *Hess: An Edge of Conspiracy*. B.B.C.2. 17 January 1990.
5. Gabel, C.A. *Conversations interdites avec Rudolf Hess*. Plon: Paris, 1988.
6. *Der Spiegel*, 21 May 1979.
7. Correspondence, April–July 1986.
8. *Flugstrecken BF110D–1*, dated 20 June 1940, with correspondence May and June 1986.
9. Interrogation of Professor Willi Messerschmitt by the U.S. Strategic Bombing Survey team at the end of the war. Air Historical Branch.
10. Costello, J. *Ten Days that saved the West*. London: Bantam, 1991.
11. Hinsley, F.H. et al. *British Intelligence in the Second World War, Vol 1*. London: HMSO, 1979. Page 555.
12. *History of No. 80 Wing*. Air Historical Branch (R.A.F.).
13. Public Record Office, *AIR28/624* Operations Record Book, R.A.F. Ouston.
14. Public Record Office, *AIR16/365* Order of Battle, 13 Group, 11 May 1941:

Squadron			Sector	Aerodrome	Aircraft
41 Squadron			Catterick	Catterick	Spitfire II
72	,,		Ouston	Acklington	Spitfire II
317	,,	(Polish)	Ouston	Ouston	Hurricane
603	,,		Turnhouse	Turnhouse	Spitfire II
43	,,		Turnhouse	Drem	Hurricane II
245	,,		Aldergrove	Aldergrove	Hurricane
602	,,		Ayr	Ayr	Spitfire
141	,,		Ayr	Ayr	Defiant

15. Letter, 30 April 1992.
16. Public Record Office, *AIR27/2079* 603 Squadron, *AIR27/442* 43 Squadron, *AIR28/861* Turnhouse, *AIR28/220* Drem, Operations Record Books.
17. Public Record Office, *AIR27/1706* 317 Squadron Operations Record Book.
18. Operational Research Section (F.C.) *Investigation of Raid 42 on 10th May 1941*, dated 18th May 1941. Air Historical Branch (R.A.F.). One difficulty here is that the names of these pilots and times are not recorded in the Operations Record Book for R.A.F. Acklington. Such omissions were frequent with these records, particularly in the early days of the war.
19. Public Record Office, *AIR27/624* 72 Squadron Operations Record Book.
20. Interview at Imperial War Museum, 25 July 1989.
21. Interview 7 May 1992.
22. The British referred to the Messerschmitt Bf110 as an Me 110.
23. Wood, D. *Attack Warning Red*. London: MacDonald & Janes, 1976. Also correspondence with Royal Observers Corps Northern Area Collection, May and June 1992.
24. Public Record Office, *AIR27/969* 141 Squadron Operations Record Book.
25. Richards, D. *Royal Air Force 1939–45*, Vol I. London: HMSO, 1953. Page 215.

Prologue

The news that Germany had lost the First World War came as a terrible shock to virtually all Germans. It meant the end of the monarchy and led to the establishment of a Republican regime which had to bear the immense unpopularity of men surrendering to enemy demands, first through the Armistice, and later through the Treaty of Versailles. Attacks against the Republican Government came from extremists of the left who wished to institute a Communist way of life, and, more important, from a fanatical right. It was openly hinted that it would be a patriotic duty to destroy a regime which had accepted unpalatable peace terms. This mood was widespread, especially amongst those who had fought at the Front. One such man was Major-General Karl Haushofer, who resolved to play his part in the destruction of the Treaty of Versailles, through his teachings in German universities.

Karl Haushofer was a patriotic German General, brought up in the traditions of the Imperial German Army. While in Tokyo from 1908 to 1911 he had learnt Japanese, made himself an expert on South and East Asia, and came to believe that the struggle for a nation's life was little more than a contest for space on the world's surface, and that the British and Japanese had appreciated this fact better than the Germans. It struck him that his countrymen had never known where their frontiers should lie, and had never had a boundary sense driven into them. When the war came he served on both Eastern and Western Fronts, rose to the rank of Major-General, and in 1918 supervised the return of the Thirtieth Bavarian Reserve Division from Alsace to Bavaria. It seemed to him that Germany was like a powerful man whose limbs had been amputated by her enemies, that the nation had been left prostrate, encircled and suffocating, and that more Lebensraum, or living space, would be the panacea for all her troubles.

Karl Haushofer acquired his degree of Doctor of Philosophy in 1913 at the University of Munich, graduating *summa cum laude* in Geography, Geology and History. In 1919 he decided that he would institute the new Science of Geopolitics, in fact the study of Political Geography seen from the point of view of the German State. It was a form of geographical Imperialism, and sought to bring about what German Nationalists thought of as a more logical arrangement of political boundaries. In his own words, 'Geopolitics wants to and must become the Geographical conscience of the State'.

Many of Haushofer's ideas came from Ratzel, Kjellen, Mahan and Mackinder, the basic ones being that the state is a biological organism which grows or contracts, and that in the struggle for space the dynamic countries swallow up the weak. In order to be self-supporting Germany must have autarchy and Lebensraum, and hence Geopolitics must become the doctrine of National Self-Sufficiency. Haushofer was a product of Bismarck's

Pursuit Aviator Lieutenant Rudolf Hess in his aircraft at the Western Front near Charleroi, 1918
(Hulton-Deutsch)

Major General Professor Karl Haushofer's old soldiers elect him leader of the Revolutionary
Committee (Martin Haushofer)

nationalist, reunified, resurgent Germany, but unlike Bismarck he had no strictly limited and precise aims as to the furthest practicable extent of German expansion. Hence German Geopolitics, if only on account of its vagueness, was never and could never be more than a pseudo-science. It was merely an attempt to set an academic stamp on claims that land in which Germans had settled was German, and that regions in which German was spoken ought to be German, or, at least, for cultural purposes, a German sphere of influence.

It was to the frustrated nationalism of a defeated country that Professor General Karl Haushofer was appealing in learned academic language. In 1921 he was appointed the Honorary Professor of Political Geography, and soon came to be known as the Professor of Geopolitics. Many of his students had come to hear him after the war, embittered that all the fighting had been in vain. Many believed the myth that the troops at the Front had been stabbed in the back by a cowardly Government. Many of them looked upon the workings of German democracy as a bottomless swamp. It was no wonder that Karl Haushofer was hailed by his disillusioned, angry and alienated students, who believed that he was giving them a sense of vision. One of these students was Rudolf Hess.

Hess, the son of a wealthy German merchant, was born on 26 April 1894 in Alexandria where he stayed for the first dozen years of his life, before being sent to school at Godesberg on the Rhine. He later served a business apprenticeship in Hamburg and went to Switzerland to study French. He reacted strongly against his father's wish that he should become a merchant, and in 1914 at the outbreak of war escaped to join the German Army as an eager volunteer. He served in the Sixteenth Bavarian Reserve Infantry Regiment, which consisted mostly of students. Under poor leadership it suffered terrible losses, but Hess and Hitler, who were still unknown to each other, came through alive. While the latter remained a Corporal, Hess rose to the rank of a Lieutenant and, after being wounded twice, became a pilot in the German Air Force in 1918.

Rudolf Hess was a fanatical young man in search of a father-substitute and a cause. He found in the course of the next few years two such substitutes, Haushofer and Hitler. The former gave him an educational training, the latter a cause. After the war Hess enrolled as a student of Economics at the University of Munich, attended the lectures of Karl Haushofer, and brooded over the downfall of his country with a burning intensity. He devoted much of his energy to the distribution of anti-semitic pamphlets, and to other policital activities, which led to the overthrow of the Socialist Republican regime in Munich in 1919. He expressed his aggressive mode of thought in a prize-winning essay on the theme 'How Must the Man be Constituted who will lead Germany back to her Old Heights?'.

He wrote: 'When all authority has vanished, only a man of the people can establish authority.... When necessity commands, he does not shrink from bloodshed.... In order to reach his goal, he is prepared to trample on his closest friends....' In 1920 Hess heard Hitler speak: he heard the voice thundering forth, and found himself wondering: 'Was this man a fool or was he the man who would save all Germany?' He decided to join the Nazi Party, and became an intimate friend of Hitler.

In 1923 he was involved in the planning of the unsuccessful Beerhall Putsch on 8 November, when he tried to protect Hitler from armed reprisal by detaining prominent members of the Bavarian Cabinet as hostages. On the next day, while Hitler was preparing to march into Munich, Hess was sent into the foothills of Southern Bavaria with his hostages, who were at one point threatened with death. When the news of the failure of the Putsch reached them Hess and his guards melted away. He made his way to Karl Haushofer's home in Munich at 30 Arcis Strasse, where he was given refuge for several weeks, and it was with Karl Haushofer's help that Hess escaped to Austria – favours which Hess would never forget.

Hess became a friend of Hitler and was frequently with him (W. G. Fitzgerald)

In due course Hitler was sentenced to five years' imprisonment in Landsberg Prison, which lasted in practice less than nine months. Hess returned, was given a very lenient sentence, and he too arrived in Landsberg, where Hitler had already started to dictate to Emil Maurice *Mein Kampf.* Hess soon supplanted Maurice as Hitler's principal secretary and typist. At this time Karl Haushofer paid a few visits to his former pupil Hess, bringing him reading material. Hess had been the Professor's personal assistant at the German Academy in Munich, and while Karl Haushofer thought that Hess's 'heart and idealism were greater than his intellect', he also regarded him as 'my favourite pupil'. During his visits to Hess in Landsberg, Karl Haushofer had occasional conversations with Hitler, and as a result certain geopolitical ideas were transmitted to Hitler either directly or indirectly through Hess. Even so Haushofer and Hitler differed in temperament, character and conviction, being from completely different worlds.

Karl Haushofer belonged to the military aristocracy and believed in government by an old-fashioned paternalistic imperial elite, and therefore he looked upon Hitler as a vulgar if resourceful upstart. Unlike Hitler, Haushofer was certainly not an extreme racialist; he had married Martha Mayer-Doss who was half-Jewish. Martha came from

23

Major General Professor Karl Haushofer with his wife,
Martha, and his sons, Albrecht (left) and Heinz (right)
(Hulton-Deutsch)

the family of George Mayer, a Jewish merchant of Mannheim, and she bore Haushofer two sons, Albrecht and Heinz. Moreover in foreign policy Haushofer wanted an Overseas Empire with a strong Germany in the Middle, South and South-East Europe. Like many German Generals he desired co-operation with Russia and competition against the British Empire for Lebensraum. Germany must not dissipate her energies by expanding South or Overseas. The Third Reich would have to gain territory in the East, and would stretch across the Russian steppes and plains. Hitler wrote in *Mein Kampf*:

> If European soil was wanted by and large it could be had only at the expense of Russia. . . . For such a policy as this there was but one ally in Europe– England. Only with England covering our rear could we have begun a new Germanic migration.
>
> No sacrifice should have been too great in winning England's friendship. We should have given up all thought of colonies and seapower and avoided competition with British industry. . . .

24

Although Karl Haushofer did not write, revise or review *Mein Kampf*, he did provide Hitler with a formula and certain well-turned phrases which could be adapted, and which at a later stage suited the Nazis perfectly. Even the vagueness of Karl Haushofer's Geopolitics would be advantageous to Hitler. In German university circles it served as a ponderous intellectual smokescreen, obscuring the aims of Nazi Foreign Policy. Meanwhile Hess's total allegiance was transferred from Karl Haushofer to Hitler. When Hitler was released from Landsberg Hess remained with him as his secretary, and his influence was great, for he had become the initiator of the Fuehrer cult. He started calling Hitler 'Der Chef', then 'Fuehrer', and soon the greeting 'Heil Hitler' became commonplace.

Most Nazis saw Hess as a coming man, as he was with Hitler almost every day, taking care of Hitler's personal affairs. Goebbels recorded in his diary on 13 April 1926 '. . . Hess: the most decent, quiet, friendly, clever reserved: Alone with Hess. Talk, He is a kind fellow'. Goering on the other hand loathed Hess as a rival and the dislike was mutual. Both Hess and Goering had been pilots, and Hess was jealous of Goering, who in the First World War had commanded the famous Richthofen Squadron. Goering pictured himself as a man of action who despised intellectuals, and in a muddled way Hess fancied himself as an intellectual expert on Geopolitics.

In the late 1920s and early 1930s Hess fulfilled two important tasks. He was good at collecting funds for the Nazi Party, and at spying on Hitler's behalf. Hess also managed the Adolf Hitler Industrial Fund, into which certain business interests paid large sums. On 15 December 1932 Hess was put in charge of a Central Party Commission, and four months later in April 1933 Hitler appointed Hess 'my deputy with the power to take decisions in my name in all questions relating to the conduct of the party'. As such Hess was able to help his old friend Karl Haushofer with the Ausland Organisations which were set up, within Germany and elsewhere, to foster contracts and comradeship between Germans in the Reich and German minorities outside.

In a sense Karl Haushofer's work with these organisations such as the V.D.A., namely the Verein für das Deutschtum im Ausland (the League for German Nationals Abroad) was merely the practical application of his geopolitical teachings in the service of

Hess, Hitler and Goering in the Burgerbraukeller, the Munich beerhall in which the Nazi veterans plotted the Beerhall Putsch (Hulton-Deutsch)

25

Pan-German Imperialism. The activities of the V.D.A. were not lost on Hitler who knew only too well that the twenty million Germans outside the Reich could be used in schemes of territorial aggrandisement for the Third Reich. On 12 February 1934 Hess established the Volksdeutsche Rat (the Council for those of German origin who were living in countries outside the Reich) with Karl Haushofer as its President. Under Hess's authority the Foreign Organisation of the National Socialist Party, the Foreign Institute and the V.D.A. began to organise Germans outside Germany.

While Hess collaborated with Karl Haushofer in guiding the work of the Ausland Organisations, he devoted all his energies to the service of Hitler. At no time was this more clear than during the Night of the Long Knives, on 30 June 1934. Between 1933 and 1934 Hitler was faced with the problems of resolving the bitterness between the SA (the Army of Nazi Stormtroopers) and the Wehrmacht (the traditional German army), and of determining the succession to President Hindenburg. Röehm, Chief of Staff of the S.A., and some of the other S.A. leaders represented those disillusioned Nazis who wanted to enrich themselves at the expense of capitalists, landlords and Civil Service bureaucrats, and Röehm wanted to reconstitute the Army under his own authority. However, Hitler had to succeed Hindenburg in order to obtain absolute power, and to do that he had to keep on good terms with the Army; this meant that the ambitions of Röehm and certain S.A. leaders would have to be curbed.

The attempts of Hitler and Hess to conciliate did not produce the intended results, and in Munich on the morning of 30 June 1934 the local leaders of the S.A. were collected, under the direction of Hess and Bormann. Roehm and his followers were arrested by Hitler, accompanied by a strong bodyguard. On the evening of the same day Sepp Dietrich, the Head of the SS Leibstandarte Adolf Hitler arrived at the Stadelheim Prison in Munich with a shooting squad. He showed Frank, the Bavarian Minister of Justice, a list of the names of 110 persons which were believed to be underlined with Hitler's pencil. Frank telephoned to Hess at the Brown House protesting, and Hess said he would approach Hitler. Hess telephoned back to say that Hindenburg had given Hitler emergency powers, and he read

Hitler and Hess (second from right) with Leni Riefenstahl, the film producer, at an open-air lunch organised by Hess in the woods near Oldenburg in Schleswig-Holstein (W. G. Fitzgerald)

At the Berghof, Berchtesgaden, Hess tells Hitler the names of stormtroopers who cannot be trusted. On 30 June 1934 they were all killed (W. G. Fitzgerald)

over the phone the names of nineteen persons who would have to be destroyed. These nineteen were summarily murdered and Roehm was dealt with later.

Of all the Nazi leaders Hess was the most retiring, and therefore his public image was less bloodthirsty than that of Himmler or Goering. There were many Germans who thought that he was an 'intellectual', an 'honest man' and 'the conscience of the Party'. It was no doubt for this reason that Hess was chosen to give a public justification for the Night of the Long Knives. The speech which he delivered at Koenigsberg on 8 July was broadcast by all German broadcasting stations:

Special thanks of the movement are due to the S.S. who in these days honouring their slogan "Our Honour is our Loyalty" carried out their duties in an exemplary manner. . . .
Who can now doubt that every youngster in the Hitler Jugend looks upon the Fuehrer as his ideal who particularly in those days acted like a heroic ideal figure of youth. . . .

27

THE TRUTH ABOUT RUDOLF HESS

Hess then touched upon the delicate subject of the guilty men:

> In an hour when the German people's existence was at stake, the extent of individual guilt
> could not be measured. Despite its harshness, it has a deep sense if mutinies in the Army are
> punished by decimation, that is the execution of every tenth man, irrespective of whether he
> was guilty or innocent.

He may have had in mind one incident in which he was involved. In Munich on the evening of 30 June, Dr Willi Schmidt, who was a music critic for the newspaper the *Muenchener Neueste Nachrichten*, was taken away from his flat by four S.S. men. A few days later a coffin was returned with his body inside, accompanied by orders from the Gestapo to keep it closed. Dr Schmid's misfortune had been to possess the same name as Willi Schmidt, a leader of the local S.A., who was shot by another group of S.S. men. When the S.S. sent the widow some money she refused to accept, and eventually Hess went to see her. He said that he was sorry about the mistake, and asked her to think of the death of her husband as 'the death of a martyr for a great cause'. He was obviously anxious that such incidents should be hushed up.

In the early 1920s two men had exercised great influence over Rudolf Hess, Karl Haushofer and Hitler. After 1923 the Professor General receded into the background and remained the paternal friend, while Hess had become one of Hitler's most fanatical supporters. By the late 1920s Karl Haushofer was no longer the major influence in Hess's life, but the two men remained close, and Hess came to know Karl's son Albrecht, a brilliant student of Foreign Affairs. In years to come this acquaintance between Rudolf Hess and Albrecht Haushofer was to result in unexpected consequences.

28

Part One

THE WORK OF ALBRECHT HAUSHOFER

'Rudi Hess and his equals are beyond help.'
Albrecht Haushofer's letter to his father, 8 June 1932

'I sometimes ask myself how long we shall be able to carry the responsibility, which we bear and which gradually begins to turn into historical guilt or, at least, into complicity . . .
There will be much violent dying and nobody knows when lightning will strike one's own house.'
Albrecht Haushofer's letter to his parents, 27 July 1934

'Perhaps we shall manage to chain the fuming titan to the rock.'
Albrecht Haushofer to Fritz Hesse after the Remilitarisation of the Rhineland, 1936

'The disappointed fury over the missed war is now raging internally. Today it is the Jews. Tomorrow it will be other groups and classes.'
Albrecht Haushofer's letter to his mother, 16 November 1938

'The one good thing is that the free countries of the world still possess a vast preponderance of power which if compelled can be used as military force.'
Letter by Marquis of Clydesdale to Douglas Simpson of the U.S.A., 1 June 1939

'There is not yet a definite timetable for the actual explosion, but any date after the middle of August may prove to be the fatal one.'
Albrecht Haushofer's letter to the Marquis of Clydesdale, 16 July 1939

Albrecht Haushofer, the troubled German patriot of partly Jewish origin who passionately wanted peace between Britain and Germany (Martin Haushofer)

ONE

Early Days

In 1933 Hess began to be influenced by Albrecht, Karl Haushofer's eldest son. Although he could not know it then, Albrecht would decisively affect the course of his life a few years later.

Because of the unwitting role he was to play, Albrecht is a person worthy of close examination; he was certainly one of the most fascinating and mysterious of all characters lurking behind the scenes of the Third Reich. It was hard for his acquaintances to judge whether he was a scholar, geographer, poet, musician, playwright, resister of Nazism or staid official in the German Foreign Office, but all who knew him agreed that he was a man of huge ability. Allen Dulles wrote that Albrecht Haushofer 'was fat, whimsical, sentimental, romantic and unquestionably brilliant'. It was said of him that his friendships were of an uncertain kind and that he would often put an end to them in a mood of angry despair. His friend Dr Carl von Weizsaecker wrote: 'He could be compared to an elephant: weighty, clever, very clever and if necessary cunning.'

Albrecht Haushofer was much closer to his half-Jewish mother than to his father, the Professor General, with whom he did not always get on well. His father at times complained that his son would never make a German soldier, and the mother often had to smooth over relations between them. His letters to his parents tell a great deal, but it is his personal letters to his mother which are the most revealing, as he confided in her in a way which he did not with anyone else.

In 1917, at the age of 14, he attended the Theresien Gymnasium in Munich, where he was a solitary figure who did not integrate with his schoolfellows, mainly because they could not keep pace with him intellectually. One of his contemporaries asked him what he wished to become and without a moment's hesitation he replied 'German Foreign Minister'. Such confidence caused irritation amongst those around him, but they recognised that he had exceptional qualities. In 1920 several of his age-group were celebrating the end of the school term and Hermann Heimpel, a friend, leaves us a glimpse of this strange man:

> Later Albrecht Haushofer made a great speech. He spoke of Germany, so full of love that it was unexpected, of the rest of the world, of stones and stars, of history and the future, with a dark seriousness as if he were carrying the wisdom of millennia and entering it in the book of the future: he spoke as if something was to happen. He appeared to be without hope, sombre and sweet. Since the others could not completely understand the speech but fully agreed with it they kept silent.

Albrecht Haushofer, as Secretary-General of the Berlin Society for Geography welcomes Swedish author and explorer, Sven Hedin at the station (Hulton-Deutsch)

In 1924 at the age of 21 Albrecht Haushofer finished his studies in History and Geography at Munich University, passed his Doctor's Degree *summa cum laude*, and submitted his thesis '*Alpine Pass States*', which was not published until 1928. Many of his father's ideas appear in it, but the word 'geopolitics' does not. Unlike his father he wished geopolitics to have the character of an exact science; it should not simply be a crude tool for political propaganda. Consequently, in most of his future writings he treated geopolitics and political geography as being on the same level.

Like many Germans he felt rootless and insecure in spite of his academic successes. He wrote to his mother on 25 May 1923: '. . . But I am sometimes troubled, young as I am, by the thought whether I shall ever find a refuge, a home, or whether I shall always be and remain a rootless person, a bird of passage . . .' In the summer of 1924 he went to Berlin and became assistant to the well-known geographer, Albrecht Penck. There, many doors were opened to him on account of his father's reputation, and he grew into his father's circle of contacts. In 1925 he became the Secretary General of the Berlin 'Society for Geography', a post which he held for the rest of his life, and in 1926 he became editor of the *Periodical of the Society for Geography in Berlin*. He lived at 23 Wilhelmstrasse, the premises of the Society for Geography, in an official flat on the top floor. During these years he travelled widely, visiting all the European countries, North and South America, the Near, Middle and Far East and the Soviet Union but it was his trips to Britain that he enjoyed most.

Politically Albrecht Haushofer was a Bismarckian patriot, with a hankering for a Constitutional Monarchy in the sense of an idealised Bismarckian State. He intensely disliked revolutionary movements, an attitude which had its roots in his memories of

Munich in November 1918. At that time an attempt had been made by a group of leftist intellectuals, led by Kurt Eisner, to seize power in Bavaria by setting up a Socialist Republican Regime. The Wehrmacht had intervened and General Ritter von Epp, a friend of Karl Haushofer, put down the revolt, but not before hostages had been shot by the revolutionaries at the Luitpold Gymnasium. On 7 November 1928 Albrecht Haushofer wrote to his parents from Berlin: 'That winter ten years ago means something to me which I shall never get rid of while I live – an inexhaustible source of hatred, distrust, anger and scorn.'

He also resented the Versailles Treaty and regarded the policy of fulfilment of the provisions of this Treaty as being too high a price for Germany to pay. As for the Treaty of Locarno of 1925, guaranteeing the frontiers of France and Belgium, he dismissed it sceptically as being 'the seal affixed to an existing situation' which would happily be broken by either side at the first opportune moment. He wanted a revision of frontiers and wrote in 1926 that a 'lively participation of the German people, constructive and formulative, was not possible if present day frontiers are to be maintained'. The Polish Corridor driving a wedge through Germany was a particularly bitter grievance to him. 'The present day solution of the Vistula problems,' he wrote, 'is unpleasant for Danzig, damaging for Germany and far from satisfying for Poland.'

Haushofer saw a future for Germany as a co-ordinating power in middle, east and south-east Europe, the area between the Baltic and the Adriatic, including the Baltic States, Poland, Czechoslovakia, Hungary and the Balkan States. Situated between two powerful neighbours, Germany and Russia, these East European countries had traditionally fallen within the sphere of influence of either Germany or Russia. As German enclaves still formed an important part of the population in each of these states, Albrecht Haushofer saw them as potential clients of Germany in the economic field.

As a southern German who had a deep attachment for the Alps, he hoped that Austria and Germany would come closer together through a process of gradual evolution, until eventually an *Anschluss* would take place. In 1931 an attempt was made at the height of the Depression to form a German-Austrian Customs Union. The plan was thwarted through the opposition of France, supported by the countries of the Little Entente, and the International Court of Justice at the Hague rejected it.

This made Albrecht Haushofer regard France as the dedicated enemy of Germany. Had not France guaranteed the frontiers of Belgium, Poland and those of the Little Entente States, and was not France preventing Germany from collaborating with Austria and from exercising a decisive economic influence in south-east Europe? Was it not symptomatic of the desire of the French Government to want to prevent Germany from ever becoming a strong European Power and to keep her isolated?

He did not consider Russia as a possible target for armed aggression, or as a potential ally. The only country with which he wished close co-operation was Britain. In a letter to his parents dated 30 July 1930, he expressed his views on both Russia and Britain in a language which few Russians would have liked:

So my first impression of Russia is one of terrible poverty and oppression, a partly purposeless, partly systematic cultural decline of enormous proportions. On the other side the accumulation of sinister power and growing economic strength (partly through ruthless exploitation of large natural resources, partly however, through an undeniably systematic large scale reconstruction) in a few entirely or nearly barbaric hands.

The national character however has not changed. The Russian is still indolent, lazy, dull, unclean and unpunctual. Many things may be recognised in many fields: and the danger must not be underestimated.

33

> To make common cause with Moscow is according to my impressions completely out of the question as long as the entire structure of our political mentality remains unchanged.

Britain fared much better in a letter dated 9 November 1939 written to his parents from London. From the way in which he expressed himself he was obviously enjoying himself, as though the seemingly self-confident British way of life was one to which he would have liked to belong, even if he did not wholly understand it.

> And now London. General impression: envy for the country which still has so many men to steer her history.
> I have at last seen almost all important leaders, to many of them I have spoken personally: e.g., Lord Allenby with whom I had a brilliant conversation for an hour without knowing who he was . . .
> Splendid the old Earl of Crawford and Balcarres, a Scot of ancient descent – one of the wisest men I ever met . . . Chamberlain who actually makes a less distinguished impression: Churchill, who has become fat and looks more like a clever clown than a Statesman . . . . The German Embassy with the young Count Bernstorff and the young Prince Bismarck makes in comparison a rather paltry impression – the welcome was exceedingly cordial.

He idealised the British two-party system of government and saw in it a complete contrast to the Weimar Republic, which had been weakened through the frequent occurrence of party political splintering (he referred to President Hindenburg as the 'sentry in front of the bankruptcy trustee's office'). He especially liked what he understood to be British flexibility and pragmatism. He believed that 'for every political aim there are hundreds of forms; but he who insists on sticking to one will be stunted'. He thought that an appreciation of this outlook had been the key to the successes of Bismarck and the British.

To Haushofer's way of thinking co-operation with Britain was essential and any war in Europe unthinkable. In any large-scale war there could not in his view be any victors – only death and destruction. In her own interests and in the interests of European civilisation Germany must achieve her aims through peaceful means.

> The peoples of Europe are in a position in which they have to get on together lest they all perish; and although one realises that it is not commonsense but emotional urges which govern the world, one must still try to control such urges. If one is forced to get on with others in a certain space, one does not have to love them. But it will be well not to exasperate one another. The risk would be too great.

In Germany he saw the weaknesses of the Weimar Regime; his play *And thus Pandurion Is Governed*, written between 1930 and 1932, deals with the unhappiness of coalition crises, and is set against the background of the French invasion of the Ruhr. He had already tried to influence diplomats and members of the Weimar Cabinets by means other than the stage. On 26 October 1929 he proudly wrote to his mother: '. . . The "People and Reich" essay has indeed attracted some attention . . . all really political people have at last recognised me as a personality in my own right, and no longer a son of my father. . . .'

On the same day he wrote a long letter to his father stating his respect and even admiration for Stresemann, the foreign minister. Albrecht had corresponded with him and regarded him as a leader of moderate nationalism.

. . . For years now Western [German] policy was made with sacrifice after sacrifice in order
to get a free hand in the East one day – now, in the few weeks since Stresemann's death, our
last means of pressure in the Poland negotiations has been thrown overboard. . . .

Everybody who sails under the direct flag of the Right is not even listened to owing to the
anxiety psychosis into which Hugenberg and Hitler have plunged the people. . . . I must
confess that four weeks ago I could not have considered how deep the desire for Stresemann's
return must be. He was certainly not a great man, but among the blind he was certainly one-
eyed. . . .

He mentioned his desire to intrigue behind the scenes and to keep on speaking
terms with Hess and the Nazis, in case any information could be gleaned from them.

I intend to have a determining voice, but not in the foreground of the platform. I am still too
young for that and the general situation is not *yet* tense enough. . . .

Do you know by any chance things about Hess, which are not confidential but none the less
interesting and which may be passed on? Please do not mention that I have asked.

It was significant that Albrecht Haushofer wrote to his father on 4 November 1929:
'What you write about the extreme right coincides with my own impressions. It may
become necessary to exert influence there one day.' On 25 February 1930 he wrote to his
mother, with a certain faith in his own ability, and with a few reservations about his father:

I wish you had borne me a little more stupid. . . . A little more convinced of the 'correctness'
of what I say – perhaps like my father who is certainly not vain, much less vain than I am myself
– who delivers his teachings only with the downright provoking conceit of conviction.

Albrecht Haushofer was doing all that he could to keep every option open, although
he had little in common with the Nazis. He did not mind mixing and collaborating with
extreme Nationalists, such as his father's friends. In November 1931 he started to work for
the *Zeitschrift für Geopolitik*, the journal which his father edited. While his father wrote the
'Reports from the Pacific World', Albrecht wrote the 'Reports from the Atlantic World'.

On 30 May 1932 Bruening's government resigned, producing in Albrecht
Haushofer a deep pessimism about Anglo-German relations and the future of Germany.
He wrote to his mother on 3 June 1932: 'It is not my fault nor that of others that today the
entire German position in the Anglo-Saxon countries is a heap of debris. . . . Let us see
how we can get through mill torrent 2, the beginning of which we now experience. I do not
think that in the end there will still exist a German Reich.'

Unlike many Germans he had no faith in or liking for Nazi ideas and ideology. On 8
June he wrote to his father that 'Rudi Hess and his equals are beyond help'. He had no
time for the Government of Papen, and wrote on 25 July: 'Mr. Von P. is a nonentity . . .
whose description of "untested efficiency" one can unhesitatingly change into "tested
inefficiency"'.

Even at this time Haushofer completely underestimated Hitler and Nazism. 'Now
we just have to await what the elections will bring. I do not believe in a swastika majority
and I have the curious idea that this possibility would be the only one of which Adolf the
Great is afraid, like a small child.' The strength of popular support for Nazism puzzled
him, and on 16 February 1932 he wrote to his parents: 'Today the Right is demagogised to
such an extent that nothing can be expected from it and experience and responsibility lie in
the middle. It is a strange situation.' He had reached the view that support for Nazism was
only a phase. He was soon to be disillusioned.

TWO

Under Hess's Protection: 1933

Albrecht Haushofer was confronted with a serious dilemma when the Nazis came to power. There were three possibilities open to him. He could oppose Nazism openly, and run the risk of being killed and of causing persecution to his family. He could flee the country and express himself without let or hindrance from abroad, or he could work for the regime in one capacity or another, in the hope of influencing the course of events in a peaceful direction.

He never seriously thought of open opposition to the Nazi regime, since any hostility might have produced a violent reaction, and have landed him in a concentration camp. Albrecht knew how ruthless the Nazis could be, and he had no reason to believe that the matter would be left there. At the very least his internment and fate would have caused great embarrassment to his family, especially to his half-Jewish mother, of whom he was very fond. He did not wish to take risks which might involve harm to her, physical or otherwise. This left him with the choice of either leaving Germany or of working for the Third Reich. The possibility of emigration was carefully considered, but it did not appeal to him, as he felt that he would be running away, and that outside Germany he would not be in a position to alter the actions of the German leaders.

The third course, that of working for the regime in the hope that he might tone it down, was an option more in accordance with his temperament and outlook. His intellectual vanity was such that he imagined he might be able to manipulate those with authority in the Reich. Yet however confident he was in his own ability, he was apprehensive. During the first months after the Nazi accession to power he adopted a waiting attitude, tinged with pessimism. In spring 1933 he wrote: 'The only consolation is very negative, that is the conviction that we are approaching such a great general catastrophe that personal catastrophes will no longer count'.

There is no doubt that he had no enthusiasm for his leaders. On 22 February 1933 he wrote to his mother complaining of Goering's threatening demands and offers to François-Poncet, the French Ambassador in Berlin, and the frustration which it caused Von Neurath, the German Foreign Minister.

> Politics for the amusement of father: Latest performance of Mr G[oerin]g: He goes to François-Poncet off his own bat, demands the return of the Corridor; if Poland responded favourably, one would assist her in conquering the Ukraine. F.-P. smiles and asks that the matter be given to him in writing. And he gets it! Two hours later a smiling Russian Ambassador shows it to the desperate Mr Von N[eura]th. These are the saviours of the nation.

36

30 January 1933. Röehm (second from left) Hitler and Hess marching to the Reichstag on the day that Hitler took his seat as Chancellor of the Third Reich (Hulton-Deutsch)

Yet he was prepared to co-operate with the Nazis as he felt that there was no turning back for Germany. On 17 March he wrote to his parents from Berlin:

As matters stand today, one has to wish them full success; because the boats are burned – a state which in itself is extremely uncomfortable – and one has to become familiar with the coastline, even if it appears to be very adventurous at first. Reasonable persons are always out of place in revolutionary periods. And that will not change so soon. . . .

He was rudely brought to his senses on 7 April 1933 when the Nazi regime passed the Civil Service Laws which excluded those of non-Aryan origin from public office within the Reich. As a person in part Jewish this news hit Albrecht Haushofer like a blow from a hammer. By German law he was at most only a second-class citizen. He may well have felt that if he chose to stay in Germany his chances of becoming German Foreign Minister were negligible, and that in the long run his career was already finished. The whole Haushofer family was affected, but Albrecht and his mother felt it most bitterly, and on 12 April Albrecht wrote to his mother:

When I examine the human side – honestly! there is not much left at all. . . . The special faith in humanity has become thin, terribly thin.

On 19 April he wrote again to his mother, expressing a sense of resignation, indifference and dread.

. . . and yet I cannot write otherwise than in a mood of a completely resigning philosophy of life, to which the individual life, especially one's own, has become indifferent and alien. . . .

37

*Martha Haushofer with leopard cubs. Being of half-
Jewish origin, only Hess's intervention saved the family
from the Nuremberg laws (Martin Haushofer)*

Desires? Hopes? You yourself see clearly enough what will yet come to pass. In small circles as well as in the large one. Why should one throw dust into one's eyes? Afterwards it will be a poor consolation that one has foreseen and known everything with clear and alert common sense. For father and for Heinz – who both have deeper roots in the soil – it will be more difficult. . . .

On 7 May his resentment at his father's passive acceptance of a racist policy bubbled over in a letter to his mother, and his intentions were almost suicidal:

I am glad about the optimism of father and of Heinz, although I do not understand it. . . . The way our German world develops I see no possibilities of activity for myself. . . .

But these are only the external things. Internally it looks like this: I now stand on a narrow strip of land which remains when one becomes indifferent to one's own existence, and when on the other hand there is no compelling reason for taking an active step towards non-existence.

I cannot really say very much regarding father's political letter. I am glad that he sees possibilities of activity for himself to a certain extent – in the same state which disqualifies his sons from the Civil Service (I have very carefully read the new Protocol to the Civil Servants' Act, I do not notice much relaxation in them). But we judge matters too differently for me to be able to say anything in respect of this attitude, in respect of his standing up or not standing up for people.

Major General Professor Karl Haushofer with young Volksdeutsch (Martin Haushofer)

You cannot plane wood without producing shavings is a very fine proverb; but when some of the shavings are personally known to you, things look very different. I only do not know whether I should envy or admire the blindness which does not see how near to us already is the blade of the plane.

On 26 May he wrote to his mother saying that he saw no future for himself, and that his position as editor of the periodical of the Society for Geography in Berlin was threatened:

And here we are back at the topic, which is unavoidable today and which I have avoided in my last letters solely for the reason that you have written to me that I should not undermine father's passably positive frame of mind. If it has to be mentioned at all, I cannot deny that now as before I take a very gloomy view of the future in general as well as of my own in particular. In this state which makes second-class human beings out of us, who in the interest of expediency should not exist, there is no activity for us. Because our position is based on the fact that our descent is either not known or ignored. That is no basis for any life-work of quality. Any position grudger – and how many of them do exist today – can have us thrown out. . . . If, for instance, the Emergency Aid Association is forced to make the granting of subsidies to journals dependent on the pure Aryan descent of the editor – a procedure which is entirely conceivable – then my position here will come to an end.

Then I shall be faced with the problem of whether to crawl away in the quiet with the remainder of my fortune and to live just as long as this remainder lasts or whether to make the attempt to find shelter somewhere abroad, which would neither be easy in practice, nor easy for me personally.

This was the first time that the thought of emigration seriously occupied him, but as a patriotic German it was unattractive, and he rejected the idea. He was in despair until June 1933, when Hitler's Deputy Rudolf Hess intervened personally. Hess issued protective letters to the two sons of the Professor General, so that the Nazis would refrain from attacking them. Hess was glad to help his old tutor and friend, who had sheltered him after the Beerhall Putsch, and he took it for granted that his sons would be patriotic Germans.

Following Hess's action, Albrecht wrote to his parents on 22 June, a long and important letter which showed that while he was prepared to work for the regime he remained basically hostile to Nazism in all its forms.

R. H. [Rudolf Hess] has not yet phoned . . . I find it touching that he engages himself so strongly in the whole matter, while on the other hand I cannot quite understand it either (seen from his angle). Because either one enacts such a Law (and in doing so, considers which class of human beings is thereby affected) or one does not enact it: if one enacts it at all, one also has to implement it.

This is, however, just a psychology, which is no longer valid today. That it is no longer valid in this case is, of course, fortunate for our family circle, especially for those members of it who are fortunate enough to have a bad memory. Unfortunately, I have a good one and I shall not forget the experience of being turned out, even though it was only a spiritual and not an actual dismissal, and even though I am now smuggled back again in the wake of H's [Hess's] peasant cunning and of father's personal authority. Because it is nothing else after all.

I am now completely clear on the point that I am fundamentally not suited for this new German world. . . . I am opposed in all essential aspects to the human type which, above all, is represented as valid in the younger generation. You know that I am not completely without passion, but it is a different passion of coldness, of stillness, of abstraction – i.e. the exact opposite of that which the emotional type ruling today can understand and need. He, whose faith in human society approximately agrees with Schopenhauer's fine parable of the porcupines – is unusable for the rulers of today.

There is no personal future for me in the new Germany, because humanly I can agree as little with the new people as perhaps Erasmus of Rotterdam could with the Anabaptists or even with the Lutheran Protestants.

Since the new state now renews the totality demand of absolutism, probably no cultural sphere free of government intervention will be left at all . . . nothing else will remain for me but a retreat into a potentially dead corner, from which in the best case a secret invisible background operation may be thought of.

In the case of geopolitics I have the strong fear that it is too near the motive of power to be acceptable to me in the long run. For the last half-year every report is an agony for me, over which I ponder for days in order to distil the necessary compromise between truth, inner conviction and the permissible.

Nothing very positive will therefore result from the friendship of R. H. [Rudolf Hess]. . . .

In the best case, I foresee for myself a state of quietness and resignation, which will undoubtedly last for years. A position publicly visible would only be a danger today, but I do not believe that it would occur to anybody to call me there. Because most of the persons in authority today do not know me and the few who know me can understandably do without me as easily as I can do without them. The best possible relationship is a friendly emphasised distance.

40

Rudolf Hess and Major General Professor Karl Haushofer. Some of Haushofer's geopolitical ideas for Lebensraum, or living space, were transmitted to Hitler by Hess and were adapted to suit Hitler's purposes

I write all this for once quite openly noting father's disappointment. . . . You, Mother, will undoubtedly understand this in every detail.

Contrary to what he wrote, something more did result from Karl Haushofer's friendship with Hess. Albrecht Haushofer received the offer of an official post in Germany as a lecturer in Political Geography at the Berlin High School for Politics through the help of Hess. He was also asked by Hess to attend talks at Danzig as the latter's representative in June 1933, and at the end of that month Albrecht wrote to his parents giving the reasons for his decision to work for the regime:

Inhibitions:
Lack in me of National Socialist philosophy of life. Lacking faith in the ability to teach and to find contact with the young generation. Compulsion to make a whole series of compromises in questions of opinion; loss of a good deal of both inner and external freedom.

Incentives:
Increased possibility of practical activity: improvement of my position in the sense of external prestige and of middle class significance of titles.

41

Compulsion to be active:

In a certain sense increase and safety of external freedom of movement, both financially as well as in respect of freedom to travel, which one must grant to the holder of this position.

You see, it is all rather muddled up, but it is, after all, a fact that the incentives are all on the side of my worldly *vita activa* – while the inhibitions are just inhibitions of my character. That I could accomplish many things better than others, that in this position a tolerably reasonable person is better than an unreasonable one, that I probably possess the necessary skill to create for myself further influence from this activity, that (and this is said really more for you than for myself, because your external need for my prestige is greater than my own) the then existing combination of external position would for quite a number of years serve as an absolutely satisfactory basis – all that I know of course. The question is whether I could manage to jump over the internal shadow, and if I do, how it will end.

He had accepted the post and would have to pay a high price for his action. He knew he would have to compromise his principles on a vast variety of issues, and that knowledge humiliated him and made him lacking in self-respect. Having accepted the post at the Berlin High School his doubts were increased rather than diminished. It appears that Goebbels, Reich Minister of Propaganda, regarded him as a Jew and referred to him as such. Albrecht at any rate wrote to Goebbels saying that his father was 'personally well-known to the Reich Chancellor and the Deputy of the Fuehrer'. Hess's 'protective' letters, to the effect that the Haushofer sons were honorary Aryans, were sent to the Ministry of Propaganda. On 22 July, Albrecht wrote to his mother about the precariousness of his own existence:

I only see very clearly, and much clearer than Father and my brother, the shakiness and insecurity of such a basis for all practical activity. What will happen if Father's friend should lose his influence one day?

When I enter the new activity, I shall have to face such a measure of sacrifice of inner conviction, of silence and of swallowing that I am unwilling further to increase this measure with open eyes by acquiring the truly false odour of a Party Member.

You, Mother, will understand that the whole matter presents for me a great inner predicament. I do not ask of Father to understand it. If the matter materialises, to which I have said 'Yes' now – then I shall pay for the external activity (and for the satisfaction of your ambition for me) a price, which is so high, that during the night it sometimes causes me long hours of wakefulness. . . .

On 5 August he wrote to his mother as a man who was trying to rationalise his position:

I have never deceived myself on the point that political life in all conceivable forms exacts compromises and sacrifices of attitude. . . .

You are quite right: we have only a choice between evils, and everything I do is, after all, but an attempt to come to terms with the present evil as best I can. . . .

Albrecht could only exist in the Third Reich provided that he concealed his real views from the Nazi High Command, and thus his relationships with senior Nazis were necessarily hypocritical. On 7 September 1933 he wrote a significant letter to Rudolf Hess, which represented a turning point in his life:

... A messenger of the Ministry for Propaganda called to bring me a letter ... in which is contained the final permission for my appointment to the High School for Politics. Now I may add a short personal word to you.

I know what I have to thank you for. It is not so much the position as such – much as it is appropriate to the possibilities of what I can accomplish – it is the deliverance from an inner plight, of the seriousness of which I cannot speak. We – my brother and I – are indebted for your intercession, to which it is solely attributable that we have not been swept onto the dump as Germans of inferior value. You will understand when I say that it is very difficult for an internally proud and sincere person to be indebted to such a degree, that he examines himself carefully before he begs or lets somebody else beg for him. I could not have accepted this extraordinary favour – not even for my father's sake – if I did not feel certain that in case of need I would be capable of full personal effort for you as a person. On the face of it perhaps all this may be very remote. It is an inner necessity for me to affirm this to myself and for once also to be allowed to express it to you.

These were words which would have their importance for both Albrecht Haushofer and Hess, and in spite of Hess's protection the subject of anti-semitism was a particularly awkward topic for Albrecht. In this connection he was in an unusual position. On the one hand it was advantageous to him that his father had a standing in Germany as an impeccably patriotic general and founder of German geopolitics: on the other hand it was a great disadvantage to him that his mother was half-Jewish, because his part-Jewish origin excluded him from all meaningful public activity – prior to Hess's intervention. Even after Hess had made him an honorary Aryan he was treated by the other Nazi leaders with reserve.

There were two strains of thought running through his mind. The strain of patriotism came from his father, who would support his country whatever it might do. The other and more sympathetic strain of hatred of all forms of violence came from his half-Jewish mother, who feared Nazism on account of its fanatical racism and vicious excesses. Although Albrecht was much closer to his mother and respected her outlook much more than that of his father, he had submitted to his father's influence, contrary to his mother's advice. He became Hess's personal adviser and by mid-1934 was installed by Hess in the Dienstelle Ribbentrop, a Nazi Foreign Affairs Bureau, under the control of Hess as the head of the Nazi Party.

As a part-Jewish person in a country which discriminated against all Jews, Albrecht Haushofer was not prepared to fight against Nazi discrimination, and run the risk of being dropped by Hess and whisked into a concentration camp. Instead he was bending over backwards to make himself acceptable as a loyal German subject, in the hope that he might mitigate the effect of Nazi racial policy.

In the spring of 1934 he wrote a laboured and cautiously worded memorandum for Hess: 'Ideas for a differentiating Solution of the Non-Aryan Problem', in which he wished to prevent discrimination against all Jews in Germany, by suggesting an annexe to the Civil Service Law of April 1933. He argued that there were Jews who should be regarded as Germans, and exceptions made in their case. Broadly speaking his suggestions would have given to established German Jewry the rights of citizenship, but not to those Jews who had immigrated into Germany within the last few decades. It may well be that he thought that this was as far as he dared go in suggesting an easing of the 'anti-semitic' legislation.

In 1933 there were about half a million Jews living within the Reich, and about one-fifth of them did not possess German citizenship. All of them were subject to discrimination after April 1933. Albrecht Haushofer in his proposals suggested that approximately two-fifths of the Jewish population in Germany, which incidentally

Summer 1935. Albrecht Haushofer in Ribbentrop's garden in Berlin. Right to left: Prince Wittgenstein, Albrecht Haushofer, Abetz (Ambassador in Occupied France between 1940 and 1944) and an unknown Frenchman (extreme left) (Martin Haushofer)

included his mother's family, should be exempted from the Civil Service Laws and should be accepted as Germans, while the other three-fifths of German Jewry, that is more than 300,000 persons, would be excluded from the rights of citizenship. Haushofer was engaged in special pleading on behalf of those in a similar predicament to himself, and he gave a brief summary of the document which he wrote for Hess a year later in a letter to his father, dated 14 January 1935:

> I have the impression that in the near future a decision in principle on the State Citizenship Act will be forth-coming in the Reich Ministry of the Interior. (Remarks of Frick, confidential information from the Ministry.) What matters . . . is the ultimate finding of a form for the exceptions deemed necessary.

Enclosure:

Should in the near future an ultimate form of non-Aryan Law in the scope of a state citizenship legislation of the Reich Ministry of the Interior ensue, it has to be examined whether the existing rules of the Civil Servants Act could not be made more flexible by a permissive provision. Such provision could look as follows. . . .

In special cases persons, who according to the Act . . . are non-Aryans and in respect of whom none of the existing saving clauses are applicable can also be recognised as Germans. Such a recognition can be granted:

(a)   in the case of children of war participants (perhaps in the case of children of holders of high war decoration);

(b)   in the case of persons who can prove that all their non-Aryan ancestors were domiciled in the present Reich territory since 1815;

44

(c)   in the case of persons who are of non-Aryan descent only in respect of one parent or grandparent, if it can be proved that among their non-Aryan ancestors of the first to the third generation there are personalities who have deserved well of the German people.

Such recognition should be granted:

(1) in cases of persons, where instances (a) (b) and (c) apply simultaneously;

(2) in cases of persons, whose recognition as Germans is proposed by one of the highest Reich authorities or by the leadership of the National Socialist German Workers Party. . . .

It is not known whether Hess reviewed with any seriousness the document which Albrecht Haushofer had previously written for him. Certainly it had no effect. Hess had no hesitation in signing the Nuremberg Race Laws and the Reich Citizenship Law. These laws dismissed all persons of Jewish origin from public office, the only exceptions being those very few like Albrecht Haushofer who were directly protected by the Nazi leadership and who were considered to be temporarily indispensable.

Albrecht Haushofer was not technically a member of the Nazi Party, but he was compromising with Nazism. He might have argued and probably did argue that it was better to save some people from discrimination, and he may have intervened personally on behalf of Jews whom he knew. Even so, these attempts were hardly more than specks of dust in a flood. In any case he was working for Hess, who was helping to direct the flow of the Nazi tide.

THREE

Personal Adviser: 1934

Albrecht Haushofer appeared to be only a lecturer in Political Geography in Berlin, but in fact behind the scenes he saw a lot of Hess, and acted as the latter's personal adviser, his policy being 'Let us educate our masters'. He gave advice to Hess on a large range of topics, three of the most important being the position of unpopular persons in the Reich, matters relating to Volksdeutsch activity with Germans outside the Reich, and Germany's relations with foreign countries, especially with Britain and the U.S.A.

On 24 August 1933 Albrecht wrote to Hess asking that Nazi threats to the life of former Chancellor Bruening should cease:

> ... A very delicate matter ... I now learn that a personality, who lives completely withdrawn in the homeland, but has still got a very great name abroad, H[einric]h B[ruenin]g, has to fear for his personal safety. ... I need not say what reactions a personal accident to B[ruening] would have abroad – Could you take care of internal restraint?

This letter may well have saved Bruening's life; and on 7 September 1933 Albrecht Haushofer wrote to Hess: 'For your intervention *in re* B. sincere thanks!'

Albrecht also tried to exert influence in Volksdeutsch affairs, in which his father and Hess were deeply involved. On 8 October 1933 he wrote to his father: 'The form of the supreme control for German nationality questions established by you in co-operation with Rudolf Hess appears to me decidedly hopeful.' On 14 October the Volksdeutsch Council appointed by Hess had its first meeting under the chairmanship of Karl Haushofer, and Albrecht became his father's representative in Berlin.

Albrecht also acted as Hess's representative on a number of occasions. Between 18 and 19 June 1934 he went as the representative of the Volksdeutsch Council to Danzig in order to induce German groups in Poland to accept a joint programme – the Zopot Agreement – and then reported back to Hess. On 19 September 1934 he arranged the first meeting between Hess and Henlein, the leader of the Sudeten German Party. It is even thought that from 1935 onwards Hitler based some of his formulations in Volksdeutsch politics on statements submitted to him by Hess and prepared by Albrecht Haushofer.

Through Hess, Albrecht attempted to settle disputes between the Volksdeutsch Council and other aggressively Nazi organisations such as the Hitler Jugend, the Ausland Organisation of the N.S.D.A.P. under Gauleiter Bohle and the S.S. under Himmler. Albrecht was opposed to Gleichschaltung or co-ordination under the Third Reich's regime, as he did not want Volksdeutsch work in countries outside Germany to be converted into Nazi Fifth Columnist activity. For this reason he attempted to resist the pressures on the V.D.A. from Nazi sources, and on 3 November 1933 he wrote to his father: 'There is no harm in your energetically intervening once again to prevent hotheads and intriguers in the Hitler Jugend from smashing up the Overseas German Youth Movement. . . .'

On 20 November 1933 Albrecht again wrote to his father, mentioning that it was difficult in a totalitarian regime for the leaders to discriminate between accurate information and false propaganda.

> I again have an appointment in the next few days with our friend Rudolf Hess. . . .
> Generally the problem of how to learn the truth is very much more burning for the leadership
> of an absolutist state than for that of a liberal one. . . .

Haushofer feared that even if Hess did learn the truth his power to act independently of Hitler was negligible, and that Hess did not have as much influence with Hitler as he had had before the Nazis had come to power. After a meeting with Hess, he wrote: 'Hess gives the impression of being full of goodwill, but I do not have the impression that this will suffice.' Yet Albrecht remained willing to collaborate with him, and in the spring of 1934 he wrote, to his father: 'Our great friend Hess is really a blessing. I recently saw him for a short while and had a pleasant discussion with him on all kinds of topics.' In contrast he wrote to his mother on the same day as though he were apologising for himself:

> The political volcano, yes I understand how you see it. But against this, without the worth of
> our friend, who is a constant source of solace amidst all the unpleasantness, we would have
> been entirely excluded, and neither insectology nor Etruscology would have saved us from
> being evicted.

He allowed himself to be caught up in abstractions, which blanketed his mind against the inhumanities inherent in Nazism. He wrote of Hess: 'There is a strange charm in his personality; whenever he is there, a friendly veil falls over all the grey and black of the present.'

Still Albrecht could see that the V.D.A. was gradually being Nazified, and that the Volksdeutsch Council, under his father, as the only relatively moderating influence, was losing its grip. In June 1934 Karl Haushofer, acting with Albrecht's approval, warned Hess that if the Volksdeutsch Council could no longer have control over the Volksdeutsch outside Europe, there would be severe repercussions in the U.S.A. and the British Dominions. On 15 August 1934 Albrecht Haushofer wrote to his father that Bohle's activities at the head of the Nazi Ausland Organisation would stir up hatred for the Germans in foreign countries:

> You can tell our friend Hess without hesitation that I too would have told him that we shall
> get a nasty foreign political swarm of wasps about our ears, if we give the all-clear to Bohle. . . .

The dispute with Bohle arose over his refusal to acknowledge the difference between Volksdeutschen (persons of German ethnic origin, but citizens of other countries) and Reichsdeutschen (German citizens living abroad). The Volksdeutschen came under the jurisdiction of Karl Haushofer and the Reichsdeutschen under that of Bohle, and Bohle was attempting to extend his own power, much to the irritation of both Haushofers. On 18 January 1935 Albrecht wrote to his father, referring to the latter's impending discussion with Hess on the possibilities of limiting the ambitious movements of Bohle:

Hitler and Hess redrawing the map of Europe. Standing on the left is Ernst Hanfstaengl, who later fled to Canada, and stooping over the table is Ribbentrop (W. G. Fitzgerald)

. . . Our superior will not get peace either, unless he puts Bohle in his place. . . .
P.S. The fact that our relationship to Ribbentrop . . . is excellent, is yet another indication as to where the source of the discord lies.

Soon after Hess told Bohle to restrict his attentions to Reichsdeutschen. Even so the Volksdeutsch Council did not succeed in co-ordinating Volksdeutsch organisations and Hess decided to reactivate it. During 1935 the Volksdeutsch Council disappeared, and soon after, in 1936, the Volksdeutsch Centre, with which the Haushofers were also connected took over the functions of the Volksdeutsch Council. This centre was a Party office established by Hess with the intention that it should co-ordinate all Volksdeutsch agencies. From the outset Bohle and the Nazi Ausland Organisation were hostile; Himmler and the S.S. were more so.

In December 1936 Karl Haushofer wrote to Hess pointing out that the substitution of S.S. and Gestapo officers for other men in the V.D.A. would have an effect of far-reaching proportions, and he suggested that Hess should obtain a personal decision from the Fuehrer. But unknown to the Professor General, Hitler had already decided to centralise control over subsidies for Volksdeutsch organisations and it is likely that Hess had received instructions which directly contradicted Haushofer's warnings. At any rate in early 1937 the Volksdeutsch Centre was superseded by a new and sinister organisation which had erupted on to the scene.

This was the Volksdeutsche Mittelstelle, V.O.M.I. (the Centre for Racial Germans), and it was controlled by one of Himmler's minions, S.S. Obergruppenführer Lorenz. In 1936 Hitler had decided that the alleged grievances of the Volksdeutschen in Austria, the Czech Sudetenland and Poland should be exploited. To do this it was necessary to have effective control over the various Ausland Organisations, and Himmler was the right man for the job as far as Hitler was concerned. 1937 was an important year for Hess and the Haushofers, for after the creation of V.O.M.I. effective control over the Volksdeutsch passed from Hess to Himmler. The overall charge in Volksdeutsch affairs still remained with Hess for a few more years, but from 1937 on the real power lay with the Reichsführer S.S. It soon became apparent that Himmler was not slow to organise the German minorities outside the Reich through V.O.M.I., so that these minorities might serve as useful pawns in any Nazi military action for extra Lebensraum.

Albrecht Haushofer was not unaware of what was happening around him, and he felt that his only security lay in serving as a useful adviser to Hess, in return for which Hess continued to protect him. On 27 March 1935 Hess sent Albrecht a copy of a letter from a Frau Schultz who was complaining about the praise given to Albrecht Haushofer's scientific work. She objected in particular to a statement Albrecht had made about Hitler's role in the Beerhall Putsch:

> On the occasion of the fiftieth anniversary of the Geographical Society in 1932 he [Albrecht Haushofer] was a guest in our house. On that occasion he declared that the Fuehrer had cowardly forsaken his comrades in front of the Feldhernhalle in 1923 and had thought only of his own personal safety. . . .
>
> I am at any time prepared to be personally answerable for the above.
>
> Heil Hitler!
> Yours faithfully,
> H. Schultz.

Hess wrote to Albrecht: 'I should be grateful to you for information as to what I can reply to this. With German salutation!' No doubt Hess was given a 'suitable' answer.

One of the main fields in which Albrecht Haushofer gave advice to Hess was on the subject of Germany's foreign relations with the Anglo-Saxon countries. On 23 August 1933 he wrote a report for Hess on an interview which he had had with Ambassador Dodd of the U.S.A. to Germany. Evidently Albrecht Haushofer foresaw the possible murder of Dollfuss, Chancellor of Austria, which he hoped to prevent:

> I have just returned from a lengthy talk with Ambassador Dodd. He tells me that he will personally do everything to effect an appeasing influence on his Government as well as on London. . . .
>
> One sentence of the talk I must quote to you literally. After having given an assurance that he would do everything to prevent or to suppress incidents, he said: 'Of course the Austrian thing can flare up any moment, and then no help that I can give will be of avail.'

Dodd was referring to the possibility of an attempt by the Nazis to annex Austria by military action, and it was an incident on 25 July 1934 which brought home to Albrecht Haushofer the hypocrisy of his position.

Both Hitler and Hess had wanted to annex Austria at the first available opportunity and plans were made either with the direct approval of Hess as Hitler's deputy or with his connivance. In view of Hess's proximity to Hitler and Himmler, and to the Ausland Organisations which had extensive contacts in Austria, and in view of the mass of information which was accumulated in the Nazi Party's headquarters at the Brown House in Munich, it is inconceivable that Hess was unaware of what was going to happen.

49

At noon on 25 July 1934 about 150 men of the S.S. Standarte 89, wearing Austrian uniforms, burst into the Chancellery in Vienna and broke into Chancellor Dollfuss's study. Dollfuss knew what they were about and dashed towards a door from his study to a secret passage which had just been blocked up. As he scrabbled desperately with his fingers at the door he was shot down, and as he lay in agony the S.S. refused to allow him either a doctor or a priest: they stood over him watching him choke to death in his own blood. At about 6.00 p.m. Dollfuss died and Austrian forces under Dr Kurt von Schuschnigg recovered control. Some thirteen of the S.S. who had murdered Dollfuss, including Planetta (one of their leaders, who claimed to have fired the fatal shot), were arrested and later executed.

Two days later, on 27 July, Albrecht Haushofer wrote to his parents from Berlin:

> I sometimes ask myself how long we shall be able to carry the responsibility, which we bear and which gradually begins to turn into historical guilt or, at least, into complicity. . . . But all of us are, after all, in a situation of conflicting obligations, from which at best fate can find a way out, and we have to carry on working even when the task has become completely hopeless.
> And now I must try to finish my geopolitics report. How, I do not know. In the evening of the day before yesterday I heard father's radio talk; I must admit it was very sinister to me to hear his sarcastic remark on Dollfuss's accumulation of offices while on the adjoining wavelength it was announced that he was dead. . . . There will be much violent dying and nobody knows when lightning will strike one's own house.

In normal circumstances Albrecht would have had no reservations about working

Major General Professor Karl Haushofer was not a member of the Nazi Party, but as President of the German Ausland organisations, he attended a memorial meeting for those who lost their lives in the Nazi movement (Martin Haushofer)

for his country as an official. Like most Germans he wanted to see a strong German leadership achieve a modification of the frontiers imposed on Germany by the Treaty of Versailles. In his outlook he has been accurately described as a 'national-liberal-conservative' and at first his attitude towards National Socialism remained ambiguous. He hesitated between acknowledgment of Hitler's effectiveness in restoring German prosperity and self-respect, and a reserve which was developing into a deep-rooted dislike of the methods of the regime. His reservations were on the grounds that its policy was racist and that its leaders were prepared to kill anyone whom they regarded as standing in their way.

He knew that, but for his father's great friendship with Hess, he would have been discriminated against along with others who were of partly Jewish origin. As a person existing under the protecting hand of Hess he was in far too vulnerable a position to protest openly against anti-Semitism and other forms of racism. He thought that any open opposition would be trampled underfoot by the brutality of the Third Reich, and therefore he was compromising. But Albrecht had no love for his leaders, and shortly before the Night of the Long Knives he had a conversation with Rudolf Pechel and Edgar Jung. Pechel, a well-known journalist, who was later sent to a concentration camp, reported that Albrecht 'condemned National Socialism and its leaders in such violent terms that Jung remarked that his own and my hatred were puerile in comparison'. In reality Albrecht was doing everything he could to camouflage himself in a world which he viewed with many misgivings. Jung was less skilful in concealing his real views and as a result was murdered by the S.S. on 30 June 1934.

Some time later Albrecht told Steinacher of the V.D.A. that Germany was nearing the abyss with ever-increasing speed, that Hess was a weakling, that Bormann held all threads in his hand and that he 'personally felt like a swindler in the Reich of the S.S.' And still he was allowing himself to be drawn more and more into political activity by Hess.

In spite of his hostility to Nazism, Albrecht thought that with his intellect and ability there was just a remote chance that he could influence and possibly 'manage' Hess and Ribbentrop, and through them Hitler, in the interests of peaceful German development. He often used to say that 'Germany could well do with a Talleyrand', and he may well have fancied himself in such a role. He probably imagined that he might be able to outwit Hitler and the Nazi leadership in much the same way that Talleyrand had doublecrossed Napoleon. Albrecht, however, had a disability in Hitler's eyes which Talleyrand did not have for Napoleon. Albrecht was of partly Jewish origin in a country whose leadership was determined to treat Jews as deadly enemies, and he could not avoid being regarded as an object of suspicion in official circles.

He saw the clouds of war gathering on the horizon and wrote to his mother on 8 August 1934 saying he believed he might have to face a choice of emigration, suicide, death, or staying behind and compromising himself to such an extent that life would become unbearable.

> There are historical necessities and I do not believe enough in miracles to expect that just in our lifetime that which has again and again been proved through millennia of human history should become invalid. Actually, nobody has ever reproached me for lacking the courage to foresee developments.
>
> I also see in this the possibilities of my own fate very clearly: there are many possibilities, but among them only few that are 'positive'. Here is a small selection of what is possible:
>
> A violent end from outside by chance or by intention;
>
> Economic decline to a point where life stops;
>
> Internal destruction through permanent time-serving;

A voluntary exit.
All that is within. . . .

He also feared that geopolitics would be used as the intellectual excuse for German expansion, not just in areas where Germans were in the preponderance, but in Europe as a whole, and he dreaded the prospect of another war:

When I then look into our geopolitics, I sometimes shudder at the way we take 'We' in the greater sense and 'We' in the smaller sense. You will, no doubt, understand what I mean.

He had hopes that the regime might eventually slow down and even abandon ideas of war, but these were very distant hopes. Besides, he was a man in continual conflict with himself, and for as long as he worked for the Nazi regime his inner conflicts were insoluble.

FOUR

Missions for Hitler and Ribbentrop: 1936–7

Hans Jacobsen wrote of Albrecht Haushofer that he 'accepted secret diplomatic missions, so that many called him *"eminence grise"* and many admired his sharp intellect while missing the human warmth, although the latter certainly was not entirely absent in him'.

During 1933 or at the latest 1934 Hess had put Albrecht Haushofer in touch with the former champagne salesman, Joachim von Ribbentrop, who was rapidly rising in the Nazi hierarchy. Hess had Albrecht appointed as an unofficial adviser to the Dienststelle Ribbentrop, a bureau under the immediate control of Ribbentrop and subject to the supervision of Hess. Albrecht was willing to work as an agent for Hess and as adviser to Ribbentrop, as he expected that in this way his chances of influencing foreign policy would be greater than in the German Foreign Office. In early 1935 he wrote a memorandum for Hess, praising the Nazi authorities whose power was used to offset the scarcity of ideas and lack of activity in the Foreign Ministry.

At the time at which Albrecht wrote this document Hitler wanted to short-circuit the German Foreign Ministry in vital negotiations with other countries, because he did not sufficiently trust its diplomats. He thus encouraged Hess and Ribbentrop to recruit a few specialists who could and would operate as the agents of a bureau which would soon become the incubator of Nazi foreign policy.

In April 1936, just after the remilitarisation of the Rhineland, Albrecht submitted a memorandum entitled 'Political Possibilities in the South East' in which he had a number of suggestions to make in relation to Czechoslovakia. He suggested that the Czechs looked upon the Germans as their principal enemy, and because the Czech nation felt itself to be endangered in the event of war the issue whether they could come to an agreement with Germany was occupying their minds as a matter of urgency. He put forward five proposals as a basis for negotiations:

1. The conclusion of a ten-year non-aggression pact.
2. A German-Czechoslovak settlement under which Germany would not raise the question of frontier revision in return for which total cultural autonomy for the Sudeten Germans would be granted.
3. Expansion of German-Czech trade.
4. The conclusion of a 'newspaper peace'.
5. Attempt to put forward joint proposals on the Hapsburg question.

53

May 1935. Major General Professor Karl Haushofer and Rudolf Hess with the King of Sweden in Stockholm (Martin Haushofer)

Albrecht Haushofer hoped that negotiations would lead to the granting of concessions for Germans living in the Czech Sudetenland, would reduce the influence of France and Russia in Czechoslovakia, and would pave the way for German development along peaceful lines.

The proposals in this memorandum interested Ribbentrop and Hitler, and in the autumn of 1936 Albrecht and the aristocrat Graf zu Trauttmannsdorff were chosen as possible envoys should secret negotiations with President Beneš of Czechoslovakia materialise. Trauttmannsdorff, acting on Ribbentrop's instructions, asked Dr Mastný, the Czech Minister in Berlin, whether talks under the name of 'cultural agreement' would be acceptable to President Beneš. The reply came back that under certain circumstances direct talks with Hitler's envoys could proceed. Trauttmannsdorff and Albrecht Haushofer were ordered to conduct the talks in secrecy, and they were strictly forbidden to have any contact with the German diplomatic mission in Czechoslovakia and with the German Foreign Minister, von Neurath.

On 18 October 1936 a meeting took place between Albrecht Haushofer and Mastný. Albrecht advanced the first four of the five proposals set out in his memorandum for Ribbentrop. Mastný went a long way to meet these demands. He admitted that the remilitarisation of the Rhineland had altered the basic tenets of Czech policy, and that while treaty obligations to Russia and France could not be disowned, they should not be interpreted with too much exactitude. Dr Mastný went so far as to accept that Czechoslovakia's borders would only be secure if steps were taken in Czechoslovakia to recognise the German nationality border, and both Mastný and Haushofer spoke about Henlein, the leader of the Sudeten German Party, in an approving manner.

Finally Mastný requested that the strictest secrecy be maintained on the German side, and asked whether Haushofer might be willing to travel to Prague to have a private and informal discussion with President Beneš. Perhaps the Czech Government felt that their Russian friends were not wholly reliable allies and that in the event of a Nazi onslaught on Czechoslovakia, the Russians might fail to come to their aid. On 13 and 14 November talks took place in great secrecy at the Hradschin Castle between President Beneš and his Foreign Minister, Krofta, on the Czech side and Albrecht Haushofer and Trauttmannsdorff on the German. Like Mastný, Beneš and Krofta were prepared to go a long way to placate the Germans, and Albrecht Haushofer's five proposals were answered as follows:

1. President Beneš stated that he was prepared to negotiate a treaty of non-aggression with the Reich. He had been friendly with Germany in the past, and wished to stress in the strongest terms that the Soviet Union could not prevent Czechoslovakia from having an accommodation with Germany.
2. On the subject of cultural autonomy for the Sudeten Germans, President Beneš, while having no admiration for Henlein, wished to satisfy the Sudeten Germans, and asked Haushofer to talk to Krofta. Beneš said that he could take up this question again when Haushofer next visited Czechoslovakia, and it emerged that the Czech Government was in favour of cultural autonomy but hostile to regional autonomy.
3. President Beneš wished to increase trade between Germany and Czechoslovakia.
4. As for a 'Newspaper Peace', such an agreement was desired. An undertaking was given that in the case of a German-Czech understanding, activity by German emigrés in Prague against the Third Reich would not be tolerated.
5. President Beneš repeated his opposition to the restoration of the Hapsburg dynasty in Austria.

Albrecht Haushofer returned to Germany, kept Himmler informed through S.S. General Karl Wolff and prepared his report for Hitler, listing German aims under two columns 'the Attainable and the Unattainable'. The 'Attainable' objectives were numbered:

1. A non-aggression pact between Germany and Czechoslovakia.
2. A neutral Czechoslovakia in the event of a Russian attack on the Reich, possibly arising out of the involvement of Germany and Russia in the Spanish Civil War.
3. A joint policy on the Hapsburg issue.
4. A Press peace and a reduction of the hostile activities of German emigrés in Czechoslovakia.
5. An agreement to increase trade between the two countries bestowing better treatment upon areas in the Sudetenland which had been adversely affected by the Depression.
6. An agreement to give cultural autonomy to the Sudeten Germans and to improve their status.

In general an agreement between the two countries would consolidate German influence in the Danube valley at the expense of French influence, would render a Russian attack on Germany more unlikely and would make a favourable impression in Britain. It might even be possible to make similar agreements with other countries in south-eastern Europe, such as Yugoslavia and Romania.

Albrecht Haushofer argued, however, that if an agreement with President Beneš was not concluded, the Czech Government might believe that the Third Reich's intentions towards Czechoslovakia were sinister. This would lead to the opposite of what was intended, and would strengthen Czechoslovakia's alliances with Russia and France. Therefore, if for some reason the Fuehrer did not wish to conclude an agreement, the talks should be continued and then be abruptly ended by raising the demands of Henlein's Sudeten German Party in the Czech Sudetenland.

From the way in which Hitler renumbered Haushofer's proposals, there is reason to believe that a neutralised Czechoslovakia, a Press peace, a reduction in the unfriendly activities of German emigrés and an agreement to double German-Czech trade appealed to him. For the time being economic advantages might be utilised. But Hitler's most important reaction – indeed his only action of vital importance here – revealed his true intentions. He put a red line through Haushofer's first suggestion for a non-aggression pact; the obvious reason being that Hitler had already decided to smash Czechoslovakia.

Furthermore, Hitler put no number opposite Haushofer's sixth aim. It was not his desire to improve the position of the Sudeten Germans. Rather he wished to exploit their grievances and use them against the Czechs.

Hitler wanted to neutralise Czechoslovakia in order to make her an easier prey, and so, as one would expect, Albrecht Haushofer was ordered to make another journey to Prague. On 18 December 1936 he and Trauttmannsdorff again met Beneš, and the conversations centred around the Czech treatment of Germans in the Sudetenland. In a handwritten note, 'Outcome of Prague', Albrecht wrote that President Beneš understood that unless the Sudeten Germans received more favourable treatment, there could be no improvement in German-Czech relations.

On 3 to 4 January 1937, Trauttmannsdorff went to Prague by himself, and after making enquiries drew up a list of the 'minimum demands' of the Sudeten Germans, which ought as he saw it to be acceptable to the Czech Government. On 11 January 1937 he sent the draft of a possible treaty to Albrecht and this was taken to Hitler. The principal piece of new information was that President Benes did not want a non-aggression pact, but rather an agreement based on the German-Czech Treaty of Arbitration signed on 16 October 1925 at Locarno. President Beneš was in essence offering:

1. That each country should respect the other's Government.
2. That both nations would collaborate in opposing the Communist bloc.
3. That attacks in the Press by one country against the other should cease.
4. That the activities of German emigrés in Czechoslovakia would be suppressed when hostile to Germany.
5. That there should be trade negotiations.
6. That there should be mutual assistance in border relations.

These points were put before Hitler, and on 19 January 1937 Albrecht wrote to his father giving an account of his interview. His words depicted the arrogance of an intellectual who thought that he could manipulate a dictator. He was flattered that Hitler chose to receive him well. In his correspondence with his parents he used Japanese code-names for certain persons, of which 'Tomodachi', meaning friend, was used for Hess, 'Fukon', meaning I will not deviate, for Ribbentrop, and 'O'Daijin', meaning Master Great Spirit, for Hitler.

> My own lecture at O'Daijin was this time really a lecture. He listened and asked intelligent questions. The final result was pleasing. Personally he was charming, in his factual attitude more peaceful, more superior than before Christmas. What I notice again and again with him – at least at those times when he adapts himself to the individual and not to mass meetings – is the powerful application of 'commonsense' in the English sense, which occasionally finds excellent formulation.
>
> The dangerous mood of war of December is at least for the moment banished. . . . O'Daijin is now in the mountains, will consider everything once again and will send for me when he is back again. I am naturally anxious to know the result. . . .

However Hitler never followed up the negotiations as Albrecht Haushofer would have liked, and the latter was instructed to let the negotiations drag on monotonously, which meant that Hitler wanted the talks to be terminated. President Beneš understood the position and wrote in his *Memoirs*:

> In the spring of 1937 Goebbels began a systematic and continuous campaign of hatred and revenge against Czechoslovakia, thus showing that Berlin, having failed to persuade us to accept its proposed agreement, had embarked on different tactics: agitation, terror and deliberately planned violence. No definitive reply ever came from Berlin, either then or later.

Haushofer had attempted to divert Hitler's policy into peaceful channels, and yet in spite of all his hopes he had merely served as a willing tool. On 20 April 1937 he wrote to his mother: 'Desires for the future? We shall be lucky if nothing happens. I do not want the next European disaster to find you still alive; nor do I wish it for father.'

In November 1936 the Anti-Comintern Pact between the Third Reich, Italy and Japan was consummated, and not long afterwards Albrecht Haushofer was sent by Ribbentrop on another mission, this time to Japan. His reports had impressed Hess, Ribbentrop and Hitler, and they wanted to be kept well informed, as well as to strengthen the German-Japanese alliance.

In any case Albrecht was suitable for another reason. His father was well known in Japan, his geopolitical writings being very popular. Many of the Japanese were fascinated by geopolitics and thought of themselves as a dynamic space-conquering people at the heart of an expanding empire. Besides, Karl Haushofer, in his writings and personal intervention had played a part in the formation of the alliance between Germany and Japan.

At the end of July 1937 Albrecht's journey to Japan and China took him via North America, and while he was in the Far East he developed a great sympathy for China and her culture. At the end of August 1937 a report was sent by him to Ribbentrop on the war between China and Japan, and he ended by saying: 'In the event of a long confrontation and of a sharp over-straining of Japanese forces together with chaos in China a situation might arise in East Asia which in every respect must be unwelcome to German policies.' He did not want Germany to be too closely involved with Japan's plans for military aggression. In September 1937 he sent another report to Ribbentrop after a short stay in the war zone surrounding Tientsin in China. In his accompanying letter he expressed sympathy for China, as though China were a possible German partner in the Far East. His actual report does not survive, but it would appear likely that he did all he could to diminish the value of a German-Japanese alliance, and advised Ribbentrop to preach moderation to the Japanese.

Haushofer left Japan, and passed his reports in December 1937 to S.S. General Karl Wolff for Himmler, addressed to the Army's General Staff, to the Navy and to the Air Ministry. On his return to Germany he had an interview with Hitler and Hess. They travelled from Munich to Freilassing in Hitler's special train, and discussed points of political interest arising out of his journey. Hitler again received him well, and listened with interest, asking a lot of perceptive questions. However, Hitler was not to be dissuaded from a pro-Japanese policy, hostile to China, and told Albrecht Haushofer that he had decided to place his 'bet on the victors'.

He must have regarded Haushofer as a useful agent and a well-informed expert supported by Hess, but it is unlikely that he trusted him to any significant extent. Conversely, while Hitler may have trusted Hess and Ribbentrop implicitly, it is most unlikely that he regarded them as experts in the same category as Albrecht Haushofer.

Hitler had good reason for not trusting Albrecht. At no time in his life did Albrecht

25 March 1935. Hitler gives his portrait to Lord Simon. Albrecht Haushofer is standing behind Hitler and his interpreter, Schmidt (Heinrich Hoffman, Munich)

become a member of the Nazi Party, and in order to avoid arousing the suspicion of the Nazi leadership he had to tread warily in trying to achieve German aims through peaceful evolution. A typical example of the veiled way in which he expressed himself was given late in 1937 when he gave a lecture in the House of Airmen in Berlin about his Far Eastern travels. At the end of his talk a young S.S. man demanded an explanation as to why it was that the German Foreign Office of which Albrecht Haushofer was the representative had been unable to prevent the outbreak of the Sino-Japanese War. Professor Rolf Italiaander described the reply:

> Tired, heavy and resigned, Haushofer got up. Had this stupid youth not understood what the gist and essence of his lecture had been? Had he not been sufficiently explicit? . . . He said in a quiet, slow and ironical voice: 'Japan and China have, as is known, thousand-year-old cultures. These are best shown in an incomparably distinguished porcelain. I would like to see the European who would be willing to play the bull in a china shop here. I, for one, would certainly refuse.'

Yet in spite of his finer feelings Albrecht knew that the negotiations for a non-aggression pact with Czechoslovakia had petered out, and that his reports from Japan, far from moderating the Japanese, had merely served as useful information for cementing the German-Japanese Axis. When all was said and done he knew that his efforts had not met with success.

FIVE

The Olympic Games, the Luftwaffe and the British: 1936–8

It was in relation to Britain and the British that Albrecht Haushofer's most important work lay. He frequently visited London, which he undoubtedly enjoyed, and as early as 1932 he had been writing reports on Britain for the German Foreign Ministry. In November 1934 he wrote home: 'The impression of London remains the same; this tradition and all this life. What a pity that in the Bulow era we missed a partnership. This is now gone and past.'

From 1934 onwards he forwarded information on Britain to Hess and he was at hand in the background when British politicians visited Germany. He was present on 30 January 1935 when Hess, Ribbentrop and Field Marshal von Blomberg had a discussion with Lord Lothian on armaments control and also on 26 March when Hitler gave a dinner in Berlin for Anthony Eden and Lord Simon, which was attended by Hess, Ribbentrop, Goering, Goebbels, Von Neurath, the foreign minister, and Schacht, the finance minister.

In April 1935 Haushofer wrote for the *Zeitschrift für Geopolitik* a 'Report from the Atlantic World' showing that he believed it was absolutely essential for Germany to live in a state of peaceful coexistence with Britain:

> The final decision on the fate of Europe – as was the case at the turn of the century – is in the hands of Britain. It must be remembered that the decision about the outbreak of war was not made in 1914 but a decade earlier when the British Empire and the German Empire, after vain attempts to establish a common course, began to drift apart. If one asks for the final reasons, one arrives at the mutual distrust for which the language of neither part found a suitable expression . . .
>
> One thing has indeed changed within a generation; while during the last years of Queen Victoria's reign, public opinion in Britain believed – and perhaps rightly so at that time – that Britain could afford to stay in isolation and not to engage in Europe's political games if these displeased her, this attitude is now of the past. Britain now knows that she cannot dodge European conflicts once these break out.

He was very anxious to avoid another German confrontation with Britain and on occasions his German friends would reproach him for compromising himself by working for Ribbentrop in Britain. Rolf Italiaander criticised him to his face, saying that it was embarrassing to see a man of his calibre collaborating with a vain charlatan like

15 July 1935. Hitler receives Members of the British Legion. Major General Professor Karl Haushofer was given honorary life membership (The Times)

Ribbentrop. Albrecht was silent and then reached for the thesis which he had written: 'Necessities and Aims – Bases of a German Policy in Europe', and read aloud one page:

> In all matters politic there are minima and maxima of the attainable. To know these limits is the iron duty of the political man. . . . . Whatever lies outside the attainable – in a wishful dreamland – is reserved for children and prophets. . . . We believe that any explosion in Europe's present situation would be very dangerous for its originator or instigator . . . Thus there is nothing else left but an attempt to reach an understanding even in questions with regard to which a revenge would seem to be much nearer human nature.
>
> There is nothing more stupid than untimely heroism. But, equally, there is nothing more stupid than an unpremeditated understanding; perhaps the granting of an advantage without any return service. One has to know what one can demand and what one can offer.
>
> It is mortifying when talking with British politicians to hear much clearer opinions about the Danzig Corridor and the chances of its removal, in comparison with those expressed by German circles who feel the fire burning their finger nails.

In 1936 Albrecht Haushofer's views on Britain assumed a greater importance when Ribbentrop was appointed German ambassador in London. This made it necessary for Albrecht to make trips to London as the agent of Hess and assistant of Ribbentrop. A few weeks after the death of the previous German ambassador in London, von Hoesch, Albrecht saw the German Embassy's public relations officer, Fritz Hesse, in London. Hesse was of the impression that Albrecht had gone to England in order to prepare the

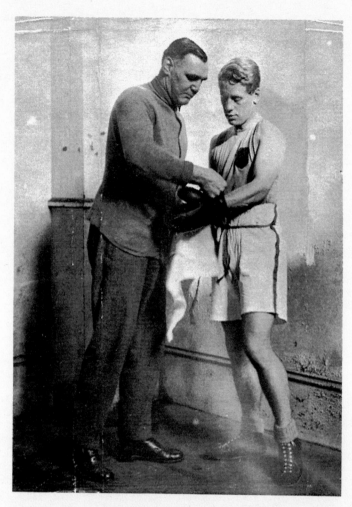

The Marquis of Clydesdale, Scottish Middleweight Boxing Champion,
having his gloves adjusted by the former English Heavyweight Champion,
Dick Smith, before the semi-final of the British Middleweight
*Championship (*The Times*)*

ground for inviting Lloyd George to visit Hitler in Germany, and also to judge how the British had accepted the remilitarisation of the Rhineland. Both Hesse and Haushofer had written reports warning Hitler of the great dangers involved in expanding the Reich through the use of armed force. Albrecht told Hesse that their reports had had a marked effect on Hitler, which was evident to anyone around Hitler when German armed forces marched into the Rhineland.

Albrecht said that at that time Hitler behaved as though he was experiencing the most anxious hours of his life: 'I would have never thought such hysterical fear and such scenes possible had I not seen them myself. If Neurath had not kept on calming him, Hitler would have quit the Rhineland. . . .' Hesse's reaction was: 'Well, that is not too bad; perhaps he will in future abstain from such unilateral actions through which he could

61

provoke a war.' Albrecht agreed that this was also his hope, however great his fears, and he replied,

> It was well that you also induced Ribbentrop to warn Hitler against a continuation of his *coups*. Hitler will keep peace for some time. But, don't forget his mentality. In a year he will only see his success and will declare all warnings stupid, cowardly and pitiful and all warners crooks. He cannot endure having shown himself weak before others. I think that the days of the Foreign Ministry are . . . numbered . . . I believe that peace is secured for the next two years . . . perhaps we shall manage to chain the fuming titan to the rock.

It was not long after this conversation that Albrecht Haushofer came into contact with a group of British M.P.s who were present at the Olympic Games in Berlin in August 1936. In view of what occurred five years later it is necessary to examine subsequent events.

The British M.P.s included Harold Balfour, Jim Wedderburn, Kenneth Lindsay, and the Marquis of Clydesdale, who became the Duke of Hamilton in 1940. Clydesdale, at one time Scottish amateur middleweight boxing champion, became in December 1929 the second youngest M.P. in the House of Commons, having been elected in a by-election. He had a good relationship with both Winston Churchill and Ramsay Macdonald as both of them were interested in aviation. His first meeting with Churchill had been as a

Clydesdale as a young pilot officer in charge of an Air Force guard of honour salutes King George V.
(Elizabeth, Duchess of Hamilton)

Clydesdale as a flight lieutenant introduces Prime Minister, Ramsay Macdonald, to 602 (City of Glasgow) Squadron (Elizabeth, Duchess of Hamilton)

13-year-old boy when Admiral of the Fleet Jackie Fisher had sent him with a message to Churchill just after the Battle of Jutland. At his school corps at Eton he had seen the Royal Flying Corps flying overhead and had thought, 'how much nicer to be in aircraft than a trench'. He joined the Auxiliary Air Force, was soon promoted and before long commanded a Guard of Honour before King George. Five foot seven inches in height, he was physically very strong and athletic in build. On several occasions in London he had been surprised to be mistaken for Lawrence of Arabia. He was a flying instructor in the Auxiliary Air Force, and in 1933 was chosen to be the chief pilot of the expedition to fly over Mount Everest. By then he had become the Commanding Officer of 602 City of Glasgow (Bomber) Squadron. He went to Berlin in August, partly to gain some picture of the direction in which Germany was moving, but mainly to see something of the Luftwaffe.

He was aware of the words of Churchill (whom he knew well in the House of Commons) written in 1935 in the book *Great Contemporaries*:

> We cannot tell whether Hitler will be the man who will once again let loose upon the world another war in which civilisation will irretrievably succumb, or whether he will go down in history as the man who restored honour and peace of mind to the great Germanic nation and brought it back serene, helpful and strong, to the forefront of the European family circle.[1]

63

Clydesdale at Heston Airport, preparing to leave for the Mount Everest Flight Expedition in 1933.
He had been selected as Chief Pilot on account of his flying skills and exceptional physical fitness
(The Times)

The question of whether Germany would choose the path of war was uppermost in his mind as Clydesdale flew his aircraft to Berlin along with his brother Geordie who unlike himself spoke German, and Jim Wedderburn the Parliamentary Under Secretary of State for Scotland.

Clydesdale was of course known primarily as an aviator. Along with his colleagues on the Everest expedition he had written the book *First over Everest*. It contained the sentence: 'A new calling has come into being which is really the spirit of the old pioneers aflame in a new form . . . transport by air, the uninterrupted navigable ocean that comes to the threshold of every man's door.'[2]

Just before arriving for his six day visit to Berlin, he had published with David McIntyre *The Pilot's Book of Everest*. Flying over the world's highest mountain in 1933 had only just been technically possible, when weather conditions were reasonably favourable. They wrote:

> Our expedition was concerned particularly with the science of flight, of geography and exploration. No man can come close to the great peaks without acknowledging a sense of awe, and understanding something of the fascinations they hold . . . We saw the mountain on both occasions in high sunshine when there were few shadows to shroud her mystery. In softer light one might expect to find something of the romance of these enormous masses of rock and ice.

3 April 1933. Clydesdale in the Houston Westland about to be sucked into a downdraught in the direction of the north-east ridge of Mount Everest (Elizabeth, Duchess of Hamilton)

Something of the mystery had been overcome and something of the unknown had been revealed; yet the Mistress of the world remains remote, immense and magnificent. The best that we could bring back was but a faint impression of her dignity and beauty.[3]

The success of the expedition had resulted in worldwide publicity and had been noticed in Germany. The *Central European Times* had written then:

The British flight over Mount Everest is a feat which will stand by itself in the history of Aviation. In point of careful and scientific preparation it is comparable with the Rear Admiral's flight over the South Pole. In point of daring and navigation skills it is only equalled by Lindbergh's crossing of the Atlantic Ocean.

The battle against winds of a force which plain-talking mortals have no conception, against treacherous up and down currents, against cold and lack of oxygen . . . is one which can only tempt men for whom the difficulty of the obstacles is but a call for further effort to overcome it.[4]

Clydesdale was accustomed to flying his own aircraft and some sixteen months before had been involved in an incident in Germany. He had been flying from Basle in Switzerland back to Britain, down the Rhine, and when the weather deteriorated he had decided to land at an aerodrome full of small aircraft. It turned out to be the aerodrome at Mannheim and his presence caused considerable consternation. This was because the aerodrome was neither more nor less than a flying training school for the Luftwaffe which, on 11 February 1935, was being developed in secret.

After an intense interrogation as to what he was doing and where he was going and being kept in a locked room for several hours, he was told that he could go to a hotel and travel on the next day. Since that time, Hitler had announced air parity with Britain and Clydesdale hoped that during his visit to Berlin he would be able to see the Luftwaffe.

The first significant occasion was the Berlin Banquet hosted by von Ribbentrop, the newly appointed ambassador to Britain. Clydesdale had met Ribbentrop a few months earlier during a dinner given by Lord Londonderry and had raised with him the fact that Germany had remilitarised the Rhineland in breach of treaty arrangements. Ribbentrop had replied that the Franco-Soviet Pact had invalidated the Treaty of Locarno and had given Germany the right to station troops up to the French frontier. On 2 May 1936 he wrote to Clydesdale:

If you should come to Germany again, let me know, as I would like to see you. If I should ever come to Scotland I should be very pleased to go and see you. In the meantime we may meet in London again. How is the Everest?[5]

At his banquet on 11 August 1936 there were more than 600 people present, with Clydesdale seated at the table of the German Minister for Labour, Ley. It has been incorrectly assumed, even by historians, that Clydesdale met Hess at the Olympic Games in Berlin. In fact this did not happen. At the Berlin Banquet, Hess was seated at a different table.

Indeed, neither Hess nor Clydesdale ever claimed to have met before the Second World War. Years later in Spandau Prison, Hess told the American Commander, Colonel Eugene Bird:

It is untrue to say that I knew the Duke of Hamilton. I had never met the man, never dined with him. If he was in the same room as I was during the Berlin Olympic Games, we never conversed. I of course knew about him and his flying.

When Bird cross-examined him on a further occasion, Hess stated correctly:

> It was the Haushofers who knew the Duke of Hamilton. Contrary to what books say since I flew, I had never met the man. Maybe I saw him across a room at a reception in Berlin and I certainly knew about him and his flying exploits. When I flew I took Haushofer's visiting card with me to present to him.[6]

All these assertions were corroborated by Clydesdale (or Hamilton as he became) and on 23 August 1980 Wolf Rüdiger Hess wrote to the author:

> I have enquired about your question a few weeks ago in London. My mother told me that indeed your father and mine *did not meet* during the Olympic Games 1936. They did according to remembrance of my mother also not meet at any other occasion before May 1941 in Scotland.[7]

However, Hess did interview one English M.P., Kenneth Lindsay, who wished to know what Hess had meant when he said that King Edward VIII was the only person who could maintain peace in Europe. Hess also welcomed the considerable numbers of those serving on the International Olympic Committee. At a later date he was under the impression that Clydesdale had been in the audience and had been a member of the International Olympic Committee lunching in his house. Baldur von Schirach, Hitler's Youth Leader, recorded in his book *Schirach and Hitler* that Hess did not know the Duke of Hamilton personally. Hess did know that Hamilton had been at the Olympic Games, and he told von Schirach that Hamilton had been at a reception Hess had given for foreign guests.[8] This was clearly a reference to the welcome that Hess had given to the International Olympic Committee.

However, Clydesdale was not a member of the International Olympic Committee and was not present on this occasion. For most of the time at the Olympic Games he was with his brother Geordie Douglas-Hamilton, who was certain that Clydesdale and Hess did not meet.

Clydesdale was present at the special dinner party given by Hitler in honour of Sir Robert Vansittart. It was well known that Vansittart as head of the British Foreign Office had the deepest reservations about Hitler, the Third Reich and the Germans, whom he believed to be preparing for war. Hitler apparently was not only impressed by Vansittart's forceful personality but also intuitively sensed his enmity and went out of his way to be accommodating for the duration of the Olympic Games.

A description of what happened was given by the journalist Ward Price. There were 150 guests present in the State Dining-Room at the rear of the Chancellor's Palace, the three tables bearing large gold candelabra arranged in the shape of a horseshoe. The room had been built out into the garden, and every detail had been approved by Hitler. The room was 120 feet long with six crimson marble pillars twenty feet high, the ceiling being a mosaic of blue and gold arranged in squares, with one large tapestry on the cream-coloured wall.

The guests were first shown into an anteroom to be introduced to Hitler, the British guests being Ward Price, Clydesdale, Lord and Lady Rennell, Lord and Lady Aberdare and Lord Barnaby.[9] Clydesdale did not speak German and Hitler did not speak English so they did not converse, but when he was introduced Clydesdale's impression of Hitler was that he looked very ordinary, just like a little bank clerk. Indeed, Clydesdale found it difficult to appreciate how he could be exercising such a mesmerising hold over the German people.

At this dinner it is certain that Hess was present, and Clydesdale believed in later years that he might have been pointed out to Hess from across the room as the British aviator who had been the first to fly over Mount Everest. Ward Price wrote that he remembered seeing Hess talk to Vansittart.

Yet in spite of the fact that Hess did not meet Clydesdale there was a tenuous and indirect connection between them. Shortly after Clydesdale arrived in Berlin his younger brother David Douglas-Hamilton, who spoke German fluently, appeared saying that he had met an interesting German.

Dr Kurt Hahn, the German of Jewish origin who had founded Gordonstoun School in Scotland, had this to say about David:

> He had worked in a Labour Camp, spoke German with many mistakes but with an astonishingly good accent; in fact I who come from the north of Germany would take him for a Tyrolean.
>
> He won the admiration of the German people for one particular reason. Like so many Englishmen in the past he acquired a love for an oppressed people and made their cause his own – the people of the South Tyrol. He was in close touch with Reut-Nicolussi, the great leader of the South Tyrolean freedom movement. He took considerable risks to acquire an intimate knowledge of local conditions. Throughout his contacts with Germany he pursued by instinct a dual policy: he showed deep sympathy and understanding with the people and at the same time his loathing of Nazi methods.[10]

The German whom David Douglas-Hamilton had met was Albrecht Haushofer. Later on, Clydesdale and some of the other M.P.s met him over dinner and tried to pick his brains. To Clydesdale he appeared as a tall man with a large body and a small head, giving an impression of being ponderous and almost clumsy. He looked middle-aged although he was in fact about thirty-three and he appeared to have a sense of humour, and an extensive knowledge of the history of Britain.[11]

He was a brilliant conversationalist, spoke in English like an Englishman and Clydesdale was impressed by the strength of his intellectual ability. He had never been a member of the Nazi Party and when somebody commented upon the importance attached by the Nazis to being 'Nordic', he tapped his nose, remarking that it was not a Nordic nose. He was reserved when speaking about the Nazi leaders, although he did cause some amusement by mimicking Ribbentrop being jealous of the other Nazi leaders, on the grounds that some of them had belonged to the Nazi Party longer than he. But when the name of Goebbels was mentioned he looked round to see whether anyone was listening, and whispered with a hiss, 'Goebbels is a poisonous little man, who will give you dinner one night and sign your death warrant the next morning'. This was no doubt an indirect reference to Goebbels's attempt to have the Haushofer sons categorised as Jews in 1933, before Hess's protection.

Albrecht Haushofer was told that the important question for the British was whether Germany was bent on a course which would plunge Europe into war, or whether there was yet an alternative prospect. He argued that with modifications to the Treaty of Versailles, Hitler would mellow and would tone down his programme. He mentioned that as well as being a university lecturer, he worked for the German Foreign Office and that he had the ear of Rudolf Hess, who as deputy to Hitler had a certain influence. As far as he was concerned he would do everything humanly possible to moderate German foreign policy.

Albrecht Haushofer introduced Clydesdale to Goering at the latter's party. Goering came across as a forceful personality with a streak of ruthlessness and brutality but not without humour. He threw out his arms saying a word of welcome.

Albrecht proceeded to interpret, and Clydesdale expressed an interest in seeing the

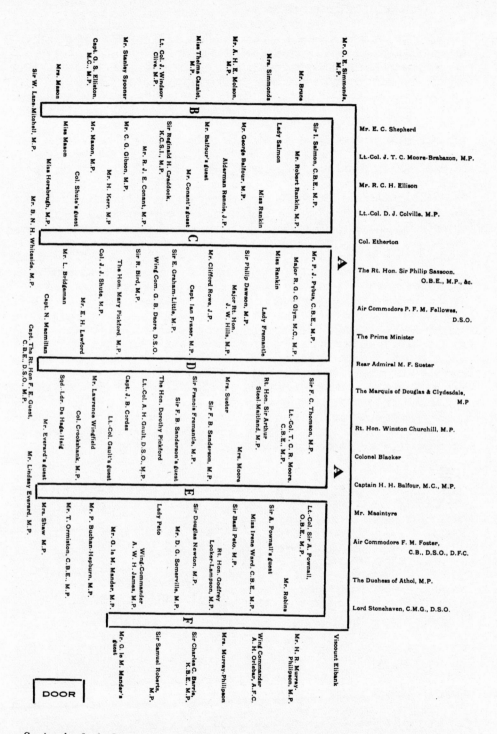

Seating plan for the Commons dinner in June 1933 in honour of the Mount Everest Flight Expedition. The Marquis of Clydesdale M.P. is seated next to Winston Churchill (Elizabeth, Duchess of Hamilton)

69

Luftwaffe. Goering at once summoned General Milch, the Luftwaffe Chief of Staff, and ordered him to lay on a tour of Luftwaffe aerodromes.

Although Clydesdale was not aware of it, he was to be given exactly the same treatment as the American aviator, Charles Lindbergh, less than one month before.12

General Milch gave a cordial greeting and offered to show Clydesdale anything he would like to see. Clydesdale remembered the curious intensity with which he added 'I feel we have a common enemy in Bolshevism'.

Clydesdale questioned General Milch closely about the state of the Luftwaffe and in due course passed the information back to Wing Commander Don, the one-armed veteran of the First World War, who was the Military Attaché at the British Embassy in Berlin.

General Milch was enthusiastic about aircraft production. In contrast to the slow rearmament in Britain, Nazi Germany was experiencing over-production. Training had been rushed and the Luftwaffe had lost a lot of prospective pilots on account of accidents.

In Clydesdale's view the German problems experienced in relation to training and recruitment were of significance. His visits were to units at Staaken and Doberitz. At Staaken he came across the Richtofen Squadron, which Goering had commanded in the First World War, but the aircraft seemed old-fashioned in their design.

At Doberitz the aircraft were more modern, and it was clear that the members of the Luftwaffe were treated as an elite group. The living conditions were more luxurious than those Clydesdale associated with armed services elsewhere. He had no doubt that air power would be a vital force if the Third Reich became involved in military operations.[13]

After these visits on 16 August 1936 Clydesdale flew his brother David down to Innsbruck in the South of Austria where he met Dr Eduard Reut-Nicolussi, the Tyrolean patriot who was opposed to the Italianisation of the South Tyrol.

The South Tyrol had been annexed by Italy after the First World War and some 230,000 German-speaking Tyroleans found themselves in an Italian district. Many of them wanted the Tyrol to be part of Austria. They disliked what they believed to be the suppression of German language and culture.

Clydesdale with 602 (City of Glasgow) Squadron which he commanded (Elizabeth, Duchess of Hamilton)

Clydesdale (right) at St Moritz beside his aircraft in which he was accustomed to flying around Europe (Elizabeth, Duchess of Hamilton)

Clydesdale regarded it as completely inconsistent for Hitler to express indignation over German minorities in the Sudetenland and the Polish Corridor and to remain silent over the subject of the South Tyroleans. The reason was obvious: Hitler was prepared to sacrifice their interests as the price to be paid for Mussolini's friendship as the leader of Fascist Italy.

At the suggestion of Dr Reut-Nicolussi, Clydesdale was taken by an emissary from Innsbruck to Bozen, to a secret meeting with the Tyrolean patriots at a lonely inn in the mountains.

Clydesdale remembered that a priest mimicked Mussolini receiving a deputation in Rome pleading for the South Tyroleans. They were ushered into the dictator's presence and after various pleasantries and mannerisms were informed that the audience was terminated. The most they received was a promise that the matters would be considered, but of course nothing happened.[14]

On 25 August Clydesdale returned to Munich and visited the Luftwaffe station at Lechfeld. He had hoped to visit one of the bombing units of the Luftwaffe but the Germans were not keen that he should do this. Lieutenant Colonel Hanesse wrote that this was impossible since the bombers were 'on their training grounds and not on their aerodrome'.[15] The Luftwaffe officers treated him with suspicion, but made it clear that they regarded the Russians as their primary enemy. The fact of most importance was that the Germans were rapidly rearming.

Clydesdale then flew north to stay with Prince Ernst August of Hanover at his castle, Schloss Blankenberg, Ernst August having been a close friend of his brother David at Oxford University. Clydesdale spent two days there before returning to Britain.[16]

71

31 July 1936. Hess welcomes forty-eight representatives of the International Olympic Committee in the Great Hall of Berlin University. Later Hess thought that Clydesdale had been in the audience, but this was not the case as Clydesdale was not a member of the International Olympic Committee (The Times)

Just over a month later Clydesdale spoke in Renfrew Town Hall as the local M.P. He said:

> Air strength was going to be the most significant force in the event of any emergency . . . One of the greatest deterrents we could have for war would be the best equipped and largest bombing force of any nation in the world.[17]

Shortly afterwards, between 12 and 14 October, Clydesdale attended a visit to German aircraft factories, having received an invitation to visit the Lilienthal Society from General Milch.

The Lilienthal Society was a German Aviation Association and lectures led on to visits to aircraft factories. Clydesdale visited the Junkers works at Dessau, and saw the construction of twin-engined bombers using diesel. These were Ju86s and later the Ju88s would be developed as bombers for the Luftwaffe. He also saw a factory where diesel engines were being made, but he was not given the figures for production. What was very

72

clear was that the Germany was rearming rapidly and that in that process Britain and France were falling behind.[18]

In January 1937 Clydesdale was skiing in Austria and wrote to Albrecht Haushofer, suggesting a meeting, in case he might glean any further information of interest. He received a reply on 7 January.

> Dear Lord Clydesdale,
>
> Your letter was a friendly surprise. Thank you for your kind wishes! My own greeting to you is probably waiting for you in Scotland: I had no idea of your being so near my Bavarian home. I am looking forward indeed to the possibility of meeting you when you pass through Germany. Our long talk in August is perhaps the most pleasant of all my 'Olympic Visitors' memories! . . .
>
> Yours sincerely,
> A. Haushofer.

On 23 January 1937 Clydesdale met him in Munich and was driven to Hartschimmelhof, the house of Karl Haushofer. The General Professor appeared as a formidable old man, who spoke English fluently, and treated Clydesdale with the most rigid politeness.

Many years earlier the General had been to Britain and India and had met the British politician, Joe Chamberlain, and also Lord Kitchener, who became Chief of the

Postcard handed to Clydesdale by Professor Reut-Nicolussi, a leader of the South Tryoleans, showing the anguish of families driven from farms by the S.S. in Hitler's attempt to appease Mussolini's Fascist Italy (Elizabeth, Duchess of Hamilton)

General Staff in the First World War. Karl Haushofer himself held a key command at the Battle of the Somme, where he was in charge of the artillery for two or three German divisions which inflicted the heaviest casualties the British Army had ever sustained.

In the background was the small and quiet figure of Albrecht Haushofer's mother. The subject of geopolitics was not discussed. It would not have been courteous, considering that one of the purposes of German geopolitics was to deprive Britain of large parts of the British Empire in the interests of German Lebensraum. Afterwards Clydesdale sent Karl Haushofer *The Pilot's Book of Everest* which he had written with Wing Commander McIntyre, and Karl Haushofer replied thanking him and saying he would review it in the *Zeitschrift für Geopolitik*.

What Clydesdale did not know was that four days after his visit to Hartschimmelhof Hess would arrive there and would be told about Clydesdale's visit and *The Pilot's Book of Everest*, which interested him greatly.[19]

Years later at Nuremberg, Karl Haushofer visited Hess and attempted to revive his memory, being on record as saying:

> Don't you remember Clydesdale, the young flyer who flew over the Himalayas - If I brought his picture to you, you would probably recognise him again – Don't you remember you liked his flying feat when he went over Mount Everest, when he dropped from 2,000 metres and he barely got away? Don't you remember that he made a very deep impression on you?[20]

Unaware of any strong impressions on Hess's part, Clydesdale wrote to Albrecht Haushofer mentioning that he had recommended his name to the Royal Institute of International Affairs, Chatham House, so that they should invite him to speak on the economic position of Germany. Albrecht replied that he would be glad to accept an invitation, provided that he could speak about the German outlook on the problem of 'raw materials and colonies' or on 'East-Central Europe'.

He also mentioned that he hoped to see Clydesdale in March 1937 when he would be in London. When he arrived Albrecht told Clydesdale that he had been sent over to Britain because Ribbentrop was in a mess, and it was his job to get him out of it.

Ribbentrop had certainly made himself an object of contempt. On arrival in Britain as Ambassador he had told the Press that he had come to warn the British about the Bolshevik menace, and that it was his intention to further an Anglo-German alliance against Russia. And further, Ribbentrop, while presenting his credentials to the King, gave the Nazi salute; and from that moment he was heartily disliked. By his behaviour he had given the British to understand that he did not expect Britain to stand in the way of German aspirations. Furthermore Ribbentrop, while Ambassador in Britain, made a special point of flying to Berlin in early November 1936 in order to sign the Anti-Comintern Pact between Germany, Italy and Japan, whose very existence implied hostility to Britain. Ribbentrop was always unpopular in Britain and was even scornfully nicknamed 'Herr von Brick and Drop'.

At least some of his unpopularity had reached Germany, and it seems that Hess sent Albrecht Haushofer to Britain in order to keep an eye on him and prevent him from becoming a laughing stock. It also appears that Ribbentrop's dislike of Albrecht dated from this time. Albrecht complained to Clydesdale that it was ironical that while von Hoesch had been popular in Britain he had been without influence in Germany, and now that Germany had sent an influential Nazi in the form of Ribbentrop the British found him thoroughly objectionable. He also said that 'Hitler understands Churchill, but he will never understand Chamberlain'.

On 29 April 1937 Albrecht gave his lecture to Chatham House in London on 'Raw Materials and Colonies: A German Point of View'. Lord Allen of Hurtwood was in the chair and introduced him with words which signified that Chatham House very much wanted to avoid the possibility of another world war. Lord Allen was quoted as saying: 'They were fortunate in having before them a very distinguished representative of the great German people, Dr Haushofer. The Institute of International Affairs was not permitted to have a corporate opinion, but it had an unanimous opinion which was that it longed to find the way to a cordial friendship with an understanding of the great people from whom the speaker came.'

Albrecht Haushofer then delivered a clever speech, without a note, and it is worth reproducing the allegory he used to depict the hatred felt by Germans for the Treaty of Versailles and for the way in which German colonies had been confiscated after the First World War:

> We have had a terrible row in the school-yard, and one of the bigger boys, with his following of smaller boys, has got a very sound thrashing, after a prolonged struggle. And the boys were angry about him. Finally he got kicked down (his enemies had been much more numerous than his friends). Lastly one boy came from another school-yard across the big water to deliver the final kick, and suddenly dashed away again, saying he did not want to have anything more to do with it.
>
> So they were going to punish the boy who had been knocked down. . . . His exotic toys, if I may use the expression, were taken away from him partly because they really did want to punish him and thought he was a very bad fellow, and partly because they rather liked his exotic toys. And so they decided to take them away.
>
> But the biggest of these boys, perhaps the toughest of them, having at least partly grown up mentally . . . and possessing quite a lot of the good things of this earth changing from the bold buccaneer into the hereditary possessor of nice things, developed a conscience. And he thought it would be a very good method of proceeding to say that the defeated boy's possessions were not taken away from him because the other boys wanted them, or because he ought to be punished, but because he was not fit to play with these toys. And so the solution was that they forced him to sign a declaration that he did not lose his nice exotic toys because he was to be punished or because the others wanted them but because he had treated them badly and was not fit to play with them.
>
> Now you see, this – for a boy – is very humiliating and he does not tend to forget such an experience.

His audience were very suspicious and were not altogether relieved when Haushofer said that 'nothing would be so fantastic as the results of another war'. After the lecture he stayed at Clydesdale's house, where he remarked that Ribbentrop was behaving with great stupidity and was becoming increasingly intransigent and unwilling to accept advice.

On 14 June 1937 Albrecht returned to London for a few days, no doubt to be briefed by Ribbentrop before leaving on his mission for Japan. In speaking to Clydesdale he left the impression of being a very worried man, as Germany was abandoning all self-restraint in her foreign policy. On 29 May Spanish Government aircraft bombed the German battleship *Deutschland* and by way of retaliation on 31 May a German naval force bombarded the Spanish town of Almeria, killing numerous civilians.

Previously the Non-Intervention Committee had been set up by the League of Nations, and a system of naval patrolling established in order to prevent acts of piracy on the high seas. A few weeks after the Almeria affair, Germany withdrew from participation in the naval patrol. These events caused much disquiet to Albrecht Haushofer, who believed that Germany was advancing steadily towards war. On 30 June 1937 he wrote from the ship *Europa*, bound for the U.S.A., a very friendly letter to Clydesdale, and this time a political note crept into it.

> My dear Douglo,
> . . . I am not leaving Europe with an untroubled mind. Our big man had been brought into the 'experiment' of collective action (and deliberation before action) not without difficulties. The breakdown may have far-reaching consequences – first psychological, then practical.
> But that can't be helped now. . . .
>
> Yours ever,
> Albrecht.

After arriving in America he wrote a report in the *Zeitschrift für Geopolitik* in August 1937. He was firmly convinced that in the event of conflict in Europe, Britain and the U.S.A. would work very closely together.

> Whether you are in San Francisco or Washington – you are aware that a fight for existence by Britain would not leave the United States in the role of impartial observers. The British

November 1937. Clydesdale and his bride, Lady Elizabeth Percy, are saluted by his brother officers after being married in St Giles Cathedral, Edinburgh (Elizabeth, Duchess of Hamilton)

Empire is just as important for America's security as the other way round. There
is no alliance between the two powers, but there exists such a profound community
of interest that both sides can pursue a policy which resembles an indissoluble
alliance. Whoever gets into conflict with Britain should know that America too will
be among his opponents, in spite of all neutrality laws.

On his return to Germany he learnt that Clydesdale was about to get married and
had sent him an invitation.[21] He wrote to Clydesdale on 27 November 1937 to express
his regrets that he could not attend the latter's wedding in Edinburgh, in what was a
warm and sentimental letter, which also showed an awareness of the historical enmity
between the Douglases and Percys, especially as Clydesdale was marrying a Percy:

> I am rather afraid you will find yourself in the midst of a terrific flood of
> congratulations – most of them thoroughly irrelevant. I do not think of this letter as
> of anything better . . . nonetheless, I am sorry I cannot have a quiet chat with you
> and shake hands . . .
> On Thursday then my thoughts – and a very strong feeling of friendship – will
> accompany your steps in St Giles Cathedral – and perhaps the spirit of history will
> have a little fun in my mind; after all it is a good thing to live in our much
> maltreated century. Please imagine what might have happened a few centuries ago:
> the heir of Douglas captured by the Percys – that would have either meant a border
> war or a northern rebellion because of the terrible ransom that might have been
> exacted by one of the Jameses or one of the Henrys.
> You are safer than many of your ancestors (at least if you don't take too many
> risks in the air – and I am sure that all your friends will have a very forceful ally in
> that respect from now on!); and at the same time you have kept up their best
> tradition; responsible leadership. – Now I can hear you say: Please – do be quiet!
> but once I am going to take advantage of being a German and therefore at liberty to
> say something that is rather un-English to say: you are bound to have a life full of
> leadership and full of love and young as we both are, I am very happy to know that.[22]

This was a letter from a man who clearly wished there to be good relations between
Britain and Germany, but he had no illusions. Attitudes were hardening in Britain,
and at the end of 1937 he wrote for the *Zeitschrift für Geopolitik*, noting that the British
were becoming increasingly hostile to Nazi Germany:

> If one has visited England in the spring of 1937, one cannot avoid the conclusion
> that neither Italy nor Japan (nor even the Soviet Union!) are considered as Public
> Enemy No.1. They (the British) are once again staring across the North Sea.

During the last week of April 1938 Haushofer visited Britain again and stayed with
Clydesdale at his home Dungavel in Scotland. He confessed that he was extremely concerned
and the tenor of everything he had to say was gloomy. He said that Ribbentrop had left
Britain (to become German Foreign Minister) an extremely bitter man, because he thought
that the British had rejected him. He caused horror amongst those present by taking out an
atlas of Europe. With one stroke of the pencil from occupied Austria to Germany he cut off
Bohemia including the Sudetenlands from the rest of Czechoslovakia. He quietly commented
'Those are the German demands'. When he was told that if Germany invaded
Czechoslovakia it was very likely that there would be war, he made no reply.

Clydesdale wrote to Lord Halifax, the British Foreign Secretary, mentioning that
Haushofer would be in London for the first week of May 1938 and might have
interesting information to impart. Halifax replied, on 3 May 1938.

My dear Clydesdale,

Thank you very much for your letter of yesterday in which you were good enough to let me know that Dr Albrecht Haushofer is in London until next Thursday evening. I should very much like to have been able to see Dr Haushofer but unfortunately I have no free time left. I am glad to say, however, that Dr Haushofer is in touch with the Foreign Office and I shall have an opportunity of hearing his views.

Yours ever,
Halifax.

On 6 May Haushofer wrote to Clydesdale from Paris:

In London Lord H. [Halifax] could not find time to see me, but I had long and I hope positive talks with two of his next collaborators. On the whole I leave England rather hopeful. If there are no real blunders made, we ought to be able to build up some sort of European stability.

On 28 May he wrote again to Clydesdale:

Having spoiled your atlas by drawing an ethnological boundary from my memory, I want to make amends. Under separate cover I am sending the most up-to-date map of German settlements in Czechoslovakia that we possess. It is based upon the official Czech census figures, therefore slightly unfavourable to the German side.

About ten days after Albrecht Haushofer had seen Clydesdale for the last time, he drew up the most important report that he ever submitted to Ribbentrop on Anglo-German relations, dated 26 June 1938:

Britain has still not abandoned her search for chances of a settlement with Germany (perhaps on the basis of German leadership, but not conquest, in South-east Europe, frontier revisions through plebiscites, West African colonies, four-power pact, armaments restriction).

A certain measure of pro-German sentiment has not yet disappeared among the British people; the Chamberlain-Halifax government sees its own future strongly tied to the achievement of a true settlement with Rome and Berlin (with a displacement of Soviet influence in Europe).

Then Albrecht came to the vital part of his report, which showed that he understood the British outlook and foresaw with great clarity the fate which Germany was approaching.

But the belief in the possibility of an understanding between Britain and Germany is dwindling fast. A new imperialism is suspected behind the pan-German programme of National Socialism (with which one has become more or less reconciled). Here the Czech question assumes the significance of a decisive test case. A German attempt to solve the Bohemian-Moravian question by a military attack would under present circumstances present for Britain (and in British opinion also for France) a *casus belli*.

In such a war the British Government would have the whole nation behind it. It would be conducted as a crusade for the liberation of Europe from German militarism. London is convinced that such a war would be won with the help of the U.S.A. (whose full participation, within days, not weeks, is anticipated) at the cost, of course, of an incalculable expansion of Bolshevism outside the Anglo-Saxon world.

78

14 October 1937. Charles Lindbergh, the American aviator, meets Rudolf Hess at a meeting of the Lilienthal Society Congress (Hulton-Deutsch)

He was saying that Germany could achieve and gain all that she required but not at the cost of war, and if Albrecht's views had been accepted, and if his suggestions had become official German policy, there would not have been a Second World War.

However, Ribbentrop was no longer interested in such arguments. He was being told facts that he did not want to hear. It appears that even now, before the Munich Agreement, neither Ribbentrop nor Hitler were prepared to understand that in the event of German armed aggression, sooner or later the British would fight in earnest, and without looking back.

Ribbentrop passed on Albrecht Haushofer's report to Hitler, and contemptuously dismissed it by adding the marginal note – 'Secret Service Propaganda'.

But Albrecht Haushofer's report that the British would fight in the event of German armed aggression was not the only sequel to Clydesdale's visit to the Olympic Games. Clydesdale had been invited to speak to the Lilienthal Society on 30 September 1936, and again on 3 August 1938 General Milch wrote to him, this time inviting him to Germany on behalf of no less a person than Field Marshal Goering himself. The translation read:

The German Academy for Aviation Research and the Lilienthal Association for Aviation Research, in which the leading personalities of German aviation research and industry are united, are jointly inaugurating about the 12th to 15th October a festival meeting in Berlin. In

Hartschimmelhof, the house of Major General Professor Karl Haushofer and his wife, Martha (Martin Haushofer)

accordance with the wish of Field Marshal Goering, in his capacity of President of the Academy and Protector of the Lilienthal Association, that this inauguration should be an assembly point for all who are active in aviation research and industry, out-standing representatives of inland and foreign aviation have been obtained to give lectures.

I take leave to invite you and the gentlemen in attendance upon you to take part in this important meeting for the international exchange of ideas in the realm of aviation. It would give me special pleasure to be able to greet you at the chief preparations for the meeting, in this respect especially at the Gentlemen's Evening for a Small Circle on the evening of 11th October and also at the opening session on the morning of the 12th October.

Your participation would do honour not only to the persons taking part but also the whole German aviation.

I have given instructions that official invitations for you and those gentlemen accompanying you should be sent by the Inaugurator and would be grateful if you would inform the General Secretary of the Lilienthal Association for Aviation Research, Furst Bismarck, Strasse 2. Berlin N.W.40 of your acceptance or refusal.

Clydesdale replies to the Lilienthal Society on 16 August, refusing the invitation as follows:

In accordance with a request which I have received from the Staat Sekretaer der Luftfahrt General der Flieger Milch, I write to inform you that it is with very great regret that I find it impossible to accept the kind invitation to attend the Meetings of the German Academy for Aviation Research and the Lilienthal Association for Aviation Research on 11th and 12th October next, owing to long-standing previous engagements in Scotland on these dates.

However, the American aviator Charles Lindbergh had accepted a similar invitation from Goering to visit the Lilienthal Society, where he met Rudolf Hess and formed the view that the Nazis were invincible in the air.[23]

Goering was not the only Nazi leader to be keenly interested in aviation: Hess, too, believed that Nazi expansionist plans depended upon Germany developing a world lead. The activities of other aviators from the U.S.A. and Britain, such as Lindbergh and Clydesdale, interested him: at that time advances in aviation had a similar appeal to the exploits of astronauts of later generations. Hess himself had hoped to be the first pilot to fly from Germany to the U.S.A. He had also come into possession of his own copy of *The Pilot's Book of Everest* by Clydesdale and MacIntyre. All this would have a relevance since there would soon come a time when Hess and Albrecht Haushofer would discuss the British.

NOTES

1. Winston S. Churchill, *Great Contemporaries*, page 261.
2. Fellows, Blacker, Etherton & Clydesdale. *First over Everest: the Honston - Mount Everest Expedition 1933*, pages 226–7.
3. Clydesdale & McIntyre. *The Pilot's Book of Everest*, pages 174, 190.
4. *Central European Times*, Zurich, 10 April 1933.
5. Hamilton papers.
6. Eugene Bird. *The Loneliest Man in the World*, pages 216, 217, 250. Professor Robert Shaw who was Lieutenant in the Highland Light Infantry, guarding Hess has said that he remembered Ivone Kirkpatrick and the Duke of Hamilton coming to identify Hess. He claimed that Hess told him that he had met Hamilton at the Olympic Games and during the discussion after Hess's interrogation Hamilton did not disagree. However this account is clearly in conflict with what Hess had said to Colonel Bird and what Hamilton believed to be the position. Hess knew that Hamilton had been at receptions at the Berlin Olympic Games in 1936 and it is quite possible that Hess might have seen him there.
7. Letter to the author.
8. Extract from von Schirach's *I Believed in Hitler*, pages 278–9 of German edition 1967.
9. *Paris Daily Mail*, 14 August 1936.
10. Hamilton papers.
11. Notes taken by the researcher Dr Campsie, whilst working for the Duke of Hamilton, after their conversations.
12. Duff Hart-Davis. *Hitler's Games: The 1936 Olympics*, page 127.
13. Manuscript of Dr Campsie.
14. Manuscript of Dr Campsie.
15. Hamilton papers.
16. Earlier in the year on 14 July 1936 Clydesdale had attended a dinner for Prince Ernst August's father, the Duke of Hanover, which was arranged by the Anglo-German Fellowship. In the Duke of Hamilton's papers, accessible at the Scottish Record Office in SRO RH4/202 in Reel 3 of the Microfilm Bundle SO19, after Hess's flight to Britain, in a subsequent libel action, there is a letter of instruction by his lawyer which stated that he had never been a member of the Anglo-German Fellowship. In fact in SRO RH4/202 Reel 1 of the Microfilm Bundle 5000 there is a receipt for membership for the year 1936. There is no evidence in his papers that he was a member after 1936, and a letter from the Secretary Conwell Evans inviting Clydesdale as he then was, to visit Nuremberg and meet Hitler was not taken up.
17. *Paisley Daily Express*, 8 October 1936.
18. Manuscript of Dr Campsie.
19. Hamilton papers.
20. Peter Padfield: Hess: *Flight for the Fuehrer* page 306, page 361 (footnote 25 to Chapter 28).
21. Hamilton papers.
22. The wedding was exceptionally large, with about 1,000 guests including Scottish Members of Parliament and European Ambassadors, though Ribbentrop, who was still German Ambassador, did not attend.
23. Kenneth S. Davis. *The Hero Charles A. Lindbergh: The Man and the Legend*, page 386.

SIX

Munich and Decline: 1938

Albrecht Haushofer remained working for Ribbentrop up to the time of Munich. On 4 February 1938 Hitler brought Foreign Office policy more directly under his own control by appointing Ribbentrop Nazi Foreign Minister. Meanwhile Austria was being threatened by military invasion. On 12 February Chancellor Schuschnigg of Austria travelled to Obersalzberg, Berchtesgaden, for his famous interview with Hitler. There Schuschnigg was battered into submission and accepted Hitler's ultimatum, which spelt the beginning of the end for Austria. The news of what had happened had not reached Albrecht Haushofer, but he knew that Germany's armoured divisions were poised to strike. He wrote to his father on 13 February:

> In the meantime the meeting at Obersalzberg has taken place without my being informed as yet of the progress. . . .
> The individual operations in the military sphere are too delicate to be confided to paper. The external form of the solution – here I completely agree with you – is masterly on the face of it. The tensions in the structure are not, however, thereby eliminated. Only the facade is really sound. . . .
> To use a medical comparison: the disease of the democracies is leprosy – that of the dictatorships is cancer.

He also included a more personal note:

> Many people send you their regards, very cordial ones from Ribbentrop, who made a calm and collected impression on me. I am very curious what effect the new facts will have on his character. . . . A man of great ambition, who has achieved the highest aim attainable, usually looks different from the way he looked at the time of his rise. . . .

Like most patriotic Germans Albrecht Haushofer supported the Anschluss but he wanted it to be realised by peaceful means and not by military invasion. During the night of 11–12 March 1938 he was in the room in the Foreign Ministry in which foreign broadcasts could be heard, along with Dr Wehofsich, the head of the Austrian section of the V.D.A. They heard that the Government of the Nazi Seyss-Inquart was in control, and it struck them that military intervention was unnecessary and undesirable. Albrecht then went to see Hess in order to ask him to persuade Hitler to countermand orders for marching into Austria on the next day, but to no avail. On 12 March the German Wehrmacht streamed into Austria.

It was Albrecht Haushofer's opinion that the Anschluss was the last step that the British were prepared to accept without serious resistance, and he viewed with concern German threats to Czechoslovakia. He knew that there were plans to use the Sudeten Germans as a springboard for ripping Czechoslovakia apart by force. On 29 March 1938 he was present as a representative of the Volksdeutsch Centre along with Ribbentrop, Weizsaecker and S.S. Obergruppenführer Lorenz of the Volksdeutsch Mittelstelle at the meeting in the Reich Chancellery, at which Henlein and the Sudeten Germans received instructions for future movements in the Sudetenland. Henlein was proving a useful puppet for Hitler's plans and the crisis between the Third Reich and Czechoslovakia loomed up, as the summer weeks passed.

Albrecht had always wanted a peaceful German-Czech settlement whereby the Sudeten Germans would be given a large measure of autonomy. He was utterly opposed to war or forcible subjugation, if only because he was convinced that Britain would fight rather than watch the growth of a threatening superpower on her doorstep. During the spring of 1938 Ribbentrop, with Albrecht, had a discussion with Nevile Henderson, the British Ambassador in Berlin. Henderson said that his Government was in principle ready to make colonial concessions in Africa and he actually laid out a map. Ribbentrop however made excessive territorial demands in such offensive language that Henderson pocketed the map and terminated the conversation. Afterwards Ribbentrop drew up a false statement on the discussion and Albrecht refused to sign it. By mid-1938 Albrecht had come to the conclusion that he had lost what influence he had ever had with Ribbentrop, that Germany had lost all hope of Britain's goodwill and that war against Czechoslovakia was very close.

On 18 August he wrote to his parents about the deterioration in Anglo-German relations:

A wise Englishman complained to me that one no longer knew in which voice to speak in Berlin; if one talked in a low voice one would be laughed at as being weak; talking in a loud voice however would be resented as intimidation. One would never be understood. Conversely one can rightly say that London's understanding for our rights lessens week by week. Correspondingly the attitude of Beneš, who believes he holds reliable trumps, stiffens. In short: everything is rapidly approaching the point at which one will no longer be master of one's decisions, but where one will be hurled down as surely as the stone which tried to roll from Partnach-Alm to Graseck without touching Partnach ravine.

Albrecht was certain that Hitler intended to go to war against the Czechs that autumn, unless he was deterred by the British Government, which he thought unlikely. A letter he wrote on 22 August 1938 to his mother explained the nature of his dilemma:

Of course I know the possibility exists that London will yet find ways to make Berlin understand the full seriousness – but our chance of reaching winter without war appears to me at best to be one to four. Once one sees matters in this light one cannot very well avoid preparing for them internally and externally I am therefore striking a balance.

Albrecht then examined the possibility of leaving Nazi Germany, but rejected this thought primarily because his mother, to whom he was deeply attached, was going to stay. There was also a subsidiary reason for not leaving. His father was in a position to protect the family from anti-Semitic outbursts through his friendship with Hess.

As long as you are still alive – and you are, after all, bound by the fact that you put into the world a second son as well, who enjoys life more than I do . . . and there is no point in fooling oneself that father's presence would not still have a high value for the further existence of this family – during that time therefore, I must not permit myself to consider a voluntary departure.

He wrote that in the case of war he could only survive if he closed his mind to even the most atrocious events.

I must, therefore, make the effort to carry on life until it is taken from me by external forces, even in conditions which would be abominable for me. I know exactly that I could survive a war in the attitude demanded from me only on one condition; that my own life has become completely indifferent to me, that no event, be it the most atrocious, could produce in me a spark of emotion. Such a transformation with the necessary speed can only take place when one prepares oneself accordingly. And I am now engaged in this internal preparation.

He finished his letter with the despairing words that the leaders of the Third Reich were determined to launch Germany into war, there being no question of any other country sparking off the conflagration.

If nothing surprising happens from the opposite side, the next four or five weeks may well still pass without an eruption. For the late autumn we have to reckon, however, with the Bohemian boiler being brought to an explosion . . .

I no longer believe that anybody or anything can stop the lighting of the fuse. And the possibility of the Bohemian conflict being localised seems to have one chance in ten. The Czechs would have to commit stupendous blunders in the next few months, or Lord Runciman would have to muster an amazing measure of power of judgment and determination.

He saw virtually no chance of war being avoided through the efforts of the Runciman Mission which had been despatched by the British Premier Neville Chamberlain to Czechoslovakia on 3 August 1938. At the time Albrecht had another conversation with Nevile Henderson, without Ribbentrop. Henderson asked him if Hitler would be satisfied if he received the Sudetenland and Albrecht told him that Hitler knew no bounds.

Haushofer thought that nothing would restrain the Nazi leaders from going to war with Czechoslovakia, unless Britain made a firm and vigorous stand, and even that would almost certainly not prevent war. At the beginning of the ensuing Munich Conference he travelled in Hitler's train, which had been sent to meet Mussolini, and later claimed that he had asked Mussolini to try to moderate Hitler. During the conference he prepared geographical maps of the proposed German-Czech frontier for Ribbentrop, and as he saw it the Munich agreement merely postponed war. He told his brother Heinz that at the end of the conference, just after the statesmen of France and Britain had left the room, Hitler turned to his entourage and remarked, 'I am still going on to Prague'. Hardly had the ink dried on the paper of the Munich Agreement, long before Chamberlain had arrived back in England supposedly bringing Peace for our Time, the treaty had been broken in all but name.

Albrecht Haushofer knew that any future war would not remain localised and viewed with pessimism the onward march of events. He had made his bid for peace in his report of 26 June 1938, and his report had been dismissed. His influence with Ribbentrop had come to an end and shortly after the Munich Conference he stopped working for him. Ribbentrop consistently told Hitler that he could base his plans for aggrandisement of the Reich on the use of military force without risking a general war, and it greatly annoyed him

10 September 1938: Hitler is cheered by 56,000 Hitler Youth with von Schirach, the Nazi Youth Leader, and Hess sitting behind him. Soon most of them would be dead as a result of Hitler's war (Hulton-Deutsch)

when Albrecht Haushofer flatly contradicted this line of thought. He resented the fact that Albrecht was primarily an agent of Hess, and only secondarily an assistant of the Ribbentrop Bureau, and the fact of Albrecht's part-Jewish ancestry rendered him untrustworthy to the Nazi apparatus.

Hitler had chosen 28 September 1938 as the date for the invasion of Czechoslovakia before Neville Chamberlain came to Munich. On that day in September Ribbentrop ordered two of his collaborators to write a report on Albrecht Haushofer, indicating that if the matter had been solely in Ribbentrop's hands Albrecht might have been removed to a concentration camp as a deviationist. It is no coincidence that amongst Abrecht's letters is a handwritten draft with numerous amendments and deletions, almost certainly intended as an excuse for Hess, who always extended his protection in such circumstances.

Regarding the occurrence of 28/9/1938, I have to say the following:
It is not quite easy to comment after five months on a conversation, the fixing of which in my memory did not appear urgent in proportion to the other duties of those days. The conversation commenced when I . . . was stopped in the passage by two gentlemen of the office with the worried question: 'What will happen?' The contrast between the former standing to attention of these gentlemen and the tone of this question provoked me to the

At Godesberg 23 September 1938 Ivone Kirkpatrick, Great Britain's expert on German affairs, watches proceedings with a wary eye. In front of him (from left to right): Schmidt (Hitler's interpreter), Nevile Henderson (the British Ambassador), Neville Chamberlain and Hitler (The Times)

ironic answer: 'Have you already got your steel helmets and gas masks ready?' To the counter remark: 'But surely there will be no war! That would be insanity!' I retorted: 'Do not say that. History is sometimes written in blood. Do you know then what the Chief really wants?'

From that moment onwards, I had the impression that in the further course of conversation it was intended to commit me to statements which were suitable for a report on me, and I confined myself to a few remarks, which left no doubt, however, that I considered a peaceful solution attainable . . . I then added that very many people now grumbled secretly, who would never have had the courage to express anxiety and deviating opinions directly. I myself had always stated my opinion to the Minister, especially relating to Britain (this being the first duty of an assistant): I therefore did not have a bad conscience. What the leadership would then decide was just whether it was to be gas masks or pipes of peace.

Albrecht stated that it had not been his intention to express contempt for Ribbentrop:

After a lapse of five months I cannot with certainty give further particulars on wording. It was decidedly not my intention to ridicule or scorn the politics of the Reich Minister. It was equally not my intention 'to cause pessimism'. Of course apart from the seriousness, the anxiety and willingness, which was no doubt felt by every German in those September days – the conversation contained indeed an element of irony, but of an irony which was directed less against the great foreign policy than against the 'attitude' of some of my interlocutors.

8 November 1938. Hitler at the name-giving party for Wolf Rüdiger Hess. Hess on far left with Major General Professor Karl Haushofer sitting in the back row, wearing a bow tie (Martin Haushofer)

In such circumstances Albrecht was in despair, especially as he believed that Hitler would never keep his word. Hitler said as much in a speech on 9 October 1938 at Saarbrucken. Nonetheless in his report for the *Zeitschrift für Geopolitik*, written in October, Albrecht inferred that in the interests of peace it was vital that Hitler should not break the Munich Agreement:

> One may perhaps consider as the most important gift to the future that strip of paper which Neville Chamberlain held in his hand on alighting from the aircraft at London: the Anglo-German peace proclamation, signed on the basis of a personal trust between the Fuehrer and Chamberlain contains more than its wording betrays, especially if one remembers that in his Berlin speech the Fuehrer clearly said that the Sudeten German territories are the last territorial claim in Europe. . . .
>
> Chamberlain with the full support of the entire Empire would have gone to war if this had become necessary. And nobody can foresee how much would have been left of the white race and of its nordic leadership if another world war had been started within European frontiers.

The Nazi leadership disregarded this warning, and it did not help Albrecht Haushofer when his father had a mild altercation with Hitler in November 1938. His father had recently attended the Convegno Volta African Congress at which colonial problems had been discussed. Afterwards, he asked Hess to arrange a meeting between himself and Hitler, and at the name-giving of Hess's son Wolf Rüdiger, Hitler and the Professor General were left together in Hess's house on the hearth before the fire. He told Hitler that further territorial demands in Europe would produce great hostility in the Western

Powers. Germany should, he argued, make an offer to Britain guaranteeing the lands alongside the Reich, promising to waive all right to Poland, provided that Britain recognised the *status quo* and returned the lost German colonies in Africa. It would be wise for Hitler to visit England, as according to his information there were circles in Britain around Chamberlain and Halifax who would be willing to consider such proposals.

Hitler eyed him stonily as though to say 'You foolish old man, you have never understood me', turned on his heel and walked out of the room without a word. Hitler was not thinking in terms of colonies in Africa. He was thinking of the eastern steppes and plains of eastern Europe and Russia, and he was prepared to risk incurring the enmity of Britain. His successes had whetted his appetite for more.

Kurt von Schuschnigg, the Chancellor of Austria before the Anschluss, told the author that the great difference between the Nazi leaders and Karl Haushofer was that they would kill for their own ends but Karl Haushofer would not – a significant difference in those times. Apart from anything else Karl Haushofer's wife was of half Jewish origin, and he and his whole family disagreed with the Nazis' racial policy. More than that they were at risk from Nazi violence, as were all those of Jewish origin.

Karl Haushofer's close friendship with Hess provided shelter for his immediate family. In a letter dated 14 November, Hess wrote:

> General a.D. Professor Karl Haushofer is unquestionably of Aryan descent. His wife Martha née Mayer-Doss is not Jewish within the meaning of the Nuremberg Laws, which I have verified from the family tree made available to me. I herewith forbid every form of molestation or search of their home.[1]

In other words Hess, for reasons of personal friendship, was setting aside the Nuremberg Laws as far as the Haushofer family was concerned. His action in so doing indicated the barbaric, weird and illogical nature of Nazi anti-semitic policy.

On 16 November 1938 Albrecht Haushofer wrote a letter of hopelessness to his mother.

> Today is the Day of Repentance and of Prayer here. This appears to me very appropriate for writing the letter requested by you. Dear Mother, why do you always so press for letters! That I am alive is evident from our telephone conversations. If I were physically ill, I would let you know. Should there be essential changes in the external order of my existence or should such be in the immediate offing, I would write about it, although such changes nowadays occur so quickly that often there remains no time for thinking or even for writing.
>
> But on what else should I otherwise write? I no longer have a private life, and if I had I would not write about it. One never knows, after all, who else reads one's letters. One cannot write about things which move one. And when one can write about them once in a while like today, when I can send the letter by my brother – what is the point of making life even more difficult for each other?

He left his mother in no doubt that it had been the intention of Hitler and Ribbentrop to destroy Czechoslovakia by having 'a nice little war' and that they no longer cared what the British would do.

> You know very well yourselves that we live in medieval circumstances, which are an insult to the gallantry of our Middle Ages; that our spiritually possessed great leaders are enraged over their failure with their nice little war (with the result that all those who in the last minute pleaded for settlement and peace are now highly unpopular), that they endeavour as far as

possible to frustrate a German-English settlement. And if you do not know it, it is perhaps better for Father's peace of mind.

He went on to deal with a subject which must have been very painful for him, since he was in the category of 'protected Jew'. On 7 November a Jewish refugee from Germany had mortally wounded Ernst vom Rath, the third Secretary of the German Embassy in Paris. On 9–10 November, with the encouragement of Hitler, Goebbels and other Nazi leaders, Heydrich at the head of the S.D., organised the looting of Jewish property throughout Germany, and the sending of Jews to prison and concentration camps. On that night countless thousands of Jewish shops and synagogues were ransacked and set on fire. This pogrom was afterwards referred to as the Kristallnacht, meaning the night of broken glass. The Government of the Third Reich imposed a fine of one billion marks upon the Jewish community, making it obvious that it wanted to expel all Jews from Germany. This naturally affected the family of Albrecht's mother. He continued:

It will be soon enough to realise what is going on, when we are all robbed or hanged. The disappointed fury over the missed war is now raging internally. Today it is the Jews. Tomorrow it will be other groups and classes.

The financial advice I gave to you yesterday is based on the contingency that perhaps as early as next Saturday, but perhaps only later, a partial capital levy will be imposed also for Aryans the financial consequences of which cannot be assessed, but which can very easily lead to a lowering of purchase power so that one may suddenly become non-liquid. The exact amount of the confiscation, which is to go by the name of 'Thank Offering', is not yet known. It will be unavoidable because public coffers are empty.

He said that all his knowledge of Britain was useless, because he had hopelessly compromised himself in British eyes by collaborating with Ribbentrop. He described a conversation, probably with Nevile Henderson.

A conversation with the British Embassy Counsellor and with a confidant of Chamberlain, who was here during these last few days, has convinced me that my personal credit and thereby my usefulness in the West in foreign political matters is now exhausted. You will, therefore, have to be prepared for the gradual ending of my chances for action. This coincides also with an inner necessity. He who constantly spits at himself becomes worthless.

About this time, just after the Kristallnacht, on 9–10 November 1938, Fritz Hesse had a meeting with Albrecht Haushofer and wrote:

I found him as pessimistic as I was myself. He told me that he had fallen into the deepest disfavour because of his warnings and that hubris ruled in Germany. 'Hitler,' he said, 'is now convinced that he can afford to do anything. Formerly he believed that we must have the maximum armaments because of the warlike menaces of the Powers striving to encircle us, but now he thinks that these Powers will crawl on all fours before him!'

Hitler had told Haushofer: 'This fellow Chamberlain shook with fear when I uttered the word war. Don't tell me he is dangerous!'

Haushofer ended by saying: 'We shall probably slither into the catastrophe we thought we had averted. I am more pessimistic than ever. It's true that Hitler does not want war, but he is ready to risk it, and this, in my opinion, is a guarantee of disaster.'

Later Albrecht again told Fritz Hesse that Hitler was certain that the British would give way. At Godesberg he had threatened Chamberlain with war and Chamberlain had made concessions. Hitler simply was not prepared to believe that Chamberlain would act differently on the next occasion. Although Albrecht was in the political wilderness for giving unwelcome advice he did not stop warning, and he wrote in the 1939 January issue of the *Zeitschrift für Geopolitik*:

> The whole of British history, the whole grim history of its conflicts with rival powers, from Spain, via Holland and France to Germany and Russia would have to be rewritten if one wanted to believe that present-day British armaments are merely bluff or that the Anglo-Saxon world could be bluffed forever. There are still political issues for which Britain (and France with her) would fight.
>
> No world power which is not in a condition of extreme decay would allow itself to be dismembered without resistance. The methods of resistance vary of course. Countries which have a long financial and economic breath are sometimes inclined to postpone military involvement for longer than other States; sometimes further than is considered right in later days by their own historians.

As Albrecht had feared, the German Army in blatant violation of the Munich Agreement occupied Bohemia and Moravia on 15 March 1939. It was now manifest to the British Parliament and public that Hitler had lied at the Munich Conference, and had played with Neville Chamberlain as a skilled fisherman plays with a salmon on a line. It brought home to British M.P.s that Hitler's dishonesty was so fundamental and endemic that never again could any meaningful negotiations be held with him or with any Germans serving under him.

Earlier that month, on 1 March, Clydesdale wrote to Air Chief Marshal Sir Cyril Newhall, the Chief of the Air Staff, asking whether he should give lectures in Germany:

> I have been approached by the Anglo-German Fellowship to give some lectures to their members in Germany, and the British Council have strongly recommended me to accept this invitation. The subjects with which it is proposed I should deal are Aviation and Physical Training and the Everest Flight.
>
> With regard to Aviation the suggestion is that I should concentrate on the AAF and make a big point of eulogising the voluntary service under democracy.
>
> As a serving officer, in the first place I should be grateful if you would let me know whether the Air Council have any objections to my giving these lectures; secondly, if there is no objection, whether there is any subject the Air Ministry would like me to insert in my lectures.
>
> I wonder if I could be given an interview with some responsible person who could advise me on these matters generally?[2]

On 8 March Air Chief Marshal Sir Cyril Newhall indicated that the Air Ministry welcomed the idea:

> Thank you for your letter of 1st March, on the subject of your projected visit to Germany. There is no objection to your giving these lectures, in fact we welcome the idea.
>
> I think it would be a good idea if you could come to the Air Ministry some day and see Group Captain Buss, the Director of Intelligence, who will be able to put forward some suggestions, such as possibly a referral on the training at Halton and Cranwell from both the moral and physical point of view. He will also be able to pass you on to any other appropriate department to enable you to get as much information as you may require.[3]

By the time that contact with Group Captain Buss took place, Moravia had been invaded and there was no question of Clydesdale going. In the wake of this aggression the threat of war was too close. On 31 March the British Government gave a pledge of Anglo-French aid for the Polish people in the event of German intervention in Poland.

Clydesdale prepared notes for a circular letter to his constituents in East Renfrew referring to the violation of the Munich Agreement:

> By this act of ruthless aggression, followed swiftly by German troops entering Memel on March 23rd and Mussolini's violent assaults on Albania on Good Friday, the Dictators have demonstrated beyond all reasonable doubt that their aim is the mastery of the continent of Europe, and there is little doubt that having achieved this we would be the next target for aggression.
>
> Consequently the Government have decided, and rightly in my opinion, that a firm stand must be made by this country if any further acts of aggression are threatened by the Totalitarian Powers against Independent states.[4]

Not long after, on 1 June, Clydesdale wrote to his American friend Douglas Simpson in Florida, summing up his personal views:

> Europe is indeed in a ghastly mess. President Roosevelt's speeches and messages to Hitler and Mussolini may well save peace. I have travelled in Germany a good deal during the past few years, and I have many German friends;[5] but I have reluctantly become convinced that Nazism is out for nothing short of world domination and in its endeavours to achieve this will go to any extreme. This regime has indeed a stranglehold on the people of Germany, and only something very drastic can remove it.
>
> I believe that firmness is the only thing that may prevent war, and it seems the only possible way to deal with a nation whose leaders base their diplomacy entirely on military strength and at the same time have no regard for international law or treaties. The one good thing is that the free countries of the world still possess a vast preponderance of power which if compelled can be used as a military force.[6]

By this time attitudes had hardened further in Britain and Germany and Albrecht Haushofer must have known with certainty that he could not prevent the attack on Poland. His failure was complete.

NOTES

1. Haushofer papers.
2. Hamilton papers.
3. Hamilton papers.
4. Hamilton papers.
5. His German-speaking friends included Dr Kurt Hahn, founder of Gordonstoun School in Scotland, whom Hitler had imprisoned; Prince Ernst August, grandson of the Kaiser who had been a student at Oxford; Professor Reut-Nicolussi, a leader of the South Tyrolean whose aspirations Hitler rejected; and Albrecht Haushofer, the German patriot of partly Jewish origin who passionately wanted peace between Britain and Germany.
6. Hamilton papers.

SEVEN

A Message of Despair:
July 1939

During 1939 Albrecht Haushofer repeated in his articles on the Atlantic World for the *Zeitschrift für Geopolitik* the warnings which he had given to the Nazi leadership. In mid-1939 he wrote that Chamberlain 'had for some months been completely cured of his Munich illusions' and that 'the final conflict between Napoleon and the other European powers was not caused by the incompatibility of real interests but by both sides looking at all treaties as scraps of paper'.

He was convinced that in any world war Germany could not defeat Great Britain, aided by the U.S.A. and Canada. He wrote in the July issue of the *Zeitschrift Für Geopolitik*:

> From watching American sources too, one reaches the conclusion that the danger of a world war is greater in Europe than in East Asia, and that one can only regard with misgivings the rapid advances in the Anglo-Saxon community. One of the pillars of this armaments community is the development of Canada into a spare part store for the British aeronautical industry. One has only to imagine what it would mean in a European war if British bombers have every European aeroplane factory within their reach, while American and Canadian factories remain immune from European or Asian attack, in order to realise the enormous advantages in the military field which Anglo-Saxon co-operation would offer to Britain in case of war.

As usual his writings were to a large extent disregarded by the Nazi leadership. Albrecht had cause for concern: his country was drifting inexorably towards war in spite of all his efforts; he was now looked upon with disfavour by Hitler and Ribbentrop, and his father was infuriating Hitler by suggesting possibilities of a better future for the Germans in the South Tyrol.

Hitler had been ready to exploit the alleged grievances of the Germans in the Czech Sudetenland and in Poland, but it was different with the South Tyrol. Since the Treaty of St Germain in 1919 the South Tyrol had come under the sovereignty of Italy, in spite of the fact that the overwhelming majority of Tyrolese were German-speaking, and would have preferred the South Tyrol to remain part of Austria. Hitler hastily disowned the Tyrolese Germans, for Mussolini's friendly attitude towards him had become evident during the formation of the Anti-Comintern Pact, and at the time of the Anschluss and Munich. Wishing to make sure of Mussolini's support, Hitler encouraged Himmler, in control of the Volksdeutsche Mittelstelle, to make plans for moving many thousands of Germans from the South Tyrol to Southern Bavaria. Hitler also ordered Goebbels, Reich Minister of Propaganda, to ban any written material in Germany which highlighted the attempts made by Mussolini's Fascists to Italianise the Germans in the South Tyrol.

Karl Haushofer, being unable to fathom the workings of Hitler's mind, recommended in his book *Frontiers* that many European boundaries should be redrawn, and that the South Tyrol more properly belonged to Germany than to Italy. On 12 July 1939 Albrecht wrote to his mother from Berlin:

> ... because of a matter, which affects Father personally and which can have far-reaching consequences in view of his tendency only to feel injustice in its full impact when it concerns a sphere which is emotionally near him. Father will one of these days be informed by the publishers that the Ministry of Propaganda has prohibited *Frontiers* since, because of its treatment of the South Tyrol, it endangers Reich politics. . . .

He advised that his father should ask Hess to intercede with Hitler, making it clear that he was prepared to make a tactful withdrawal from public activity.

> I must add, however, that I am very doubtful whether Tomodachi [Hess] will achieve anything against Dr G. [Goebbels], not perhaps because of the latter's special malice, but because O'Daijin is at this moment in such an over excited state . . . that he immediately sees red at the word South Tyrol and starts to rage. . . .
>
> Here now my analysis of the general situation, which is based on the innermost information (just as last year, when I after all knew, not only 'assumed', since the beginning of June, that October had been fixed by the highest authority as the deadline by which the Czechs question must be 'settled' with all, including military, means).
>
> Until the middle of August nothing will happen. From the middle of August onwards everything is to be prepared for a sudden war. Now as before O'Daijin wants only a local war and he is wavering as last year since he is not sure whether the West will remain quiet.
>
> The difference compared to last year is only that this time the West is taken more seriously, and that the deadline has not been fixed with the same determination as last year. Instead the will to fight on the opposite side is stronger, our own economic situation worse and the prospect of finding more favourable conditions, perhaps next year, is diminished. The state of danger is, therefore, at least just as acute.

He felt that he had to escape from the Berlin atmosphere at least temporarily, taking with him some of his students on a journey abroad.

> I have very seriously considered whether to go on my excursion. But it is perhaps a last chance and I have to get out of this asphyxiating atmosphere once again, otherwise I shall burst. . . .

On the same day, 12 July, he wrote another letter to his father pleading with him to be careful:

> Matters are bad – but I must tell you that O'Daijin sees red in this matter. . . . Opposition on the south alpine question is, therefore, at present dangerous in the extreme.

He than made a comment of dissatisfaction about Britain in general and Clydesdale in particular, saying that English reactions were making themselves felt in a 'very painful form', which showed that he must have been watching developments in Britain closely. It is easy to understand what Albrecht Haushofer meant by looking at *Hansard* for 10 July 1939, when Clydesdale asked the Prime Minister two questions concerning the South Tyrol. In view of the fact that Hitler had begun to remove the Germans from the South Tyrol to Germany, Clydesdale wanted a recommendation to be made by the Prime Minister to Hitler, that he should remove the Germans from Danzig to Germany, and thereby avoid the expectation of war. Clydesdale also asked the Prime Minister whether he would remind Hitler and Mussolini 'that by their settlement of the South Tyrol, where alone in Europe a simple frontier revision is possible, they have not got a leg to stand on in demanding territory elsewhere'. R. A. Butler, Under Secretary of State for Foreign Affairs, replied evasively on behalf of the Prime Minister.

On 19 July 1939 Clydesdale again asked the Prime Minister:

If in view of the fact that South Tyrol was the only place in Europe where frontier revision provided a simple solution of the racial problem, but that Herr Hitler apparently preferred settling this problem by a scheme to remove the German population from their land, he [the Prime Minister] would take steps to obtain detailed information regarding the case of other German demands?

Mr Butler replied that the Government would 'bear in mind the possible application of these principles to other areas'.

Clydesdale asked in his Supplementary Question:

Has the Rt. Hon. Gentleman on his present information any reason to suppose that Herr Hitler would prefer war rather than settle his other demands by a similar scheme of the kind in operation in the South Tyrol? Moreover, does he think that Herr Hitler and Signor Mussolini have initiated a new principle of settling racial problems by negotiation rather than war, or, on the other hand, in view of the fact that South Tyrol is inhabited by about the oldest German population, is Herr Hitler merely for the sake of expediency acting as treacherously to his own people as he acted to the Prime Minister at Munich?

Mr Butler again replied:

'Honourable members must draw their own conclusions.'

Clearly Clydesdale's point had been made.

Albrecht knew that the tone of these remarks meant that there would be general war if Germany invaded Poland, and while on holiday with his students he sent Clydesdale the following letter which is worth quoting in full since it reveals so clearly his attitude to the world situation.

Cruising the Coast of Western Norway.
July 16th, 1939.

My Dear Douglo,

I have been silent for a very long time – partly from outside, partly from inside reasons. The outside reasons are easily and quickly stated: having told some very unpopular truths after my last return from England, and having pulled my full weight with the forces of moderation on our side during the weeks before Munich, I had to move very carefully afterwards. I did not want to find myself waking up one morning with an appointment as Consul General to Paramaribo (I dare say such a place exists somewhere in South America).

The inside reasons are less easily put down. But I think I can make them clear at least to you. We have had more than one talk on the Versailles Treaty and its aftermath. You know how I feel about it. I have always regarded it as a failure on the side of British farsightedness – to put it mildly – (but you may blame the French!) that concessions and revisions mostly came too late. I fully admit that the critical years were 1931/32. One third of the concessions to Germany that you allowed to be taken later on without agreement, offered in 1932 – and Germany would never have taken the revolutionary plunge she took in 1933. But that is old history.

After the National-Socialist advent to power there remained one hope: that – after having done away with most (if not all) of the Versailles grievances by rather violent and one-sided methods – the great man of the regime would be prepared to slow down, to accept an important (though not an all-dominating) position in 'the Concert of Europe'. It may have been an unreasonable hope – knowing the man as we know him – but – realities being what they were – it was the only hope one could act upon. Now – I cannot entertain that hope any longer; and that is my reason for writing and posting this letter somewhere on the coast of Western Norway, where I am taking a few short weeks of rest.

I just want to give you a sign of personal friendship – I do hope that you will survive whatever may happen in Europe – and I want to send you a word of warning. To the best of my knowledge there is not yet a definite time-table for the actual explosion, but any date after the middle of August may prove to be the fatal one. So far they want to avoid the 'big war'. But the one man on whom everything depends is still hoping that he may be able to get away with an isolated 'local war'. He still thinks in terms of British bluff, although the Prime Minister's and Lord H's [Halifax's] last speeches have made him doubt – at least temporarily; the most dangerous thing is that he is racing against time: in more than one sense.

Economic difficulties are growing, and his own feeling (a very curious and remarkable one) that he has not a very long time of life ahead of him, is a most important factor. I could never adapt myself to the idea that any war might be inevitable; but one would have to be blind not to realise that war may be very near.

So the question: what *can* be done? gets all the more important. But perhaps I should have added a few things about the psychological position in the mind of the German people before trying to answer that question. On the merits of their present government, the Germans are less united than at any date since 1934. But if war breaks out on the Corridor question, they will be more solidly behind their present leader than over any case that might have led to war in these last years. The territorial solutions in the East (Corridor and Upper Silesia) have never been accepted by the German nation, and you will find many and most important Englishmen, who never thought them to be acceptable – and said so! A war against Poland would be not unpopular.

World war of course is quite another thing: but few people in Germany realise that they would be up against a world war. I should just mention one more point: 'encirclement' has proved to be a most efficient weapon of inside propaganda. Pre-war memories (and war-blockade experiences) have risen in many minds – and the idea that England wants to 'hem in' Germany on every side has got very deep into the German mind (even there, where it is *not* 'Nazi'). Of course there are difficulties. That hateful South Alpine deal is making a big, though naturally subterranean, stir.

But war against Poland would – for the first weeks at least – unite, not disintegrate the German nation. And that is – at least to my feeling – all-important; not because I might hope that a united German nation might win the war: I am very much convinced that Germany cannot win a short war and that she cannot stand a long one – but I am thoroughly afraid that the terrific forms of modern war will make any reasonable peace impossible if they are allowed

95

to go on for even a few months. Therefore we simply have to stop the explosion. Another European war, another Treaty of Versailles, another total revolution all over Europe – well – I need not say what it would mean for Europe as a whole.

Now to the core of the question: what can be done? Very little from inside Germany. Even now at least something from England.

Something on the tactical side: Your 'inside' people know how to put a certain amount of pressure on the big man in Rome: they ought to start that pressure fairly soon. Something of the more general type: It is not enough for England to advertise herself as the big boss in the fire brigade, or to organise a fire insurance company with other nations (some of them – viz. Poland – not quite above playing with fire themselves). What Europe needs is a real British peace plan on the basis of full equality and with considerable (but strictly mutual) safeguards on the military side. I realise to the full that a strong system of safeguards will be necessary if your people are to be persuaded to meet even the slightest German wishes regarding European or colonial territory. But as long as your Government has not lost sight of the second part of their original programme – full security and peaceful change through negotiation – they might be able to test the second part early enough to secure a positive effect. I cannot outline what might be an acceptable compromise in detail.

I cannot imagine even a short-range settlement without a change in the status of Danzig and without some sort of change in the Corridor. Possibly a long-range settlement between Germany and Poland would have to be based upon considerable territorial changes combined with population exchanges on the Greek–Turkish model (people in England mostly do not know that there are some 600,000–700,000 Germans scattered through the inner (formerly Russian) parts of Poland!) – but if there is to be a peaceful solution at all, it can only come from England and it must appear to be fair to the German public as a whole.

Even now – after the present rulers of Germany have given ample provocation – your people would be wise not to forget that they refused a plebiscitarian solution in the Corridor (and subsequently the Poles drove some 900,000 Germans out of their former German provinces!) and that they prevented one in Upper Silesia.

Last September Mr Neville [Chamberlain] had the trust of the majority of Germans. If you want to win a peace without – or even after – a war, you need to be regarded as trustees of Justice, not as partisans. Therefore – once more – if you can do anything to promote a general British peace and armaments control plan – I am sure you would do something useful. . . .

I am rereading this letter and should like to add something of a personal kind. You will realise that I have written this letter with the utmost frankness because I know that you realise the risk I should be running if the existence of this letter should become known. . . . Therefore, I wanted to add what may seem very curious to you: please destroy this letter after reading it – and destroy it most carefully. But perhaps this is unfair: so I give you freedom for your own discretion to show this letter personally either to Lord H [Halifax] or to his Under Secretary Mr B [Butler] – if you see fit of course – under one condition: that no notes should be taken, my name never be mentioned, and the letter be destroyed immediately afterwards.

As a sign that you have received this letter I only ask for some non-committal picture-postcard (to my normal address, telling me that you are well. If you have seen fit to show the letter you might add something about your family. . . . I do hope we may meet again.

Yours very sincerely,

A.

After returning to Berlin he wrote to his parents on 13 August: 'One differs from the scoundrels and fools by the lack of present-day joy – from the others by the lack of hope for the time beyond the cataclysm. . . .' His despair was apparent and Carl von Weizsaecker, a friend, wrote of him:

Please Destroy this letter after reading it —
and destroy it most carefully. But perhaps
this is unfair: So I give you freedom
for your own Discretion to show this letter
personally either to Lord H. or to his
Under-Secretary Mr. B. — If you see fit
of course — under one condition: that
no notes should be taken, my name
never be mentioned, and the letter be
destroyed immediately afterwards. — As
a sign that you have received this
letter I only ask for some non committal
picture - postcard   to my normal adress)
telling me that you are well. If you
have seen fit to show the letter you
might add something about your family...
I do hope we may meet again ——
                    Yours ever sincerely
                                A.

The letter forecasting the date of Hitler's war from Albrecht Haushofer to the Duke of Hamilton, dated 16 July 1939, which was read by Churchill, Halifax and Chamberlain. In sending this letter, Albrecht Haushofer ran the risk of execution (Elizabeth, Duchess of Hamilton)

When it proved impossible to prevent Hitler's war, the outcome of which he foresaw, he sank into a year-long bitterness and pessimism which lay like lead on him and his friends.

He omitted no single step which seemed to offer hope, although he entertained no hope. When we younger people told him that we believed in the future and in present events being perhaps a means of purification, all he could say was that he saw nothing but senseless destruction, that perhaps we might live in such a future but for him there was no place in it.

On 22 August 1939 the news came through that the Nazi–Soviet Pact would be signed, and Walter Stubbe, Albrecht's assistant, recorded that Albrecht was standing against a desk, with two young students beside him and the *Times Atlas* page of the Soviet Union open in front of him:

> I just heard Haushofer say: 'Now they have concluded a friendship, but in four weeks at the latest we shall have a war. Then the madman in his drunkenness will overrun the West and Alfred Rosenberg will get what he wants: he will gorge himself in the Sarmatian steppes and it will be the end of Europe.'
>
> Then something unexpected happened: with a cry of despair at such sombre visions, Wolfgang Hoffman [one of his favourite students] shouted, 'You damned pessimist!' Haushofer seemed to collapse: he left the room and uttered a moan, 'You know best, of course'.

Meanwhile in Britain Albrecht Haushofer's letter had arrived just after Clydesdale had been asking further questions in the House of Commons as to whether the German population in Poland could be removed to Germany in the same way as the German population in the South Tyrol was being transplanted to Bavaria and elsewhere.

On his return from the House of Commons Clydesdale found Albrecht Haushofer's letter waiting for him. The first half of it was of interest because it confirmed his suspicions that Hitler was determined to have war. As for the second half of the letter containing proposals as to what Britain might do, he considered it to be quite useless. Clydesdale saw Albrecht Haushofer as a very able man who was trying to reconcile his patriotism with his hatred of war, but was finding it impossible. He interpreted this letter as a message of despair.

Albrecht Haushofer continues to teach his students the art of making maps (Martin Haushofer)

Shortly after, in late July 1939, Clydesdale approached Winston Churchill after Question Time in the House of Commons and asked to see him alone, whereupon Churchill asked him round to his flat that evening. Churchill, being a backbencher, was still in the political wilderness, but he always had time to listen. Clydesdale arrived at his house while Churchill was in the bath, and Churchill emerged wrapped in a large bath towel. Clydesdale handed him Albrecht Haushofer's letter. Churchill sat down and read it very slowly with so much concentration that his cigar went out. Eventually he thrust the letter aside and sighed: 'There is going to be war very soon,' to which Clydesdale replied, 'In that case I very much hope that you will be Prime Minister.' Churchill did not deny that this would happen and merely shook his head saying, 'What a hell of a time to become Prime Minister.'

After this interview Clydesdale showed the letter to the Foreign Minister, Lord Halifax, whose comment was 'Hitler is out for world hegemony', and via Lord Dunglass (who as Sir Alec Douglas-Home would be a future Prime Minister), to Neville Chamberlain, as he thought it important to let him know that war against Poland was imminent. Having done this Clydesdale reclaimed the letter, and sent a non-committal postcard about his family to Albrecht Haushofer.

A month later, on 1 September 1939, German armed forces swamped Poland and after the expiry of the British ultimatum to Germany, Neville Chamberlain committed Britain to war against Nazi Germany on 3 September. Afterwards Churchill was asked in the Lobby of the House of Commons by Clydesdale how long he thought the war would last, and Churchill replied several times, 'Until the end of Hitler.'

The conquest of Poland followed within a few weeks, and many in Britain were surprised at the relative lack of activity in the first months of what came to be known as the 'Phoney War'. There was immediate demand for a statement of British War Aims, on the grounds that every attempt should be made at the outset of the war, in so far as it was possible, to separate the German people from Hitler. This demand came from a variety of different men, including William Temple, Archbishop of York and later Archbishop of Canterbury, Clydesdale, A. D. Lindsay, the Master of Balliol, and Arthur Salter. Their hope was to encourage any potential German Resistance to Hitler in Germany, by announcing that as soon as Hitler and the Nazi leadership had been destroyed there would be room for negotiation.

On 2 October 1939 the Archbishop of York broadcast on the B.B.C. on 'The Spirit and Aims of Great Britain in War', and expressed this point of view:

> Men are taking up a hateful duty: the very fact that they hate it throws into greater relief their conviction that it is a duty. . . . Our purpose is to check aggression, and bring to an end the perpetual insecurity and menace which hang over Europe spoiling the life of millions as a result of the Nazi tyranny in Germany. . . .
>
> It seems to me that the achievement of our purpose is possible only if two conditions are fulfilled. The first is that we should make no terms with Herr Hitler or his Government not because it is undemocratic, which is Germany's concern and not ours, but because it is utterly untrustworthy. The second is that the terms which we make with an honourable German Government shall be arrived at in such a way as to show that we have sought no kind of advantage for ourselves and no humiliation for the German people. . . .

Clydesdale, who was still an M.P. at this time, believed that a statement of British war aims was desirable so that men of goodwill in Germany would know what Britain was trying to accomplish and under what circumstances Britain would make peace. For example, it had to be made clear that no negotiation would be considered as long as the

Conference on the new struggle with the British Empire by sea, land and air at Hitler's home, the Berghof at Berchtesgaden. Hitler looks at Hess who is standing (W. G. Fitzgerald)

Nazis were in power. Equally he believed that if the Nazis were driven from power and succeeded by an honourable government willing to renounce Hitler's ill-gotten gains, then the major war aim would be achieved and negotiation of a just settlement could begin.

He had hoped to send a letter to *The Times* from young M.P.s who were serving officers in the three fighting services. He obtained the advice of Lord Halifax on the drafting of the letter, and he expressed regret that the Prime Minister had sent a message through Lord Dunglass to him that it was undesirable technically for serving officers to make a statement of this kind. He would therefore send the letter under his own name, with all references to the fighting services deleted. The letter ran:

Sir, Many like yourself, have had the opportunity of hearing a good deal of what the men and women of my generation are thinking. There is no doubt in any quarter, irrespective of party, that this country had no choice but to accept the challenge of Hitler's aggression against one country in Europe after another. If Hitler is right when he claims that the whole of the German nation is with him in his cruelties and treacheries, both within Germany and without, then this war must be fought to the bitter end. It may well last for many years, but the people of the British Empire will not falter in their determination to see it through.

But I believe that the moment the menace of aggression and bad faith has been removed, war against Germany becomes wrong and meaningless. This generation is conscious that injustices were done to the German people in the era after the last War. There must be no

100

repetition of that. To seek anything but a just and comprehensive peace to lay at rest the fears and discords in Europe would be a betrayal of our fallen.

I look forward to the day when a trusted Germany will again come into her own, and believe that there is such a Germany, which would be loth to inflict wrongs other nations such as she would not like to suffer herself. That day may be far off, but when it comes, then hostilities could and should cease, and all efforts be concentrated on righting the wrongs in Europe by free negotiations between the disputing parties, all parties binding themselves to submit their disputes to an impartial equity tribunal in case they cannot reach agreement.

We do not grudge Germany Lebensraum, provided that Lebensraum is not made the grave of other nations. We should be ready to search for and find a just colonial settlement, just to all peoples concerned, as soon as there exist effective guarantees that no race will be exposed to being treated as Hitler treated the Jews on November 9th last year. We shall, I trust, live to see the day when such a healing peace is negotiated between honourable men, and the bitter memories of twenty-five years of unhappy tension between Germany and the Western democracies are wiped away in their responsible co-operation for building a better Europe.

> Yours truly,
> Clydesdale
> House of Commons.

Similar letters and publications followed from Sir Arthur Salter, the Bishop of York, Sir Norman Angell, Lord Eustace Percy and the Master of Balliol. It was thought that at the beginning of the war a statement of British War Aims urging Germans to destroy Hitler might have been accepted as an incentive to moderate Germans. It was believed that such a statement would have meant no more than the taking out of an insurance policy against an event which might never happen. No emphatic statement of War Aims however was ever made by Neville Chamberlain's Government. Clydesdale's letter, along with the other letters and articles, had no effect on British Government policy but it does provide one of the connecting links in this story.

It came to the notice of Sir Frederick Ogilvie, the Director-General of the B.B.C., that on the 10.15 p.m. German News on 6 October 1939, Clydesdale's letter had been quoted. It is very likely that one of the Haushofers or Hess learnt about it, and that a sentence in the letter appealed to Hess, namely 'We shall I trust live to see the day when such a healing peace is negotiated between honourable men'. To the Nazis honour implied loyalty. It was not for nothing that the motto of the S.S. was 'Our honour is our loyalty' and Hess's loyalty to Hitler was beyond doubt. Hess would have been the first to have considered himself an 'honourable man', and would not have paid attention to the rest of Clydesdale's letter, which he would not have liked.

Albrecht Haushofer, on the other hand, would have understood Clydesdale's letter and would have appreciated that the war between Britain and Germany would be waged until Hitler and all that he represented had been destroyed – with or without the help of the German people. The issue was a clear-cut one for Clydesdale and the British, but it was not so simple for Albrecht who was a man writhing within himself, torn and tormented.

What happened to Albrecht between the outbreak of war and the end of 1940 is a long story. Basically he was collaborating with embryonic dissident circles in preparing peace plans. Many of those concerned were later associated with the German Resistance to Hitler. His public work in 1940 involved teaching at the University of Berlin or working part time for the Foreign Office under Ribbentrop. During the same year he began to work with men who would be associated with opposition to Hitler, namely Johannes Popitz, Karl Langbehn, a lawyer, and Ulrich von Hassell, the former German Ambassador in Italy.

Popitz had been Prussian Minister of Finance in 1932, and after Goering became Premier of Prussia had tried to influence the latter, with as much lack of success as Albrecht Haushofer had had with Ribbentrop. Popitz belonged to the Wednesday Society in Berlin, which included some fifteen persons who had made outstanding contributions to academic science. Through Popitz Albrecht became acquainted with the Wednesday Society. Hassell belonged to it, as did General Beck who had resigned as Chief of Staff of the German Army in 1938.

Associated with these men were Dr Carl Goerdeler the ex-Mayor of Leipzig, General Oster of Admiral Canaris's Abwehr (the German counter espionage service), and a number of high-ranking officers including Witzleben and von Truckow. Many of them believed that only a severe military disaster would induce German generals to act against Hitler.

As for Albrecht's views, after the outbreak of war he revealed them to a colleague in the Foreign Office, Fritz Hesse, who recalled that:

Haushofer called Hitler and his circle scum, his collaborators gangsters, and with an unsurpassed sharpness and malice enumerated the personal weaknesses of individuals. Since Haushofer himself had, at least for some time had the role of adviser and was then, as was usual, dropped by Hitler, his remarks bore the stamp of authenticity.

Haushofer argued with me that once the die was cast the war with Britain would be fought to the bitter end, and that there was no chance of an agreement with Hitler . . .

Haushofer also agreed with me that the patriotic pressures exerted on all Germans, the Gestapo terror and the indecision of political generals made it appear impossible that any internal action for the removal of the Hitler regime could succeed during the war. This we fully agreed, already at the beginning of the great struggle, that Germany's chances of an understanding with the opponents would only present themselves after Hitler's downfall.

It was in these circumstances that Albrecht prepared a peace plan which was submitted through one of his pupils, H.W. Stalmer, who had a Foreign Office job in the German Embassy in Spain, to the British Embassy in Spain but without results. The British refused to enter into discussions.

With his hatred of all forms of violence Albrecht was in the position of a man who did not want to fight against Germany and did not want to fight for her. Indeed Albrecht Haushofer was a man who did not want to fight at all.

As an ambitious, if troubled, German patriot he had refused to leave Germany before the outbreak of war and was now relying on the strength of his wits. He had one foot firmly planted in the German Resistance to Hitler, and his other firmly planted in the Nazi camp, both as assistant of Ribbentrop and as personal adviser to Rudolf Hess.

He talked about his dealings as 'sailing through troubled waters' and when questioned by friends as to the expected outcome of his hopes for peace he would say, 'one can only foresee three or four moves in a game of chess with any degree of accuracy.'

His uncertainty was not without cause, for with Hitler there could be no half measures. Those who were not with him were against him, and Albrecht was not with him. In 1940 Albrecht was playing a double game.

At this point it is appropriate to leave Albrecht Haushofer and return more closely to the career and fortunes of Hitler's personal deputy, the head of the Nazi Party, Rudolf Hess.

Part Two

THE HESS-HAUSHOFER
PEACE FEELERS

'I cannot imagine that cool, calculating England will run her neck into the Soviet noose instead of saving it by coming to an understanding with us.'
Rudolf Hess to Dr Kersten, *c.* 24 June 1940.

'It must be realised that, even in the Anglo-Saxon world, the Fuehrer was regarded as Satan's representative on earth and had to be fought. . . .
'As the final possibility I then mentioned that of a personal meeting on neutral soil with the closest of my English friends: the young Duke of Hamilton, who has access at all times to all important persons in London, even to Churchill and the King.'
Albrecht Haushofer's Tutorial to Hess, 8 September 1940.

'The whole thing is a fool's errand.'
Albrecht Haushofer to his parents, 19 September 1940.

'I replied that if a peace agreement was possible, the arrangement could have been made before the war started, but since Germany chose war in preference to peace at a time when we were most anxious to preserve peace, I could put forward no hope of a peace agreement now.'
Wing Commander the Duke of Hamilton's response to Deputy Fuehrer Rudolf Hess, 11 May 1941.

'Do you mean to tell me that the Deputy Fuehrer of Germany is in our hands? . . . Well, Hess or no Hess I am going to see the Marx Brothers.'
Prime Minister Winston Churchill to Wing Commander the Duke of Hamilton, 11 May 1941.

'England should give Germany a free hand in Europe, and Germany would give England a completely free hand in the Empire. . . . Germany had certain demands to make of Russia which would have to be satisfied, either by negotiation or as the result of a war.'
Rudolf Hess to Ivone Kirkpatrick, 1.30 a.m. 13 May 1941.

ONE

Hess's Decline and Hitler's Peace Offers

Towards 1939 Hess's influence with Hitler was declining. It is sometimes said that Hess's character was different from that of Nazi leaders like Goering, Himmler and Goebbels. He was certainly more loyal and less intelligent. His loyalty to Hitler secured for him a position of great power, as head of the Nazi Party, and his lack of intelligence led to his gradual decline, a process which became noticeable in 1937 with the rise of Himmler, Goering and Bormann.

In the 1920s Hess had been Hitler's closest friend. Hitler had been an insignificant corporal in the Great War, while Hess had been an officer, and his unqualified admiration had given Hitler a certain self-confidence, for he felt that Hess's loyalty meant recognition by the German officer class. Hitler also believed that if his speeches passed Hess they would easily go down with a German mass audience, since, as Hitler said, a mass audience is apt to follow the lowest common denominator.

Hess himself was a man longing for domination by a stronger will. His close friendship with Hitler made him into a hard and ruthless Fascist, prepared to do anything on Hitler's behalf, as he had shown during the Night of the Long Knives. Because his loyalty to Hitler was absolute he was quite unlike Himmler and Goering. Consequently, Hess had not sufficient imagination to be a prime mover of Nazism. He was the devoted follower, implementing Hitler's will in Hitler's wake. Content to reflect the lustre of his leader, diverting all light away from himself, he was a pale carbon copy of his Fuehrer. Inseparable from Hitler in the Reichstag and elsewhere, he had become almost an adjunct of Hitler's personality.

Hitler had a great affection for Hess as his closest and most devoted friend, and, as such, he wanted to reward him. He found administration tiresome and was glad to delegate. In April 1933 he appointed Hess as his Deputy with power to make decisions in his name in all matters of Party leadership.

Hess in return helped to extend Hitler's power in many ways. He appointed a University Commission of the Party and on 18 July 1934 the Nazi League of German Students was directly subordinated to him. He also sent circulars for the German Industry Adolf Hitler Fund to organisations such as Krupps, so that the necessary funds could be acquired 'for the unified execution of the tasks which fall to the lot of the S.A., S.S. and other political organisations'.

In the early years after his accession to power Hitler found Hess's work satisfactory, and on 27 July 1934 he increased Hess's authority by compelling all Nazi leaders to present drafts of laws to Hess for his preliminary sanction. Through Hess he wished to keep a check on other Nazi leaders.

It looked as though Hitler might make Hess his heir. However, in 1934, after visiting Hess's house near Munich, Hitler said that he had decided not to make him his successor because Hess's house had displayed a lack of taste for art and culture. Consequently Goering was appointed Hitler's successor over Hess's head, Hess remaining Hitler's personal Deputy.

Towards the end of the war, Hitler would say, 'If anything happens to me Germany will be left without a leader. I have no successor. The first, Hess, is mad. The second, Goering, has lost the sympathy of the people; and the third, Himmler, would be rejected by the Party.' But in 1934 Hess was very close to Hitler. At the Nuremberg Rallies, Hess would recite to the countless thousands of Stormtroopers, 'The Party is Hitler. But Hitler is Germany, just as Germany is Hitler. Hitler! Sieg Heil!'[1]

Hitler may not have felt until later that Hess was deficient in other respects, for his new job was more demanding than that of being simply Hitler's secretary. At the Brown House in Munich, Hess at the head of the Nazi Party had control over at least nineteen departments, his Chief of Staff being Martin Bormann.

Three of the most important departments under Hess were in Berlin. Todt's Department for Technical and Organisation Questions had considerable control over German industry and was responsible for the construction of autobahns, so that panzer divisions could move with maximum speed throughout the Reich. Another was the Foreign Department dealing with the Nazi Party's Ausland Organisation under Hess's protégé, Gauleiter Bohle, and perhaps the most important department was the Dienststelle Ribbentrop.

Hess, as the head of the Nazi Party, was responsible for bringing in vicious legislation against those who were anti-Nazi and those of Jewish, or of part-Jewish origin. On 20 December 1934 he signed a decree entitled 'Laws against Treacherous Acts towards the State and Party'. Article 1 imposed penalties upon anyone making utterances which harmed the prestige of the Nazi Party or Nazi State, and Article 2 made it illegal for anyone to make malicious statements about the Party or its leading personalities. Hess and Himmler saw to it that this decree was rigorously enforced.

Hess brought in many of the Nuremberg Race Laws, along with Frick, the Reich Minister of the Interior, and Goering. On 14 November 1935 he signed the decree which deprived all Jews of their right to employment in government offices and of their right to vote. On 15 September he signed the Law for the Protection of Blood and Honour and under that decree and under the Reich Citizenship Law he went on to issue the necessary legislation for the carrying out or the supplementing of those laws. Another decree signed by him forbade Jews to marry or to have extra-marital relations with Germans.

In one of his speeches Hess quoted Treitschke's saying 'All justice is political'. Hess certainly made it so. He had set in motion the wheels which culminated in the mass murder of Jews. In a speech in Berlin to the officers of the German Wehrmacht on 16 January 1937 he spoke proudly about Nazism as a forceful movement which had been 'enabled to obliterate Jewish poison in all spheres'. The actual obliteration was carried out by Himmler and his men. Like Hitler, Hess was content to leave the matter to Himmler. On 9 June 1934 Hess decreed that the Nazi Party's Intelligence Service should be absorbed by the S.S., the Security Service of the Reichsführer S.S. being established as 'the sole political news and defence service of the party'. Again, on 14 December 1938 Hess issued a decree that control over the S.D. (the Secret Service of the S.S.) should be transferred to Himmler's S.S. To express solidarity with his

Hess takes to wearing the uniform of an S.S. Obergruppenführer. Hitler, flanked by Goebbels and Hess, receives the Nazi salute at a rally in Berlin (Hulton-Deutsch)

accomplice Himmler, Hess accepted the honorary position of Obergruppenführer in the S.S.

Hess encouraged Germans to look upon themselves as a master race, and in his speech on 16 January 1937 he declared:

> As at home, abroad too Germans are being instructed in National-Socialist ideology. . . .
> They are being re-educated to a proud sense of being German, to cohere among themselves,
> to respect one another, so as to make them realise that they stand higher than any other
> national group. . . .

The methods which Hess used for encouraging Germans to 'cohere' to the Reich can be discerned in the events leading up to the Anschluss. Through the Ausland Organisation Hess had been in touch with the illegal Nazi Party in Austria from 1933 onwards. In the autumn of 1934 he appointed Reinthaler as leader of the peasants in the Austrian Nazi Party. In 1936, Hess and Goering had meetings with the Austrian Nazi Seyss-Inquart and on 25 January 1938 the Austrian Government discovered his underhand game. On that day the Austrian Police visited the headquarters of the Committee of Seven in Vienna, which was in fact the head office of the illegal Nazi Party. There they picked up documents initialled by Hess which gave instructions for the staging of a revolt in the spring of 1938. According to this plan the German Wehrmacht would enter Austria as soon as Austrian troops tried to put down the revolt, to prevent German

107

7 April 1938. Hess salutes the tomb of Holweber in the Vienna cemetery. Holweber had been executed for murdering Chancellor Dollfuss of Austria (Associated Press)

blood being spilt by Germans. There was no need to put this or any similar plan into operation, as the Austrian Government capitulated.

On 12 March 1938, the morning that German troops marched into Austria, Hess and Himmler were the first Nazi leaders to appear in Vienna. On the next day, 13 March, Hitler, Goering, Hess, Ribbentrop and Frick signed the Anschluss Law for a 'free and secret plebiscite', to determine the question of reunion with Germany, the results of which were predetermined, with Himmler's S.S. organising the polls.

On 24 July 1938 Hess and Himmler made a point of being present at the celebrations held on the anniversary of the murder of Dollfuss. Four years before, Hess and Hitler had disowned the revolt which had caused Dollfuss's death. At that time no reference had been made by Hess to the fact that thirteen Nazis, including Planetta, had been executed for their share in Dollfuss's murder. Yet on 24 July 1938 Hess proudly commemorated the unsuccessful Putsch by laying a wreath at the grave of the murderers and by eulogising them. 'Wherever in all the world National Socialists march, these dead comrades march with us.' As a final touch, on 20 May 1938 Hess signed a decree extending the anti-semitic Nuremberg Laws to Austria.

In spite of Albrecht Haushofer's part-Jewish ancestry Hess had made an exception in his case, because his old friend Karl Haushofer had sheltered him after the Beerhall Putsch, and Hess was glad to repay his debt of gratitude by protecting the Haushofer family. Karl Haushofer spoke highly of the intellectual ability of his son Albrecht, and

*18 May 1936. Hess in Leipzig's Exhibition Hall. Note the unconscious
symbolism of the Sword of Damocles over Hess
(Hulton-Deutsch)*

Hess was willing to consider Albrecht's technical reports on Volksdeutsch matters and
Foreign Policy as well as on other topics including science and education. Albrecht
however had no share in the formulation of Nazi policy. He could influence Hess only on
matters of detail. Any line of policy emanating from Hitler was accepted absolutely by
Hess and rational argument was impossible.

Nonetheless Hess was gradually declining in importance, and this became
noticeable in 1937. His loss of influence was mainly due to the rise of Himmler and of
Bormann in the Nazi Party. In 1937 the Volksdeutsche Mittelstelle was created and, with
S.S. General Lorenz at its head, was effectively controlled by Himmler. Although Hess
was still senior to Himmler his position was static, while Himmler's domain was rapidly
growing. At the same time Hess's influence in the Nazi Party was declining, because Hitler
was coming to realise that his Deputy was not an efficient or competent administrator.

*20 April 1939. On the occasion of Hitler's birthday, Hess presents Hitler with fifty original letters of Frederick the Great on behalf of the Nazi Party (*The Times*)*

More and more work was undertaken by Bormann, who wheedled his way into Hitler's confidence by managing the Adolf Hitler Industrial Fund for Hitler's private uses. Putzi Hanfstaengl wrote: 'Hess gradually became a nobody, a flag without a pole. Even Hitler once said to me of his Deputy: "I only hope he never has to take over from me. I would not know who to be more sorry for, Hess or the Party." '

On top of this Hess, according to Hanfstaengl, 'was already becoming highly peculiar and went in for vegetarianism, nature cures and other weird beliefs. It got to the point where he would not go to bed without testing with a divining rod whether there were any subterranean water-courses which conflicted with the direction of his couch.'

It was no wonder that he was beginning to lose his place in the Nazi hierarchy to Himmler and Bormann. Even Ribbentrop had become a more powerful figure than Hess. The Dienststelle Ribbentrop had rapidly grown in numbers from about fifteen in 1934 to more than three hundred in 1937. It had become the boiler-room of Nazi diplomacy, and after Ribbentrop became Foreign Minister Hitler listened only to him when considering whether the British would tolerate the German enslavement of one country after another. Ribbentrop's advice to Hitler in 1938 and 1939 had been that the British would either not fight at all when Poland was attacked, or would not fight seriously when confronted with a *fait accompli*.

Hess did not question Ribbentrop's policy, because it was the policy of Hitler, whom Hess always supported. On 27 August 1939 Hess spoke of the exceptional restraint exhibited by Hitler towards Poland, and on 30 August he became a member of the Council of Ministers for Defence of the Reich. His intimacy with Hitler remained unaltered and on 1 September he was reappointed Hitler's successor after Goering, whilst the German army was invading Poland. On the same day Hess rang Karl Haushofer and told him that

21 June 1940. The Nazi High Command leaves after the French signing of the Armistice at Compiegne. From left to right: General von Brauchitsch, Admiral Raeder, Hitler, Goering, Hess and Ribbentrop (Associated Press)

there would be a short thunderstorm, and the General Professor replied that one could not know how big a flood might follow, and that he who rode a tiger could not jump off.

Two days later, on 3 September, Hess was beside Hitler when Hitler's interpreter Schmidt read out the British ultimatum, demanding withdrawal of German armed forces from Poland. Hitler turned to Hess and said, 'My book has been written in vain.' Sixteen years before, Hitler had dictated to Hess, whilst writing *Mein Kampf*, 'No sacrifice should have been too great in winning England's friendship.'

After the fall of Poland, Hess was involved in the administration of the occupied territories. In September and October 1939 he signed decrees incorporating Danzig and German-occupied Poland into the Reich and on 12 October he signed another decree creating the administration of German-occupied Poland. He aided Himmler in the recruiting of the S.S., which was already providing numerous extermination squads, and whose Waffen S.S. units were in his opinion more suitable than other units for policing the occupied eastern territories.

Hess had no feelings of humanity towards the Poles. He had been involved in the formulation of penal laws for the Poles in the occupied eastern territories, based on the premise that the Pole was less susceptible to the infliction of ordinary punishment than other human beings. Hess therefore wanted them to do the heaviest forms of labour in concentration camps.

Yet Hess never put the British into the same category as the Russians or any other people in Eastern Europe. He approved when Hitler offered a peace conference to the British Empire from the Reichstag on 6 October 1939, saying that if the opinions of Mr Churchill and his followers were to prevail, this statement would have been his last. As a matter of fact it was only his first and it was promptly rejected by Neville Chamberlain, as the Germans showed no signs of withdrawing from the occupied territories. As Ciano caustically wrote, the only voices in Britain in favour of the conference suggested by Hitler were Lloyd George and Bernard Shaw, proving that the British considered Hitler's proposals to be quite unacceptable.

As the Western democracies had rejected his peace overture, Hitler turned his attention to the destruction of France in the spring of the next year. After demolishing the French armed forces, however, Hitler stopped his Panzer divisions from attacking the British Expeditionary Force at Dunkirk on 24 May 1940. General Guenther Blumentritt described Hitler's words:

> He then astonished us by speaking with admiration of the British Empire, of the necessity for its existence and of the civilisation that Britain had brought into the world. . . . He said that all he wanted from Britain was that she should acknowledge Germany's position on the Continent. . . . He concluded by saying that his aim was to make peace with Britain. . . .

The next weeks characterised Hitler's love-hate attitude towards the British. On 18–19 June 1940 Ciano recorded that Hitler 'makes many reservations on the desirability of demolishing the British Empire, which he considers, even today, to be an important factor in world equilibrium'. On 7 July again Ciano wrote that Hitler was 'rather inclined to continue the struggle and to unleash a storm of wrath upon the English. But the fatal decision has not yet been reached and it is for this reason that he is delaying his speech, of which, as he puts it, he wants to weigh every word.' Hitler had for some time been thinking of invading Britain, but he was only toying with the idea, partly because he did not want to run the risk of failure and partly because he intensely disliked the sea. He had even told Field Marshal Rundstedt, 'On the land I am a hero; on the sea I am a coward.'

Hence Hitler made his famous peace offer to the British Empire on 19 July 1940

19 July 1940. Hitler sits next to Hess after making his peace offer to Britain from the Reichstag. Left to right: Hess, Hitler, von Neurath and Goebbels (UPI)

from the Reichstag. Before and after he spoke he sat beside Rudolf Hess, to whom he paid a standard tribute. He started by saying that he had warned Britain and France in his former peace offer of 6 October 1939, and that a small clique of British warmongers were keeping the war alive.

> For this peace proposal I was abused and personally insulted. Mr Chamberlain, in fact, spat upon me before the eyes of the world, and following the instructions of the instigators and warmongers in the background – men such as Churchill, Duff Cooper, Eden, Hore-Belisha and others – declined even to mention peace, let alone to work for it. . . .

With words flowing with sarcasm he poured scorn on the British resolve to fight whatever the consequences.

> In the opinion of British politicians their last hopes, apart from allied peoples consisting of a number of kings without a throne, statesmen without a nation and generals without an army, seem to be based on fresh complications which they hope to bring about, thanks to their proven skill in such matters.
>
> A veritable 'wandering Jew' among these hopes is the belief in the possibility of a fresh estrangement between Germany and Russia. . . .

He said that any such hope was based on a false premise and he then reverted to his

113

constant theme that it was only this small war clique in Britain which was causing the war, and that the British people were longing for peace:

> Mr Churchill ought perhaps, for once, to believe me when I prophesy that a great Empire will be destroyed, an Empire which it was never my intention to destroy or even to harm. I do, however, realise that this struggle, if it continues, can end only with the complete annihilation of one or other of the two adversaries. Mr Churchill may believe that this will be Germany. I know that it will be different.
>
> In this hour, I feel it to be my duty before my own conscience to appeal once more to reason and common-sense in Great Britain as much as elsewhere. I consider myself in a position to make this appeal since I am not the vanquished, begging favours, but the victor speaking in the name of reason.
>
> I can see no reason why this war must go on. . . .
>
> Possibly, Mr Churchill will again brush aside this statement of mine by saying that it is merely born of fear and of doubt in our final victory. In that case, I shall have relieved my conscience in regard to the things to come. . . .

Winston Churchill regarded Hitler's peace offer as a gross affront, and did not condescend to reply. On 22 July the peace offer was casually rejected out of hand by Lord Halifax in a routine broadcast.

Even so Hitler had no heart for invading Britain, especially as he had clearly made up his mind to attack and annex large parts of Russia. The date alone for the Russian venture had to be fixed, and Hitler was persuaded that an attack in the autumn of 1940 was not practicable. His commanders were having to restrain him, because Hitler's mind was adopting a new mould. He thought that Britain was refusing to make peace because she was hoping for help, above all from Russia, and that if Russia were smashed Britain could no longer have this hope and would therefore have to make peace. As Halder noted on 31 July 1940 after further talks with Hitler:

> Britain's hope lies in Russia and the United States. . . .
> Russia is the factor on which Britain is relying most. . . .
> With Russia smashed, Britain's last hope will be shattered. . . .
> Decision: Russia's destruction must therefore be made a part of this struggle. Spring 1941.
> The sooner Russia is crushed the better.

It has been suggested that Hess may not have known that Hitler was going to attack Russia. However there is a certain amount of evidence on this point from high-ranking Nazi sources which appears to point solely in one direction. Otto Dietrich, Hitler's Press Officer, wrote that Hess was one of the few who knew about the plan to attack Russia, and that Hitler was very much afraid in the latter half of May 1941 that Hess would give away the outline of this plan to the British. Fritz Hesse, Ribbentrop's Press Officer, recorded that Himmler too was very anxious lest Hess after his flight might betray to the British the Fuehrer's intentions towards Russia. Walter Schellenberg, one of Himmler's most senior Intelligence Officers, was also aware of the concern of Hitler and Himmler, and wrote in his memoirs that Hess certainly knew about Hitler's decision to attack Russia.

Albrecht Haushofer was in the secret as well and while the preparations for the Russian campaign were made from August onwards under the heavily camouflaged order entitled Aufbau Ost or 'Reconstruction East', Hess was becoming more and more impatient. He had been kept in constant touch by Walter Warlimont of Hitler's Operations Staff in the OKW (Armed Forces High Command). Warlimont related that as

13 November 1940, Berlin. Hess shaking hands with Molotov, the Soviet Foreign Minister, during the time of the Nazi-Soviet Pact (UPI)

Chief of the Section it was his responsibility to keep Hess in the picture as to the most recent military developments. As Deputy Fuehrer of the Third Reich and as a member of the Council of Ministers for the Defence of the Reich, Hess obviously had to be kept informed. He probably knew about the decision to attack Russia months before Hitler issued his order for Operation Barbarossa on 18 December 1940.

Indeed Hess may well have known about Hitler's decision to invade Russia before anyone else. In June 1940, during the French Campaign, Hitler and Hess had a lengthy conversation, and Hess later admitted to Lord Simon that the plans for his Secret Mission stemmed from this date. Presumably this was the conversation referred to by Dr Kersten, Himmler's doctor, in his diary entry for 24 June 1940. Hess was in an excitable condition, suffering from stomach pains, and in the course of his treatment from Kersten spoke about an era of Franco-German co-operation. When Kersten brought up the British question, pointing out that they were a stubborn people, Hess replied:

> We'll make peace with England in the same way as with France. Only a few weeks back the Fuehrer again spoke of the great value of the British Empire in the world order. Germany and France must stand together with England against the enemy of Europe, Bolshevism. That was the reason why the Feuhrer allowed that English Army to escape at Dunkirk. He did not want to upset the possibility of an understanding. The English must see that and seize their chance. I can't imagine that cool, calculating England will run her neck into the Soviet noose instead of saving it by coming to an understanding with us.

Hess had already made up his mind to restore himself in Hitler's personal esteem. He would help to make peace with Britain so that together Germany and Britain might oppose Russia, which Hess had described as 'the enemy of Europe'. His political aim was an open secret. He had laid it down as Hitler's secretary in *Mein Kampf* in 1923.

> If European soil was wanted by and large it could be had only at the expense of Russia. . . . For such a policy as this there was but one ally in Europe – England. Only with England covering our rear could we have begun a new Germanic migration.

The only conclusion to be drawn is that Hess's immediate objective was to get Britain out of the war, so that Hitler's long-term aims for the establishment of a German Empire in the east could be realised. And so it was that the idea of a secret mission to the British came to germinate in the mind of Rudolf Hess.

NOTE

1. Alan Bullock, *Hitler and Stalin: Parallel Lives*, pages 983, 385.

TWO

A Tutorial for Hess:
8 September 1940

On 31 July 1940 Hitler told his commanders that an attempt must be made to finish preparations for the invasion of England by 15 September. There were several major complications however. The German Navy was inferior to the British Navy and had been severely mauled in the Norwegian campaign. Moreover the Luftwaffe, while numerically superior to the Royal Air Force, was quite unable to gain control over the air, and both the British Navy and R.A.F. wasted no time in harrying the German Invasion Fleet. On 17 September Hitler acknowledged that the R.A.F. had not been defeated and decided to postpone Operation Sea Lion indefinitely.

During this time Rudolf Hess was attempting to discover whether the British might be susceptible to a peace feeler. For this purpose he sought the advice of Karl Haushofer, and had an eight-hour meeting with him on 31 August. The conversation was described by the Professor General in a letter to Albrecht on 3 September:

> I was rewarded, for it brought me a meeting with Tomo [Rudolf Hess] from 5 o'clock in the afternoon until 2 o'clock in the morning, which included a three-hour walk in the Grunwalder Forest, during which we conversed a good deal about serious matters. I have really got to tell you about a part of it now.

According to Karl Haushofer, Hitler was making preparations for launching an invasion against Britain, but was hoping for a peaceful way out and Hess was wondering whether a peace feeler could be made through a British intermediary in a neutral country.

> As you know, everything is so prepared for a very hard and severe attack on the island in question that the highest ranking person only has to press a button to set it off. But before this decision, which is perhaps inevitable, the thought once more occurs as to whether there is really no way of stopping something which would have such infinitely momentous consequences. There is a line of reasoning in connection with this which I absolutely must pass on to you because it was obviously communicated to me with this intention. Do you, too, see no way in which such possibilities could be discussed at a third place with a middle man, possibly the old Ian Hamilton or the other Hamilton?

117

The photograph of the Duke of Hamilton as shown in The Pilot's Book of Everest *which Hess had read (Elizabeth, Duchess of Hamilton)*

The last two persons mentioned were both known to Karl Haushofer. General Sir Ian Hamilton, the veteran of the Gallipoli Campaign in the 1914–18 war, had once had lunch with Hitler and Hess, and Karl Haushofer had met the Duke of Hamilton (then Marquis of Clydesdale) once, before Munich.

Karl Haushofer told Hess that there was a good opportunity to send 'well disguised political persons' to Portugal for a meeting with a British contact, while the Portuguese were holding their centennial celebrations. The Professor General added in his letter to Albrecht that an old friend, Mrs Roberts, had just sent a message of greetings to the Haushofer family. Her address was c/o Post Box 506, Lisbon, and he felt that a channel to the British might be opened up through her, and 'that no good possibility should be overlooked'.

Albrecht had been prepared by his father, and was in due course summoned by Hess to Bad Godesberg for a lengthy talk on 8 September. Hess had his reasons for calling Albrecht. He disliked Ribbentrop and knew that the Reich Foreign Minister had rejected the advice of Albrecht Haushofer, whom Hess had appointed to the Dienststelle Ribbentrop in order to keep Ribbentrop in check. He knew too that Ribbentrop had advised Hitler that it would be safe to tear Poland apart on the basis that the British would not fight seriously and that Hitler had acted on this information in disregard of the views expressed in Albrecht Haushofer's reports. He now turned to Albrecht in the belief that Albrecht knew a great deal more about the British than Ribbentrop. After the meeting Albrecht drew up the following memorandum.

TOP SECRET   Berlin, 15 September 1940.

ARE THERE STILL POSSIBILITIES OF A
GERMAN-ENGLISH PEACE?

On 8 September, I was summoned to Bad G. [Godesberg] to report to the Deputy of the Fuehrer on the subject discussed in this memorandum. The conversation which the two of us had alone lasted two hours. I had the opportunity to speak in all frankness.

I was immediately asked about the possibilities of making known to persons of importance in England Hitler's serious desire for peace. It was quite clear that the continuance of the war was suicidal for the white race. Even with complete peace in Europe Germany was not in a position to take over the inheritance of the Empire. The Fuehrer had not wanted to see the Empire destroyed and did not want it even today. Was there not somebody in England who was ready for peace?

First I asked for permission to discuss fundamental things. It was necessary to realise that not only Jews and Freemasons, but practically all Englishmen who mattered, regarded a treaty signed by the Fuehrer as a worthless scrap of paper. To the question as to why this was so, I referred to the ten-year term of our Polish Treaty, to the Non-Aggression Pact with Denmark signed only a year ago, to the 'final' frontier demarcation of Munich. What guarantee did England have that a new treaty would not be broken again at once if it suited us? It must be realised that, even in the Anglo-Saxon world, the Fuehrer was regarded as Satan's representative on earth and had to be fought.

If the worst came to the worst, the English would rather transfer their whole Empire bit by bit to the Americans than sign a peace that left to National Socialist Germany the mastery of Europe. The present war, I was convinced, shows that Europe has become too small for its previous anarchic form of existence; it is only through close German-English co-operation that it can achieve a true federative order (based by no means merely on the police rule of a single power), while maintaining a part of its world position and having security against Soviet Russian Eurasia. France was smashed, probably for a long time to come, and we had opportunity currently to observe what Italy is capable of accomplishing. As long, however, as German-English rivalry existed, and in so far as both sides thought in terms of security, the lesson of this war was this: every German had to tell himself: we have no security as long as provision is not made that the Atlantic gateways of Europe from Gibraltar to Narvik are free of any possible blockade. That is: there must be no English fleet. Every Englishman, must, however, under the same conditions, argue: we have no security as long as anywhere within a radius of 2,000 kilometres from London there is a plane that we do not control. That is: there must be no German Air Force.

There is only one way out of this dilemma: friendship intensified to fusion, with a joint fleet, a joint air force, and joint defence of possessions in the world – just what the English are now about to conclude with the United States.

Here I was interrupted and asked why, indeed, the English were prepared to seek such a relationship with America and not with us. My reply was: because Roosevelt is a man who represents a Weltanschauung and a way of a life that the Englishman thinks he understands, to which he can become accustomed, even where it does not seem to be to his liking. Perhaps he fools himself – but, at any rate, that is what he believes.

A man like Churchill – himself half-American – is convinced of this. Hitler, however, seems to the Englishman the incarnation of what he hates that he has fought against for centuries – this feeling grips the workers no less than the plutocrats.

In fact, I am of the opinion that those Englishmen who have property to lose, that is, precisely the portions of the so-called plutocracy that count, are those who would be readiest to talk peace. But even they regard a peace only as an armistice.

I was compelled to express these things so strongly because I ought not – precisely because of my long experience in attempting to effect a settlement with England in the past and my numerous English friendships – make it appear that I seriously believed in the possibility of a settlement between Adolf Hitler and England in the present stage of development.

I was thereupon asked whether I was not of the opinion that feelers had perhaps not been successful because the right language had not been used. I replied that, to be sure – if certain persons, whom we both knew well, were meant by this statement – then certainly the wrong language had been used. But at the present stage this had little significance.

I was then asked directly why all Englishmen were so opposed to Herr von Ribbentrop. I suggested that in the eyes of the English, Herr von Ribbentrop, like some other personages, played the same role as did Duff Cooper, Eden and Churchill in the eyes of the Germans. In the case of Herr von Ribbentrop, there was also the conviction, precisely in the view of Englishmen who were formerly friendly to Germany that – from completely biased motives – he had informed the Fuehrer wrongly about England and that he personally bore an unusually large share of the responsibility for the outbreak of the war.

But I again stressed the fact that the rejection of peace feelers by England was today due not so much to persons as to the fundamental outlook above.

Nevertheless, I was asked to name those whom I thought might be reached as possible contacts.

I mentioned among diplomats, Minister O'Malley [British Minister to Hungary] in Budapest, the former head of the South Eastern Department of the Foreign Office, a clever person in the higher echelons of officialdom, but perhaps without influence precisely because of his former friendliness towards Germany; Sir Samuel Hoare [British Ambassador to Spain], who is half-shelved and half on the watch in Madrid, whom I do not know well personally, but to whom I can at any time open a personal path; as the most promising, the Washington Ambassador Lothian [British Ambassador to the U.S.A.], with whom I have had close personal connections for years, who as a member of the highest aristocracy and at the same time as a person of very independent mind, is perhaps best in a position to undertake a bold step – provided that he could be convinced that even a bad and uncertain peace would be better than the continuance of the war – a conviction at which he will only arrive if he convinces himself in Washington that English hopes of America are not realisable. Whether or not this is so could only be judged in Washington itself; from Germany not at all.

As the final possibility I then mentioned that of a personal meeting on neutral soil with the closest of my English friends: the young Duke of Hamilton who has access at all times to all important persons in London, even to Churchill and the King. I stressed in this case the inevitable difficulty of making a contact and again repeated my conviction of the improbability of its succeeding – whatever approach we took.

The upshot of the conversation was H's [Hess's] statement that he would consider the whole matter thoroughly once more and send me word in case I was to take steps. For this extremely ticklish case, and in the event that I might possibly have to make a trip alone – I asked for very precise directions from the highest authority.

From the whole conversation I had the strong impression that it was not conducted without the prior knowledge of the Fuehrer, and that I probably would not hear any more about the matter unless a new understanding had been reached between him and his deputy.

On the personal side of the conversation I must say that – despite the fact that I felt bound to say unusually hard things – it ended in great friendliness, even cordiality. . . .

At this time Albrecht was working for the members of the still embryonic German Resistance to Hitler as well as for the German Foreign Office and Hess. He was walking a tightrope, and it appeared to him that Hess was the only Nazi leader who would and could be of assistance to him, and further that he was the only Nazi leader at that stage whom he could use. As a patriotic German Albrecht believed that any peace with Britain was better than no peace. He was trying to open up a channel to Britain on Hess's behalf with, as he believed, Hitler's knowledge, and he had put forward Hamilton's name as a desperate man clutches at a straw. Albrecht knew that the British were in no mood for Nazi peace feelers, but by a strange irony had given Hess the name of the person whom Hess would approach. He had told Hess that his friend the Duke of Hamilton had access at all times to all important persons in London, although Hamilton had in fact been called up before the outbreak of war and was serving full-time with the R.A.F. in the east of Scotland. Nevertheless, once the idea had been put into the mind of Rudolf Hess nothing in the world would get it out.

THREE

The Peace Feeler:
23 September 1940

There has been some doubt amongst historians as to whether Hitler knew that Hess was trying to make contact with the British through asking Albrecht Haushofer to send a written communication of some kind. However, it appears from several sources that Hitler did know that Hess was going to try and make some such form of contact. Hewel, Ribbentrop's liaison man with Hitler, told Fritz Hesse that Hitler was using Albrecht Haushofer for making contact with the British, and that Haushofer had connections with Britain through the Swiss Professor, Carl Burckhardt. Frau Hess was more definite: she wrote that her husband tried to get in touch with prominent circles in Britain through Albrecht Haushofer via Spain or Switzerland, with Hitler's knowledge. As for Albrecht Haushofer himself, he had written in his memorandum on the possibilities of a German–English peace that Hess had given him the impression that their conversation as to how to make contact with the British by letter had been conducted with Hitler's prior knowledge. He also wrote that the chances were that he would not be required to take any action unless agreement on the subject was reached between Hitler and Hess.

According to Otto Dietrich, Hess did have a conversation with Hitler. He asked Hitler whether his policy towards Britain remained unchanged and Hitler told Hess that he still desired an Anglo–German understanding. The most that can be assumed from these sources is that Hitler gave a measure of approval to Hess to make enquiries through Albrecht Haushofer. It may well be that Hitler did not wish anyone else to know that such enquiries were being made with his approval. Be that as it may, Hess in due course took action. He got in touch with the Haushofers.

He knew that notwithstanding Karl Haushofer's refusal to join the Nazi Party, his teachings on geopolitics had provided Hitler's expansionist policies with a cloak of intellectual respectability. On 27 August 1939 Hitler had written to Karl on the German Chancellor's headed paper:

> Esteemed Professor, may I convey my sincerest congratulations upon the occasion of your 70th Birthday.
>
> At the same time I confer upon you the Order of the Eagle of the German Reich, with the dedication 'To the important German Geopolitician' in recognition of your achievements in the field of Geopolitics.
>
> With best wishes for your continued work and well-being I remain with German greeting, Yours, A. Hitler.[1]

On 10 September 1940 Hess wrote to Karl Haushofer referring to the letter of 3 September (see above [page 117]) which the General Professor had sent to Albrecht. Obviously Hess had been toying with the mechanics of opening peace feelers.

The prerequisite naturally is that the inquiry in question and the reply would not go through official channels, for you would not in any case want to cause your friends over there any trouble.

It would be best to have the letter to the old lady, with whom you are acquainted, delivered through a confidential agent of the A.O. [Ausland Organisation] to the address that is known to you. For this purpose Albrecht would have to speak either with Bohle or my brother.[2] At the same time the lady would have to be given the address of this agent in L. [Lisbon] or if the latter does not live there permanently, of another agent of the A.O. who does live there permanently, to which the reply can in turn be delivered.

As for the neutral I have in mind, I would like to speak to you orally about it some time. There is no hurry about that since, in any case, there would first have to be a reply received here from over there.

Meanwhile let's both keep our fingers crossed. Should success be the fate of the enterprise, the oracle given to you with regard to the month of August would yet be fulfilled, since the name of the young friend and the old lady friend of your family occurred to you during our quiet walk on the last day of that month.

With best regards to you and to Martha,

Yours, as ever
R[Rudolf] H[Hess]

From the tone of his letter Hess was evidently quite determined to make a peace overture and Albrecht after seeing it wrote to his parents from Berlin on 18 September 1940, pointing out that it was not as easy as Hess imagined to make contact with a person such as Hamilton in a country with which Germany was at war. Also he did not wish to endanger their friend Mrs Roberts who would have to see that a message was conveyed from Portugal.

In the midst of a rather intensive activity only these lines for today as acknowledgment of the letter in question, I shall consider the whole case again for another twenty-four hours and will then write to T. [Hess] directly. It really can not be done in the way he imagines. Still, I could formulate a letter to D.H. [Douglas Hamilton] in such a way that the conveyance in no way endangers our old lady friend. Above all, I have to make it clear to T. once again that without the permission of his authorities of the highest responsibility my ducal friend can just as little write to me as I can do it the other way round. . . .

On the next day, 19 September, Albrecht wrote to Hess mentioning that he had seen the latter's letter to his father.

TOP SECRET

My dear Herr Hess,

Your letter of the tenth reached me yesterday after a delay caused by the antiquated postal service of Partnach-Alm. I again gave a thorough study to the possibilities discussed therein and request – before taking the steps proposed – that you yourself examine once more the thoughts set forth below.

I have in the meantime been thinking of the technical route by which a message from me must travel before it can reach the Duke of H [Hamilton]. With your help, delivery to Lisbon can of course be assured without difficulty. About the rest of the route we do not know. Foreign control must be taken into account; the letter must therefore in no case be composed in such a way that it will simply be seized and destroyed or that it will directly endanger the woman transmitting it or the ultimate recipient.

In view of my close personal relations and intimate acquaintance with D.H. I can write a few lines to him (which should be enclosed with the letter to Mrs R. without any indication of place and without a full name – an A would suffice for signature) in such a way that he alone will recognise that behind my wish to see him in Lisbon there is something more serious than a personal whim. All the rest, however, seems to be extremely hazardous and detrimental to the success of the letter.

Let us suppose that the case were reversed: an old lady in Germany receives a letter from an unknown source abroad, with a request to forward a message whose recipient is asked to disclose to an unknown foreigner where he will be staying for a certain period – and this recipient were a high officer in the air force (of course I do not know exactly what position H. holds at the moment; judging from his past I can conceive of only three things: he is an active Air Force General,[3] or he directs the air defence of an important part of Scotland, or he has a responsible position in the Air Ministry).

I do not think that you need much imagination to picture to yourself the faces that Canaris or Heydrich would make and the smirk with which they would consider any offer of 'security' or 'confidence' in such a letter if a subordinate should submit such a case to them. They would not merely make faces, you may be certain! The measures would come quite automatically – and neither the old lady nor the Air Force officer would have an easy time of it! In England it is no different.

Now another thing. Here too I would ask you to picture the situation in reverse. Let us assume that I received such a letter from one of my English friends. I would quite naturally report the matter to the highest German authorities I could contact, as soon as I had realised the import it might have, and would ask for instructions on what I should do myself (at that, I am a civilian and H. is an officer).

If it should be decided that I was to comply with the wish for a meeting with my friend, I would then be most anxious to get my instructions if not from the Fuehrer himself, at least from a person who receives them directly and at the same time has the gift of transmitting the finest and lightest nuances – an art which has been mastered by you yourself but not by all Reich Ministers. In addition I should very urgently request that my action be fully covered vis-à-vis other high authorities of my own country, uninformed or unfavourable.

It is no different with H. He cannot fly to Lisbon – any more than I can! – unless he is given leave, that is unless at least Air Minister Sinclair and Foreign Minister Halifax know about it. If, however, he receives permission to reply or to go, there is no need of indicating any place in England; if he does not receive it, then any attempt through a neutral mediator would also have little success.

In this case the technical problem of contacting H. is the least of the difficulties. A neutral who knows England and can move about in England – presumably there would be little sense in entrusting anyone else with such a mission – will be able to find the first peer of Scotland very quickly as long as conditions in the Isle are still halfway in order. (At the time of a successful invasion all the possibilities we are discussing here would be pointless anyway.)

My proposal is therefore as follows:

Through the old friend I will write a letter to H. – in a form that will incriminate no one but will be understandable to the recipient – with the proposal for a meeting in Lisbon. If nothing comes of that, it will be possible (if the military situation leaves enough time for it), assuming that a suitable intermediary is available, to make a second attempt through a neutral going to England, who might be given a personal message to take along. With respect to this possibility,

I must add, however, that H. is extremely reserved – as many Englishmen are toward anyone they do not know personally. Since the entire Anglo–German problem after all springs from a most profound crisis in mutual confidence, this would not be immaterial.

Please excuse the length of this letter; I merely wished to explain the situation to you fully.

I already tried to explain to you not long ago that, for the reasons I gave, the possibilities of successful efforts at a settlement between the Fuehrer and the British upper class seem to me – to my extreme regret – infinitesimally small.

Nevertheless I should not want to close this letter without pointing out once more that I still think there would be a somewhat greater chance of success in going through Ambassador Lothian in Washington or Sir Samuel Hoare in Madrid rather than through my friend H. To be sure, they are – practically speaking – more inaccessible.

Would you send me a line or give me a telephone call with final instructions? If necessary, will you also inform your brother in advance? Presumably I will then have to discuss with him the forwarding of the letter to Lisbon and the arrangement for a cover address for the reply in Lisbon.

With cordial greetings and best wishes for your health.

Yours etc.

A.H.

On the same day Albrecht drafted a letter to Hamilton and wrote to his parents. With his letter to his parents he enclosed Hess's letter to his father, his own reply to Hess, the draft of his letter to Hamilton, and the memorandum on the possibilities of a German-English peace:

Enclosed I am sending you some responsible documents:

Firstly the letter of T. to father.

Secondly my reply to T., which has already been despatched and which I hope has your belated approval.

Thirdly the draft of a letter to D. [Hamilton], which I keep for myself and shall also not show to anybody, with the request for you to examine whether it contains any danger for the potential lady conveyer. I think actually that it sounds harmless enough. I have purposely fitted in the reference to the "authorities" over there as a safeguard for the lady conveyer and for the recipient. Therefore, your honest opinion, please, and corrections, if necessary.

Fourthly a record in writing of what I said in G. [Godesberg] on the eighth – as vindication before history (to be kept in your custody).

The whole thing is a fool's errand – but we cannot help it. According to our latest news the Union agreements between the Empire and the United States are about to be signed. . . .

On 23 September 1940 Albrecht wrote to Hess that the letter to Hamilton had been despatched via Alfred Hess.

My dear Herr Hess:

In accordance with your last telephone call I got in touch with your brother immediately. Everything went off well, and I can now report that the mission has been accomplished to the extent that the letter you desired was written and despatched this morning. It is to be hoped that it will be more efficacious than sober judgment would indicate.

He also wrote to his father on the same day enclosing a copy of the letter to Hamilton which by this time had probably been revised, and he admitted that the responsibility for sending it lay with Hess.

Enclosed a copy of a short significant letter, which is perhaps better kept in your custody than in mine. I have now stated clearly enough that this is an action the initiative of which has not rested with me.

Now to English matters. I am convinced, as before, that there is not the slightest prospect of peace; and so I don't have the least faith in the possibility about which you know. However, I also believe that I could not have refused my services any longer. You know that for myself I do not see any possibility of any satisfying activity in the future.

If the 'total victory' from Glasgow to Capetown were to be achieved for our savages, then the drunk sergeants and the corrupt exploiters will call the tune anyhow; experts with quiet manners will not be needed then. If it is not achieved, if the English succeed in delivering the first blow with American help and in creating a long protracted war equilibrium with the aid of the Bolshevist insecurity factor, then, however, there will sooner or later be a demand for the likes of us – but in conditions in which little enough will be left to salvage any more. . . .

He wrote that his only hope of being able to influence affairs in Germany was that there would be a far-reaching change. The head of the Foreign Office, Ernst von Weizsaecker, was in a similar position to himself. If there was no such change, then such men as Himmler's minion, Lorenz, would have the supremacy, and Albrecht would be in for a thin time.

I can only have a political future if in the end I am proved right with my Cassandra voice. . . . I recently talked with old Weizsaecker about the same topic. We occupy similar positions. He too tells himself that he would come into his own, only if external circumstances arose, which would deprive him of all pleasure in this activity: i.e. if he is proved right with his similar Cassandra reputation. Otherwise he could just as well go as myself: in that case the Lorenz types would have the greater historical justification on their side. . . .

Albrecht had admitted in this letter that there was no chance of peace with Britain. He must have read Churchill's broadcast of 11 September 1940, in which Churchill had summarised the opinion of the British on Hitler:

This wicked man, the repository and embodiment of many forms of soul-destroying hatred, this monstrous product of former wrongs and shame, has now resolved to try to break our famous island race by a process of indiscriminate slaughter and destruction. What he has done is to kindle a fire in British hearts, here and all over the world, which will glow long after all traces of the conflagration he has caused in London have been removed. He has lighted a fire which will burn with a steady and consuming flame until the last vestiges of Nazi tyranny have been burnt out of Europe. . . .

Albrecht was looking for compromises, where there were none to be made, and on 2 October 1940 he wrote to his parents:

I now wait – without much confidence – for a chance of still being able to influence in some way or other the suicidal course of the struggle of the white master races with the modest powers of reason.

But we have, at least on our part, done what was possible.

A little later he wrote to his mother on 25 November:

You know I do not easily forget and I am heavily weighed down by my share in the great collective guilt. . . .

126

Lord David Douglas-Hamilton, the Duke of Hamilton, Lord Geordie Douglas-Hamilton, and Lord Malcolm Douglas-Hamilton, taken in 1940: the only four brothers in the Royal Air Force to be professional instructors and Squadron Leaders (Elizabeth, Duchess of Hamilton)

He seems to have felt that the sending out of a peace feeler to Britain on Hess's behalf was never more than a completely forlorn hope.

NOTES

1. Haushofer papers.
2. Hess's brother Alfred had been earmarked to be future Gauleiter of Egypt, and he would have been if the Germans had won the battle of El Alamein.
3. In fact he was not an Air Force General, but a Wing Commander whom the Secretary of State for Air, Sir Archie Sinclair, would ask to be an honorary Air Commodore on 23 November 1940.

FOUR

The British Secret Service

On 2 November the Examiner in the Ministry of Information Censor's Department intercepted a letter, possibly a few hours after the letter had been received in Britain. On 6 November the original was sent to MI5 and a photostat copy was transmitted to the Foreign Office. The letter was dated 23 September 1940 and had been sent from a person who signed himself 'A' via a Mrs V. Roberts in Lisbon, Portugal. Mrs Violet Roberts had married Ainslie Roberts and was his widow. His son, Maxwell Roberts, had worked in the British Embassy in Berlin and had lost his life in a car accident in 1937.

The sender obviously intended that it should be forwarded to the Duke of Hamilton. It was a strange letter, and Hamilton did not learn about its existence until five months after it had been sent. During the interval the British Secret Service were probably making enquiries as to who 'A' was, and after a great deal of time, and possibly effort, they must have discovered that it was one Albrecht Haushofer who had close connections with the German Foreign Office.

On 22 November, from Room 055 of the War Office used by MI5, a letter was sent to Mr Hopkinson, Secretary to Sir Alexander Cadogan, Head of the Foreign Office. All it said was:

> A letter dated 23 September 1940 written by somebody named 'Dr A.H.', obviously a German, to the Duke of Hamilton was intercepted by the censor and copies sent to MI5, the Foreign Office and I.R.B.
>
> We are pursuing enquiries into this case, but meanwhile I should be grateful to know if you have taken any action. I propose to forward the letter to the Duke of Hamilton provided you do not object.

A Foreign Office official, in a note on the MI5 letter dated 4 December, commented with a wry sense of humour:

> We don't seem to come into this very much and no doubt the Duke of Hamilton will be tickled to death to receive in December a letter which was addressed to him on September 23rd.
>
> I see that Dr A.H. says that 'letters will reach me fairly quickly; they would take some 4 or 5 days from Lisbon at the utmost in the following way . . .', but perhaps MI5 does not step in that direction.

Hopkinson had already taken this into account when he replied on 7 December on the subject of the intercepted letter 'written in September by someone, presumed to be a German, to the Duke of Hamilton'. At this stage there was no great or pressing interest in the letter, and neither MI5 nor the Foreign Office had any inkling that any senior Nazi, or indeed any Nazi, leader might be involved. Hopkinson's reply to MI5 ended with the words:

> We have not done anything about it ourselves and we have no objection to the letter being allowed to go on to its destination if you think this worthwhile in view of the length of time which has elapsed since it was written.

Accordingly Hamilton received a letter dated 26 February 1941 from Group Captain F. G. Stammers, O.B.E. The latter asked whether Hamilton might be in London in the near future, as he was anxious to have a chat with him on a certain matter, in his office in the Air Ministry at Houghton House, the late London School of Economics. Halfway through March 1941 Hamilton visited Stammers and was asked what he had done with the letter which Albrecht Haushofer had written to him. Hamilton thought that he was referring to the letter sent by Albrecht Haushofer in July 1939, which had been deposited in the vaults of a bank. It soon became clear that they were talking about different letters whereupon Stammers pushed across the desk a photographed copy of the intercepted handwritten letter which Hamilton had not seen before. It ran:

B. Sept. 23rd.

My dear Douglo,

Even if there is only a slight chance that this letter should reach you in good time, there is a chance, and I am determined to make use of it.

First of all, to give you a personal greeting. I am sure you know that my attachment to you remains unaltered and unalterable, whatever the circumstances may be. I have heard of your father's death. I do hope he did not suffer too much – after so long a life of permanent pain. I heard that your brother-in-law Northumberland lost his life near Dunkirk – even modern times must allow us to share grief across all boundaries.

But it is not only the story of death that should find its place in this letter. If you remember some of my last communications in July 1939, you – and your friends in high places – may find some significance in the fact that I am able to ask you whether you could find time to have a talk with me somewhere on the outskirts of Europe, perhaps in Portugal. I could reach Lisbon any time (and without any kind of difficulties) within a few days after receiving news from you. Of course I do not know whether you can make your authorities understand so much, that they give you leave.

But at least you may be able to answer my question. Letters will reach me (fairly quickly; they would take some four of five days from Lisbon at the utmost) in the following way: double closed envelope: inside address: 'Dr A. H.' Nothing more! Outside address:

'Minero Silricola Ltd.,
Rua do Cais de Santarem 32/1
Lisbon, Portugal'.

My father and mother add their wishes for your personal welfare to my own. . . .

Yours ever,
'A'.[1]

Hamilton was surprised to read this letter, as it had never occurred to him that Albrecht Haushofer would attempt to make contact with him during the war. Stammers

129

explained that the Intelligence authorities were of the opinion that Haushofer was a significant person, who had close connections with the German Foreign Office. They also thought that it might be of considerable value to make contact with him. Hamilton told Stammers that, as far as he knew, Haushofer had been sent over to Britain by the German Foreign Office in order to control Ribbentrop, that he had found this a hopeless task and that in any case he was not a man of war.

On 28 March, Group Captain Stammers wrote to Hamilton:

> I never thanked you for your kind assistance in giving me information regarding the subject of your call at the Air Ministry. You promised that you could let me have a certain letter which was sent to you from Norway which was lying in your bank. I have not yet had this letter and would be very grateful if you could send me a copy of it.

This was a reference to Albrecht Haushofer's letter of 16 July 1939 sent before the outbreak of war. On 6 April, Hamilton replied thanking him for his letter:

> The letter you mention is from a friend of mine whom we discussed at our last meeting. If the terms of this letter were disclosed to the authorities in his own country, he would probably be in very serious trouble. He has asked me to destroy the letter after reading it and 'destroy it most carefully'. He, however, gave me freedom of my own discretion to show it to the then Foreign Secretary on one condition – that no notes be taken and his name never mentioned, and the letter destroyed immediately afterwards.
>
> My only object in showing this letter to anyone would be because it might be of some national service.
>
> I hope to be in London again within the next three weeks and would be glad to show it to you.[2]

Following this letter Hamilton received a Postagram asking him to report to Group Captain D. L. Blackford at the Air Ministry, on 25 April at 11.30 a.m. Hamilton duly appeared, and had a conference with Group Captain Blackford and Major Robertson. They were eager that Hamilton should volunteer to go to Portugal in order to acquire all information possible from Albrecht Haushofer. Hamilton said reluctantly that he would of course go if he was ordered, and he was told that for this type of job people volunteered and were not ordered. He would be given time to consider the proposition and the technical arrangements of getting him there and back could easily be laid on.

On 26 April Hamilton saw Lord Eustace Percy, the Rector of the University of Newcastle, as he wished to ask the advice of someone for whose integrity and discretion he had the utmost respect. Percy had worked for the Foreign Office, had later served as a Cabinet Minister under Baldwin and had resigned in 1936 when Hitler remilitarised the Rhineland. He had been appalled that the British Government considered that the British Armed Forces were militarily too weak to repel the German invading forces. He now advised Hamilton to proceed with caution on certain conditions. Two days later, on 28 April, Hamilton wrote to Blackford:

> I am prepared to go, if you wish it, but I think I must make two conditions: I should not, of course, like to hold any communication with X without the knowledge of and consultation with H.M. Ambassador at my destination. I presume that there will be no difficulty about this, and, to avoid any possible misunderstanding or delay at my destination, I would suggest that I should be authorised to explain the position to Sir Alexander Cadogan, at the Foreign Office, before I leave.

I must be able to explain to X why I am answering his letter after a delay of seven months. It would be dangerous to allow him to believe that the authorities had withheld his letter from me last autumn and had now released it and had asked me to answer it. That would give the impression that the authorities here had 'got the wind up' now, and want to talk peace. May I therefore have an explanation of the circumstances in which the letter was withheld from me last autumn?

For a number of reasons this letter was not appreciated. First it looked as though Albrecht Haushofer was making some sort of peace overture, and the Intelligence authorities were only interested in extracting technical information as to the plans and intentions of the enemy. Indeed, when a section of the German Resistance to Hitler was making a peace feeler to Britain via Josef Mueller through the Vatican, Churchill had sent a minute to Eden, insisting that it must be made clear to the Papal Nuncio that the British did not wish to make any enquiries as to terms of peace with Hitler, and that British agents had been 'strictly forbidden to entertain any such suggestions'.

Secondly, Hamilton had demanded that he should see the Head of the British Foreign Offlce and the British Ambassador in Lisbon, which meant that if anything went wrong it would be harder for the British to disown him, as is usually the case with unsuccessful agents.

Thirdly, the British Intelligence authorities had already burnt their fingers badly over the Venlo Incident when two British agents, Captain Payne Best and Major R. H. Stevens, were kidnapped over the Dutch border on 9 November 1939. They had expected

Hess was a skilled aviator and is here seen showing Hitler one of his early private aeroplanes
(W. G. Fitzgerald)

to meet members of the German Resistance to Hitler, and were shaken to discover that these 'representatives' turned out to be agents of Himmler, and included Schellenberg. This had proved embarrassing to the British, as Goebbels's propaganda machine used their capture to maximum effect. In the present case it was not clear who Albrecht Haushofer represented, and in the light of the Venlo incident it was certainly possible that he might be a double agent.

Lastly, Hamilton's letter had raised the point that the British Secret Service had apparently been inefficient in withholding a letter for five months, and Secret Service organisations do not like questions being asked about their inadequacies, nor about their methods.

Many years later Major Robertson recalled the events which took place at the Air Ministry meeting and which subsequently caused MI5 to reject any further contact with Albrecht Haushofer.

Major Robertson was in charge of operations dealing with double agents in MI5 and was invited to advise on this aspect of the case. He recollects that he advised against proceeding with the case from the double-agent standpoint. During the conversations about it, none of them had any knowledge that Hess was involved, or that Albrecht Haushofer was advising Hess. Indeed no great significance was attached to Albrecht Haushofer's letter.

Major Robertson believed that the delay in dealing with the letter was because it was lost or mislaid, or had got into the wrong file. Indeed, B Division of MI5 had recently changed its address, causing an administrative upheaval. However, the effect of the delay was that it was much more difficult to answer Albrecht Haushofer's letter. With an overture of that nature, a response had to be made straight away to be effective. Otherwise the recipient of the reply would be suspicious. Accordingly his advice was emphatic that this matter should be dropped.

Major Robertson enjoyed a close and friendly relationship with Air Commodore Boyle, who had been very helpful to him in double-cross operations. Indeed the two men enjoyed a close rapport, and on 3 May 1941 Group Captain Blackford wrote to Hamilton on Air Commodore Boyle's behalf:

SECRET   3rd May 1941
Dear Hamilton,
1. Thanks for your letter dated the 28th April. I am sorry not to have been here when you came to London, but I had a casualty in the family and was compelled to go away for a bit.
2. I have discussed your letter with Air Commodore Boyle and he agrees with you that this may not be the right time to open up a discussion, the nature of which might well be misinterpreted.
3. You will realise, of course, that the Air Ministry are in no way concerned with the policy question involved and are only concerned with the problem whether or not it is practicable to open a channel with your assistance. I have, however, put your views to the Department concerned and I know they will receive careful consideration.
4. In my own view the delay which has occurred makes it extremely difficult to find a watertight excuse for action at the present time, and although quite a good one has been suggested on the lines of an enquiry from you as to why your previous letters have not been answered, it might not carry conviction and so have undesirable political consequences.
5. Incidentally, the delay was in no way due to any fault of Air Intelligence, another department having mislaid the papers.
6. It is Air Commodore Boyle's view that in the present circumstances a move of the kind suggested could not be made without Cabinet authority, and with this I agree. In the

circumstances, will you, therefore, regard the matter as in abeyance. I will let you know at once should it come forward again.

7. Air Commodore Boyle has asked me to thank you for the trouble you have taken in this connection.

8. Should you be passing through town any time I hope you will find it possible to come in and see me and have lunch with me if you can spare the time.

9. I am sending copies of this letter to Air Commodore Boyle and Captain Robertson.

Yours sincerely,
D. L. Blackford.

Hamilton replied to Blackford on 10 May.

I fully appreciate the position and will regard the matter as in abeyance until I hear from you that it has come forward again. I also realise that the Air Ministry is in no way concerned with the policy question involved, and that it was not the fault of the Air Intelligence but another department for the papers having been mislaid.

As regards the opening up of the channel, I am of the opinion that a very good opportunity may have been missed owing to the delay. I must admit I do not like the suggestion already made, which you mention, on the lines of an enquiry from me as to why my previous letters have not been answered. Quite apart from the undesirable political consequences which might be caused by failing to carry conviction, on the other hand X might think that either the British authorities or the German authorities had withheld a letter to him, either of which might also have an undesirable effect.

If the proposition materialises and I am asked to go, I think that probably the best way of overcoming the difficulty would be if I adopted the following procedure.

I would write to X – 'I did not reply to your letter last autumn because I saw no opportunity of leaving this country at that time. It appears now that I may have a chance of arranging a meeting with you abroad some time during the next month or two. If you would still like to see me, will you let me know.' I would then wait for a reply before starting, so that I would only have to leave my service duties for the minimum time and avoid the appearance of waiting anxiously on his doorstep.

Many thanks for your kind invitation to come and see you and have lunch. I should very much like to accept, if I am able to come to London in the near future.

Hamilton never received a reply to this letter for later on the same day, 10 May 1941, R.A.F. Fighter Command Radar Stations picked up a single enemy aircraft flying across the North Sea towards Lindisfarne, and at 22.25 hours the Royal Observer Corps identified it as a Messerschmitt 110, shortly after it had crossed the Northumbrian coast. While the British Secret Service and R.A.F. Intelligence were proceeding with slow and heavy tread something had happened which rendered their actions irrelevant.

NOTES

1. General Professor Karl Haushofer's grandson, Martin Haushofer, told the author that 'Minero Silricola Limited' was an accommodation address for the Abwehr, the German Secret Service. It appears that this point had not been picked up by MI5 in 1940.
2. Hamilton papers.

Hess ready to fly his Me110

FIVE

The Leap into the Dark: 10 May 1941

Back in Germany Hess's influence with Hitler had declined to an all-time low. The American Under Secretary of State, Sumner Welles, wrote after an interview with Hess on 3 March 1940:

> Notwithstanding the impression so often given me previously that Hess possessed a powerful and determining influence in German affairs, the effect he made upon me at the time was that of a man who had only the lowest order of intelligence. . . .
>
> It was so obvious that Hess was merely repeating what he had been told to say to me . . . and that he had neither explored the issues at stake nor thought anything out for himself, that I made no attempt to enter into any discussion with him.

Nobody was more aware of the situation than Hess himself. There was no question of his being disloyal in any circumstances; and, as Albrecht Haushofer explained to Rainer Hildebrandt:

> Hess leads a conventional bourgeois life but as soon as Hitler in some form enters his subconscious he automatically becomes liable to mental excesses. . . .
>
> During the first years I tried to warn Hess of the dangers which he could avoid and proved to him in black and white Hitler's mistakes. . . . Hess saw all this and was determined to intervene where necessary. At the end of our talk he said, 'I will ask the Fuehrer; I am sure he will understand and will turn everything to the best'. . . .
>
> It is Hess's dream to be able by some great mediating act to save the Reich for Germany, for his friends and first of all for Hitler, his idol. Hess is a Parsifal, and all injustice committed by Hess is in fact due to his bondage and under a kind of hypnosis.

It was to be expected that Hess would feel that he could not play his part in saving the Third Reich by remaining tied to office work. In September 1939 he asked Hitler for permission to fly with the Luftwaffe at the Front. Hitler refused and demanded an assurance from Hess that he would not fly again, whereupon Hess promised not to fly for one year. By September 1940 Hess felt free from his promise. During the same month he tried to put out his peace feeler to Britain through Albrecht Haushofer. However, as this letter never received a reply, Hess thought that he would make another attempt, this time without the knowledge of his wife and the Haushofers, and above all without the knowledge of Hitler. He would embark on a personal unauthorised mission of a secret and dramatic kind.

He must have known about the suggestion which Goering had made to Hitler just after Britain's declaration of war against Germany. Goering then said, 'We must fly to Britain and I'll try to explain the position. . . .' When Hitler was informed he had said to Goering, 'It will be of no use, but if you can, try it.' For a long time the rumour had persisted that Goering might fly over to Britain, but Goering was not sufficiently enthusiastic about the possibility of success.

Hess, however, took a different approach. He had always regarded Goering as a rival and with cause. In 1940 Hitler and Hess had conversed for many hours. Afterwards Hitler said to Speer: 'When I talk with Goering, it's like a bath in steel for me: I feel fresh afterwards. The Reich Marshal has a stimulating way of presenting things. With Hess every conversation becomes an unbearably tormenting strain. He always comes to me with unpleasant matters and won't leave off.' Hess knew that Goering had always managed to outshine him and was Hitler's first Deputy Fuehrer while he was only the second. After the fall of France, when Hitler made his peace offer to the British Empire, he had made Goering a Marshal of the Reich and merely complimented Hess as a loyal follower. Hess may well have felt that here was an opportunity to outshine Goering, by following the suggestion which Goering had not followed up himself.

It occurred to Hess that the making of a peace overture by original means would be welcomed by the British as a sporting gesture. He was influenced by the example of the American Colonel Charles Lindbergh who had been the first man to fly solo across the Atlantic from west to east. Hess had wanted to be the first man to fly the Atlantic solo from the east to the west, but in the end his plans fell through. It was left to Hess to win, in 1934, the annual air-race round the Zugspitze, the highest peak in Germany, a feat of which he was very proud; and after it Lindbergh warmly congratulated him. Hess had never met the Duke of Hamilton as he had met Lindbergh but he had read the *Pilots' Book of Everest* by Hamilton and Group Captain D. F. McIntyre and it had appealed to him. If Hamilton had been the first pilot to fly over Mount Everest and Lindbergh was the first aviator to fly solo across the Atlantic, he, Hess, would be the first pilot to fly from Germany to Britain with an offer of peace in the midst of a great world war.

The Swedish author and explorer Sven Hedin had incorporated a suggestion in his book *Ohne Auftrag in Berlin* that if Hitler had flown over to Britain during the war, had offered to shake hands and come to a 'reasonable' agreement, the British would have been suitably impressed. The British author Peter Fleming had written very differently on the same theme in a comic vein in *The Flying Visit* adding that if Hitler had parachuted into Britain nobody would have been able to believe it. Hess, however, was not to know about Peter Fleming's book, and he made his preparations. He went to Professor Messerschmitt at Augsburg airport, and with his permission made frequent practice flights in a Messerschmitt 110. On Hess's orders extra fuel tanks were fitted to the aircraft as well as radio equipment and Hess's secretary, Hildegard Fath, obtained secret weather reports about conditions over Britain and the North Sea.

The mission was kept a closely guarded secret but one person learnt about it, almost by mistake. In January 1941 Hess and his Adjutant, Karl Heinz Pintsch, went to Augsburg airport, and Hess told him that if he had not returned from his flight within four hours Pintsch was to open the letter addressed to him and to deliver the other letter personally to Hitler. Some four hours later Pintsch opened the letter and read to his horror that his superior had flown to Britain. He was not much relieved when Hess's aircraft suddenly reappeared. On this occasion Hess had had to turn back on account of bad weather.

Pintsch has given an account of the consequent conversation between himself and Hess, which should be treated with caution as it was told many years later, but its broad outline is clear. Hess took Pintsch into his confidence, because he was afraid that his plans would be given away. He explained that Hitler had no designs on the British Empire, which was the reason for not invading Britain after Dunkirk. The enemy of the Third Reich was Russia and Hitler wanted to expand in the east. Therefore it was essential to get Britain out of the war, or else Germany might soon be fighting the dreaded war on two fronts against most of the world, including the U.S.A. as well as Russia and Britain. The Anglo-German situation, so Hess thought, needed a personal approach. Naturally there was an element of risk, but nothing in comparison with what he might achieve if success were to smile upon him. He would save millions of lives and the future of the Third Reich. He would fly to the Duke of Hamilton's home, show him Albrecht Haushofer's visiting card, and ask to see the King.

Pintsch decided to be discreet, and it may be that others in Germany guessed that Hess had something in mind. Shortly before he made his final flight Hess told Count Schwerin von Krosigk, Hitler's Finance Minister, that the Russians alone were benefiting whilst the British and Germans were at each other's throats. He could not understand why the British had not responded to Hitler's offer of peace, and could not see why they had not understood that Bolshevism was the menace threatening Europe and that Hitler had no demands to make of Britain. He felt certain that if the matter were properly expounded to the British, it would be possible to conclude an agreement.

Winston Churchill gave an accurate analysis of Hess's motives in his *History of the Second World War*.

He knew and was capable of understanding Hitler's inner mind, his hatred of Soviet Russia, his lust to destroy Bolshevism, his admiration for Britain and earnest wish to be friends with the British Empire, his contempt for most other countries. No one knew Hitler better or saw him more often in his unguarded moments. With the coming of actual war there was a change. Hitler's meal-time company grew perforce. Generals, admirals, diplomats, high functionaries, were admitted from time to time to this select circle of arbitrary power. The Deputy Fuehrer found himself in eclipse. What were party demonstrations now? This was a time for deeds, not for antics. . . .

Here, he felt, are all these generals and others who must be admitted to the Fuehrer's intimacy, and crowd his table. They have their parts to play. But I, Rudolf, by a deed of superb devotion will surpass them all and bring to my Fuehrer a greater treasure and easement than all of them put together. I will go and make peace with Britain. My life is nothing. How glad I am to have a life to cast away for such a hope! . . .

Hess's idea of the European scene was that England had been wrested from her true interests and policy of friendship with Germany, and above all from alliance against Bolshevism, by the warmongers, of whom Churchill was the superficial manifestation. If only he, Rudolf, could get at the heart of Britain and make its King believe how Hitler felt towards it, the malign forces that now ruled in this ill-starred island and had brought so many needless miseries upon it would be swept away. . . .

But to whom should he turn? There was the Duke of Hamilton, who was known to the son of his political adviser, Haushofer. He knew also that the Duke of Hamilton was Lord Steward. A personage like that would probably be dining every night with the King and have his private ear. Here was a channel of direct access.

Just as some in Britain hoped that the German people might be separated from Hitler, so it was, Hess thought, that the British people, if encouraged, might be separated

6 November 1940. Wing Commander the Duke of Hamilton acts as a pall bearer to Squadron Leader Archie MacKellar, Scotland's greatest fighter pilot in the Battle of Britain (Bulletin)

from Churchill. Hess knew that he was taking a considerable risk, but he well appreciated that nothing could have been more in Hitler's interests than to get Britain out of the war before the attack on Russia was launched. If he was successful he would be acclaimed as a popular hero in Germany.

On the whole he hoped to be back from his secret mission before too long. On 9 May 1941, one day before he made his flight, he wrote to Reichleiter Darré.

I am contemplating an extensive journey and I do not know when I shall be back. I therefore cannot as yet tie myself down to a fixed date. I shall get in touch with you again after my return. . . .

138

On the next day, Saturday, 10 May 1941, he put on the uniform of an Oberleutnant in the Luftwaffe, went to Augsburg, obtained the Me 110 with the extra fuel tanks attached to it, left a letter for Hitler with his adjutant, and took off into the evening air, on a long and remarkable flight. By a strange paradox the most loyal and unimaginative of Nazi leaders was attempting a daring deed.

In setting out in this way, Hess was making a number of fundamental mistakes:

Firstly, he had not gauged correctly what the British reaction would be to a Nazi peace initiative. It would have made sense from his point of view to have discovered the answer through enquiries in a neutral country such as Portugal or Switzerland. If he had, he would have discovered that the British were united in their opposition to Nazi aggression and had every interest in securing Hitler's defeat.

Secondly, he was choosing Hamilton, who had been an M.P. until the death of his father and was therefore no longer in the House of Commons. As a serving officer, Hamilton was effectively out of politics. Therefore an approach to him was an inept move.

Thirdly, Hamilton was a supporter of Churchill as his supreme commander and any message to him from Hess would reach Churchill within twenty-four hours of his arrival in Scotland. His letter to *The Times* in October 1939 had been sent 'with the intention of strengthening the moderate opinion in Germany against the Nazi regime'.[1]

The only aspect in which Churchill's views differed from those of Hamilton was the emphasis the latter placed on encouraging a potential resistance to Hitler. Churchill's view was that if someone got rid of Hitler so much the better, but it was not worth spending emotional capital and time on people who might be wholly unable to deliver. His thinking was moving in the direction of the formula of unconditional surrender. Whether it might have made any difference to encourage a potential resistance to Hitler at that stage must remain one of the unanswered questions of history.

In 1940 there were no obvious or outward signs of any German resistance to Hitler, and the British were fighting off the threat of invasion. Hamilton had been a controller with 11 Group of Fighter Command. He was sent to France on 17 May 1940 by Air Chief Marshal Sir Hugh Dowding to make contact with the R.A.F. squadrons in France. He flew out there in a Magister and had the experience of being narrowly missed by bombs when on the ground. He reported back to Dowding that the Germans were pouring through the French defences and that there was chaos everywhere. For this report, he was Mentioned in Dispatches, since it confirmed Dowding's wishes to retain the bulk of Fighter Command at home in preparation for the Battle of Britain.

At the outset of that battle Hamilton was made Station Commander of Turnhouse, and on 15 August his Fighter Sector was involved in combat with a force of about 100 bombers sent to attack Newcastle. As a result of the brilliant tactics of Squadron Leader Archie MacKellar, DSO, DFC, and other squadron commanders, the Luftwaffe suffered heavy losses.

On 14 October he visited 602 (City of Glasgow) Squadron, his old squadron stationed in the Tangmere area, and was very pleased to learn that the pilots had shot down about eighty Luftwaffe aircraft in the Battle of Britain. At that time and over the next six months, the possibility of a major German peace initiative never entered his mind.

On Saturday 10 May 1941 Hamilton was on duty in the operations room of the Turnhouse Sector when the track of a Messerschmitt 110 was reported by the Royal Observer Corps. Hess had flown north over Germany and then over the North Sea, on a track in the direction of the Shetland Islands, before turning west on a course for Dungavel House, the residence of Hamilton in Lanarkshire. His aircraft had been picked up by radar when out to sea at about 15,000 feet. Soon afterwards it went into a dive and was plotted by sound and bearing by the Royal Observer Corps post at Embleton, a short distance inland from the coast. It then lost further altitude rapidly and was spotted at about 50 feet by the post near Chatton at 20.25 hours. At this point it was about 20 km inland and probably travelling in excess of 300 m.p.h.

Hamilton understood that when the aircraft flew west over Britain and the Ouston Fighter Sector to the south of his own sector, fighter aircraft were directed to intercept it. In fact, as Roy Conyers Nesbit shows in his Introduction, three Hurricanes were in the air but were being flown by Polish pilots on a training flight. The records show that it was two Spitfires from Acklington in Northumberland which were immediately ordered to intercept. No Spitfire from Scotland was sent up, but a further Spitfire was scrambled from Acklington. Hamilton was aware that later an R.A.F. Defiant nightfighter was also scrambled; he thought this was based at Prestwick, but the records show it took off from nearby Ayr. Nevertheless no interception was made.

Hess had flown west unimpeded in the gathering darkness and, having climbed, passed very close to Dungavel House. To check his bearings he continued to the Ayrshire coast, turned and flew back, while climbing further in order to bale out. He was closely pursued by the Defiant but parachuted out a few minutes before the nightfighter could attack.

The question has been asked as to how Hess managed to elude the British defences. There were several reasons for this:

Firstly, Hess arrived at dusk over a relatively lightly defended part of the English

Late 1940. Wing Commander the Duke of Hamilton welcoming to Scotland young pilots from the Empire who had volunteered for active service (The Herald)

coast, in terms of both ground and air defences. Although he was picked up by radar when out over the North Sea, his track was confused with that of the two Spitfires vectored to intercept him, so that he escaped attack by them.

Secondly, the radar did not operate inland. Instead, tracking of enemy aircraft once the coast was crossed depended on the Royal Observer Corps. Although the R.O.C. posts reported the Messerschmitt and its speed extremely accurately, the R.A.F. did not believe them at first, for the normal role of such an aircraft was that of a long-distance fighter and there seemed no purpose in such a flight. Instead, they thought that the aircraft must be a Dornier bomber, which was slower than the Me 110, and made arrangements accordingly.

Thirdly, none of the aircraft which tried to intercept Hess were fitted with airborne interception radar. Although some of the R.A.F. nightfighter squadrons further south, which were bearing the brunt of the fighting at this stage, had been fitted with this new equipment, it had not been supplied to the aircraft of 13 Group.

Fourthly, although the night sky was clear and with a full moon, there was some low-lying mist which hampered the spotting of a low-flying aircraft from above, especially against the dark hills over which Hess flew. The pilot of the third Spitfire from Acklington which was sent up at 22.20 hours did not spot the Messerschmitt, although Hess later stated that he understood that a Spitfire was only about five km behind him at one stage.

Fifthly, Hess was lucky in baling out shortly before the Defiant nightfighter closed with him, for it was only a few miles away and by this time he had climbed. The tactic of these nightfighters was to fly low and look upwards for enemy aircraft silhouetted against the night sky, and this squadron had achieved notable successes in the previous few days by employing this method, in spite of the absence of airborne radar.

Thus it was that Hess penetrated the British fighter defences.

He flew back along the route which he had just taken, and made preparations for parachuting. He found great difficulty in getting out of the Messerschmitt, and in fact only managed to extricate himself from the aeroplane after a half-roll when it was flying upside down. He hurt his ankle on landing near the farm of Eaglesham, and was found getting out of his parachute harness by David McLean. He was taken into McLean's house and was treated with firmness and kindness as is the custom in the west of Scotland.

He was dealt with as a prisoner of war, and was collected by the Home Guard. Whilst at the Home Guard H.Q. Major Graham Donald, the Assistant Group Officer of the Royal Observer Corps in Glasgow, saw the prisoner, who was looking 'slightly fed up'. Hess said he was called Hauptmann Alfred Horn, and that he had 'a secret and vital message for the Duke of Hamilton, and that he must see the Duke at once'. Alfred Horn was, in fact, Hess's brother-in-law, the brother of his wife. This suggestion that he should meet Hamilton caused a great deal of merriment, but the Home Guard realised that their captive was serious, since he had a map with the home of Hamilton, Dungavel House, marked in red on it.

Whilst in the custody of the Home Guard, a member of the Polish Consulate in Glasgow, named Battaglia, asked the prisoner questions in the presence of some fifteen to twenty members of the Home Guard.

The prisoner repeated that he had a message for the Duke of Hamilton. When asked whether he knew the Duke of Hamilton, he replied, 'I saw him at the Olympic Games in Berlin, and we have a friend in common'. This was no doubt a reference to the dinner given by Hitler for Lord Vansittart, attended by 150 people, at which Hess had not met Hamilton but had seen him across the room. The so-called friend was Albrecht Haushofer, but Hess did not mention his name. When asked what the message was about, Hess replied that it was in the highest interests of the British Air Force.[2] Battaglia recalled

11 May 1941. The wreckage of Hess's aircraft guarded by the Cameronians and the police
(The Herald*)*

several people remarking on the prisoner's resemblance to Hess. However, at that time the prisoner's identity was unconfirmed.

Major Donald, thinking that the prisoner's face looked very familiar, asked him if his name was Alfred Horn, and suggested that his name might be Rudolf Hess. At this Hess jumped and gave 'a forced laugh', and everyone else laughed. Major Donald then telephoned the duty controller of his sector, and asked him to pass on to the Wing Commander that 'the prisoner was a refugee of sorts, who had an important message for him, and that if the name Alfred Horn meant nothing to him, then the real name was Rudolf Hess.'

However, the full message was not passed on in this form, possibly because it appeared incredible. In the early hours of the morning the R.A.F. sector controller at Turnhouse Airport telephoned Hamilton asking him to come to the operations room. Hamilton was then confronted with the surprising information that the pilot of the Me 110 which had flown across Scotland, and had recently crashed in flames, had asked personally for him and had given his name as Hauptmann Alfred Horn. By this time Hess had been handed over to the Army who had taken him to Maryhill Barracks in Glasgow, where at times he was in the custody of Corporal William Ross, a future Secretary of State for Scotland.

Hamilton made arrangements with the intelligence officer, Flight Lieutenant Benson – whose duty it was to interrogate captured German aircrew – to leave for Glasgow early the next day. In general, R.A.F. interrogation officers liked to interview prisoners as soon as possible after capture, but this did not necessarily extend to getting station commanders up in the middle of the night to see every new prisoner of war.

At this time Hamilton was very short of sleep, there having been raids during the past three nights which had kept him extremely late in the operations room. That night, the

House of Commons itself had been bombed, many bombers had been shot down, and this German pilot was now in safe custody.[3]

Hamilton returned to his home near the airfield. The thought that the German pilot might be making a political initiative did not occur to him. Remembering that he had noted down the names of the Luftwaffe officers he had met during the Olympic Games in 1936, he looked through the list. Horn's name did not appear so Hamilton returned to bed, somewhat puzzled, but in readiness for what the next day might hold in store.

NOTES

1. Public Record Office: INF1/912/HN07083.
2. Public Record Office: F01093/11.
3. Letter dated 11 September 1991 from Air Historical Branch, Ministry of Defence.

SIX

Hess, Hamilton and Churchill: 11 May 1941

On Sunday, 11 May 1941, Hamilton, together with the R.A.F. Interrogating Officer, arrived at Maryhill Barracks at 10 a.m. Hamilton first examined the personal effects of the prisoner, which included a Leica camera, a map, a large number of medicines, photographs of the prisoner and a small boy, and the visiting cards of General Professor Karl Haushofer and his son, Dr Albrecht Haushofer. These cards at once made Hamilton think that Oberleutnant Alfred Horn had a knowledge of the letter from Albrecht Haushofer which had so greatly interested the Intelligence authorities.

Contrary to what has sometimes been suggested, the personal effects did not include any written peace proposals. There is evidence from Bohle, who worked for Hess with the German Ausland organisations, that Hess asked him to prepare peace proposals in Germany. Bohle asserted that under instructions he helped translate them into English.[1] If so, no records of them exist. No doubt Hess memorised the proposals, and may have destroyed the records before his flight, the preparations for which he made in great secrecy.

Accompanied by the Interrogating Officer and the Military Officer on guard, Hamilton entered the prisoner's room. Hess was in bed still suffering from the leg injury caused by his parachute landing the night before. Hamilton had no recollection of having seen him before, and the prisoner immediately asked that Hamilton should speak to him alone. The other officers were requested by Hamilton to withdraw, which they did. The most accurate account of what followed is given in Hamilton's report to the Prime Minister:

> The German opened by saying that he had seen me in Berlin at the Olympic Games in 1936, and that I had lunched in his house.[2] He said, 'I do not know if you recognise me, but I am Rudolf Hess.' He went on to say that he was on a mission of humanity and that the Fuehrer did not want to defeat England and wished to stop fighting. His friend Albrecht Haushofer told him that I was an Englishman who he thought would understand his (Hess's) point of view. He had consequently tried to arrange a meeting with me in Lisbon. (See Haushofer's letter to me dated September 23rd, 1940.) Hess went on to say that he had tried to fly to Dungavel and this was the fourth time he had set out, the first time being in December. On the three previous occasions he had turned back owing to bad weather. He had not attempted to make this journey during the time when Britain was gaining victories in Libya, as he

144

thought his mission then might be interpreted as weakness, but now that Germany had gained successes in North Africa and Greece, he was glad to come.

The fact that Reich Minister Hess had come to this country in person would, he stated, show his sincerity and Germany's willingness for peace. He then went on to say that the Fuehrer was convinced that Germany would win the war, possibly soon but certainly in one, two or three years. He wanted to stop the unnecessary slaughter that would otherwise inevitably take place. He asked me if I could get together leading members of my party to talk over things with a view to making peace proposals. I replied that there was now only one party in this country.

He then said he could tell me what Hitler's peace terms would be. First he would insist on an arrangement whereby our two countries would never go to war again. I questioned him as to how that arrangement could be brought about, and he replied that one of the conditions, of course, was that Britain would give up her traditional policy of always opposing the strongest power in Europe.

I then told him that if we made peace now, we would be at war again certainly within two years. He asked why, to which I replied that if a peace agreement was possible, the arrangement could have been made before the war started, but since Germany chose war in preference to peace at a time when we were most anxious to preserve peace, I could put forward no hope of a peace agreement now.

He requested me to ask the King to give him 'parole', as he had come unarmed and of his own free will.

He further asked me if I could inform his family that he was safe by sending a telegram to Rothacker [Hess's aunt], Hertzog Str. 17, Zürich, stating that Alfred Horn was in good health. He also asked that his identity should not be disclosed to the Press.

It was the German radio which made the first public announcement about Hess's departure. On the evening of Monday 12 May the Germans broadcast that Hess, 'apparently in a fit of madness', had taken possession of an aircraft contrary to Hitler's orders and had disappeared. It was only after this broadcast that the British Press realised that the mysterious parachutist who had landed in Scotland was Hess.

At the first meeting Hamilton gained the impression that Hess, far from being mad, was a man of self-confidence who had numerous proposals to make which would have been highly favourable to the Nazi leadership, although certainly not to anyone else. Hess at one point said that the buying of fifty second-rate destroyers from the U.S.A. was a pointless exercise, because if Britain made peace such contracts with the U.S.A. would be unnecessary.

He also told Hamilton that while he had arrived without Hitler's knowledge, he knew how Hitler's mind worked so well that he could say with complete certainty what Hitler's peace terms would be, and what conditions Hitler would be prepared to accept in order to finish the war. By this time Hamilton had heard quite enough – certainly at that stage. His report continued:

Throughout the interview, Hess was able to express himself fairly clearly, but he did not properly understand what I was saying and I suggested that I should return with an interpreter and have further conversation with him.

Hess then asked 'Will you please have me moved out of Glasgow, as I am anxious not to be killed by a German bomb', and Hamilton left him. Hamilton's report ended:

From Press photographs and Albrecht Haushofer's description of Hess, I believed that this prisoner was indeed Hess himself. Until this interview I had not the slightest idea that the invitation in Haushofer's letter to meet him (Haushofer) in Lisbon had any connection with Hess.

Albrecht Haushofer had previously described Hess as a dark, swarthy man with eyes sunken into his head and a sallow complexion. The prisoner answered this description, and Hamilton had now to consider how the matter should be best reported. The situation was one without precedent, and King's Regulations provided no guide.

Hamilton collected some of the photographs of the prisoner and told the officer commanding that the prisoner was probably very important, and that a strong guard should be put over him. He went quickly to visit the site of the crashed aircraft, to check out the German pilot's story, and confirmed that it was an Me110. He drove back to R.A.F. Turnhouse in the afternoon to dictate his report.

Mrs Pyne was then a W.A.A.F. clerk in the operations room, dealing with the normal routine correspondence of a fighter station, and remembered the Commanding Officer making several telephone calls including one to the officer in charge of the Group. She remembered him being somewhat on edge, and when he dictated his report to Pearl Hyatt, he was pacing up and down. It was clear that what the German prisoner had said had come as a great surprise and a shock to him. He drove back to Turnhouse aerodrome in the afternoon, when he collected the letter which Albrecht Haushofer had written in July 1939. Having obtained leave from his Air Marshal, he rang up and asked to see Sir Alexander Cadogan, the head of the Foreign Office. The official at the other end of the phone acted with all the superciliousness of which the British Civil Servant is a master. As Sir Alexander was a very busy man, if it was a matter of the greatest importance an interview might be fitted into his programme in a couple of weeks' time. At that moment Jock Colville, the Prime Minister's Private Secretary, walked into the room of the Private Secretary in question, and heard that the Duke of Hamilton wanted the head of the Foreign Office to motor down to Northolt and meet him. Colville took the telephone and Hamilton demanded to see the Prime Minister without delay, as there might be something very important to report. Hamilton was comforted with the information that the Prime Minister was at that time more accessible than the head of the British Foreign Office. He said he would be at Northolt within two hours and asked Colville to make the necessary arrangements.

He went quickly across the aerodrome, to collect from the Station Commander's house the letter which Albrecht Haushofer had written to him in July 1939. While there he told his wife briefly what had happened. He explained to her later that he had told her in case he was shot down or did not get through on his way to Northolt. He showed her a photograph of himself which the prisoner had brought on his flight and said, 'I think he is Hess.'

At that moment his wife said, 'There is Cyril'. A family friend, Squadron Leader Cyril Longsden, had arrived with his children for tea with the Station Commander's wife, on time at 4.00 p.m. However, Hamilton was in a hurry since he wanted to get his information through as soon as possible. He left immediately to choose a suitable fighter aircraft to fly south.

Jock Colville gave his own account of the unfolding of events. He had spent the night of 10–11 May, which was perhaps the heaviest night of the Blitz, at 10 Downing Street and in the early hours of the morning had a curiously vivid dream centring on Peter Fleming's *Flying Visit*, which he had read some months before, and also on reports that Goering had been flying over London with the Luftwaffe to witness the damage which German bombs

Jock Colville as a young fighter pilot. But on 11 May 1941, as the Prime Minister's Private Secretary, he had great influence (Mrs Harriet Bowes-Lyon)

were causing. So strong was the impression left by this dream that it was still very much in his mind when he spoke to Hamilton on the telephone later the next morning. Hamilton said that something extraordinary had taken place, but declined to reveal what this extraordinary event was. All he did say was that it was like something out of an E. Phillips Oppenheim novel, and Colville, with his strange dream still in his mind, asked: 'Has somebody arrived?' There was a pause and then Hamilton replied 'Yes'. Colville thereupon rang up the Prime Minister, and received instructions not to go to Northolt, but to have Hamilton diverted directly to Kidlington and Ditchley.

Winston Churchill records in his *History of the Second World War*:

On Sunday May 11, I was spending the weekend at Ditchley – presently a secretary told me that somebody wanted to speak to me on the telephone on behalf of the Duke of Hamilton. The Duke was a personal friend of mine, and was commanding a fighter-sector in the East of Scotland, but I could not think of any business he might have with me which could not wait till morning. However the caller pressed to speak with me, saying the matter was one of urgent Cabinet importance. . . . I therefore sent for him.

147

The cloisters of the House of Commons were bombed on the same night and at the same time as Hess flew to Britain on 10 May 1941 (Hulton-Deutsch)

Hamilton took off for Northolt in a Hurricane, and assembled his thoughts as he flew. He knew that Albrecht Haushofer must have played a large part in what had happened, because he himself had never had any connection with Hess before. He simply could not believe that Albrecht Haushofer could or would have sent Hess to see him. He recalled that years before Albrecht had once said casually to him that he hoped one day Hamilton might meet Hess. Yet Hamilton had never imagined that a meeting would take place in such circumstances. Although Hamilton could not know about it, neither had Haushofer, and Hamilton's astonishment was as nothing in comparison with the shock experienced by Albrecht. Indeed at the same time as Hamilton was flying to see Churchill, Albrecht Haushofer was being taken to Hitler.

When Hamilton landed at Northolt he was given a message to fly on to Kidlington, near Oxford. The Prime Minister's car was waiting to take him to Ditchley Park, the country home of Ronald Tree where Tree's son was acting as host to some thirty guests, including the Prime Minister, Brendan Bracken and Sir Archibald Sinclair, the Secretary

Prime Minister Winston Churchill gives the victory sign (Hulton-Deutsch)

of State for Air. They were finishing dinner and Churchill welcomed Hamilton with great enthusiasm and asked him for his news. During the day information had been coming in concerning the heavy air raid on London during the night before, when the House of Commons had been hit by incendiary bombs and had been severely damaged. Adversity stimulated the Prime Minister, and he could not have been in more exuberant spirits or in better form, especially as thirty-three German bombers had been shot down in the last twenty-four hours. As the room was full of guests Hamilton replied that he must communicate his news to the Prime Minister in private. Accordingly the guests automatically withdrew, leaving the Prime Minister, Hamilton and Sir Archibald Sinclair. Hamilton then explained that a German pilot had arrived in Scotland, had given the name of Oberleutnant Alfred Horn to everyone else, and had then told him personally that he was Rudolf Hess.

Hamilton had the impression that Churchill was looking at him sympathetically, as though he were suffering from war strain and hallucinations. On 15 May Churchill made

149

the frank admission to the House of Commons: 'In view of the surprising character of the occurrence I did not believe it, although I was very interested when told in the course of Sunday.' Churchill then asked Hamilton very slowly and with great emphasis: 'Do you mean to tell me that the Deputy Fuehrer of Germany is in our hands?' Hamilton replied that the man had certainly declared himself to be Hess. He then produced the photographs of the unidentified prisoner and assured him that the photographs were of the German he had interviewed that morning. Churchill looked at them and said, 'Well, Hess or no Hess I am going to see the Marx Brothers.'

By the time that the film-show was finished the Prime Minister had decided that it was necessary to go into the matter thoroughly, the time being about midnight. For the next three hours Hamilton went through every detail and was asked every conceivable type of question.

Hamilton explained that it was his personal view that the German was Hess, as he answered Albrecht Haushofer's description. He again showed Churchill the letter which Albrecht Haushofer had sent in July 1939 as well as a copy of the letter sent by Haushofer in September 1940. In the light of these letters it was clear that Hess's flight involved a peace offer, and that Hess was stating terms which would be acceptable to Hitler, although the flight was made without Hitler's knowledge.

It was, furthermore, Hamilton's impression that the prisoner was an energetic, fanatical and stupid man, and that he had come to certain definite conclusions, one being that the British were losing the war and another that the British had been cowed by the bombing of their civilian population. Hamilton also said that Hess, if he was Hess, had said that Mr Churchill would not be very sympathetic to his point of view. After a momentary pause Churchill replied, 'By God I would not.'

Hamilton was sworn to secrecy, and felt that Churchill was not entirely clear as to how the matter should be explained, for Hess's peace overture could not have been made in a more unconventional and unexpected way. At any rate it was decided that Hamilton should come up to London with the Prime Minister on the following day.

On the morning of 12 May the news of Hess's arrival had not broken, although there was some speculation around Glasgow and also East Renfrew, which Hamilton had represented as an M.P. until early 1940. The three cars left Ditchley for London at about 9.15 a.m. At one point speeding at 70 m.p.h. through a built-up area, a police car gonged the Prime Minister's car – whereupon without slackening speed a much louder gong resounded from somewhere in the depths of Churchill's car, and the police car immediately withdrew.

On arrival at 10 Downing Street, Churchill told the Foreign Secretary, Anthony Eden, the bare essentials and said that the prisoner must be identified. He then passed Hamilton over to Eden, who took him to the Foreign Office. The story was repeated, and was accepted with astonishment, or not accepted, as the case may be. Eden called in his German expert, Ivone Kirkpatrick, later permanent Under Secretary for Foreign Affairs. Kirkpatrick accepted the news very much as a matter of course, and it was arranged that he and Hamilton should fly to Scotland, so that Kirkpatrick might identify the German.

That evening Hamilton flew Kirkpatrick north in a D.H. Rapide and on landing heard that an announcement had just been made on the German wireless that Deputy Fuehrer Rudolf Hess was missing. This dispelled any doubt in their minds as to the identity of the German prisoner. At Turnhouse aerodrome they received instructions from the Secretary of State for Air to proceed with all possible speed to Buchanan Castle in Drymen, where the prisoner had been moved under armed guard, in order that identification should be made as soon as possible.

They arrived at Drymen after midnight and went in to interview the prisoner. At one

Wing Commander Lord Geordie Douglas-Hamilton, Chief Intelligence Officer of R.A.F. Fighter Command in 1940 standing behind Sir Archie Sinclair, Secretary of State for Air and Balfour, Minister for Air in the Air Ministry. On 12 May 1941 he lunches with the Duke of Hamilton and is told of the extraordinary appearance of Hess in Britain (Imperial War Museum)

o'clock on the morning of 13 May 1941 Kirkpatrick was summoned to the telephone. The Foreign Secretary had been unable to bear the suspense any longer. Kirkpatrick explained that the German had been talking for more than an hour and had said nothing. He still had no idea why he had come to Scotland, but there was no doubt that it was indeed Rudolf Hess. Within hours a statement was issued from 10 Downing Street, that the German officer who had parachuted out of an Me 110 in Scotland had been identified as Hitler's Deputy Rudolf Hess, and on 13 May the story broke in the Press. Meanwhile Ivone Kirkpatrick had returned to the interview, but like Sir Alexander Cadogan he was 'a very busy man', and he behaved as though this particular episode in the war was an infernal bore.

151

NOTES
1. Evidence of Bohle at the Nuremberg War Trials and also referred to in the Goebbels Diaries for 1941.
2. This was probably a reference to the dinner given by Hitler in honour of Lord Vansittart in Berlin during the Olympic Games, where Hess may have seen Hamilton across the room, but this dinner was not given in Hess's house. Hess was probably confusing the dinner in honour of Lord Vansittart with the lunch he gave in his own house to the International Olympic Committee.

SEVEN

Hess's Peace Terms: 12–15 May 1941

On the way to Drymen, Kirkpatrick described the Nazi leaders to Hamilton, and said that of all of them Hitler was by far and away the worst. Behind all the bombast, histrionics and hysteria Hitler remained the most treacherous, calculating and cold-blooded devil in the world. It was an extraordinary scene which ensued. Kirkpatrick and Hamilton were treated to a speech in German by Hess, delivered from copious notes, which for the first hour consisted of a long eulogy of Hitler. Kirkpatrick sat looking like a sphinx.

During this interview Hess probably made a more complete statement of his ideas, hopes and aims, than at any other time. His views are recorded in detail in Kirkpatrick's first report to the Prime Minister, which gave a truer picture of what actually took place than the lighthearted account in his memoirs, *The Inner Circle* written years later.

Hess started [Kirkpatrick reports] by saying that he must go a long way back in order to explain the chain of circumstances which had led to his present decision.

Its origin lay in an English book called *England's Foreign Policy under Edward VII*. The author of this book who was an impartial and reputable historian,[1] admitted that from 1904 on, England's policy had been to oppose Germany and back France in the certain knowledge that this would lead to a conflict with Germany. Thus England was responsible for the war in 1914.

After the war came the Treaty of Versailles and the failure of the British Government to accord to the democratic system in Germany those concessions which would have enabled it to live. Hence the rise of Hitler and National Socialism.

Having given the interpretation of history accepted by the Nazis, he turned to more recent events. He said that Hitler had tried to negotiate the Anschluss through peaceful means, and after failing was forced to occupy Austria, as it was the wish of the Austrian people.

The Czechoslovak conflict was caused by the French trying to make Czechoslovakia an air base against Germany, and Hitler had to smother this attempt. Hess declared that Chamberlain's intervention at Munich had greatly relieved Hitler, but as the British and French had tried to arm the remainder of Czechoslovakia, Hitler had been compelled to act against this menace to Germany.

Sir Ivone Kirkpatrick, the British Foreign Office expert on Germany, who correctly identified Rudolf Hess (Hulton-Deutsch)

England had then caused the Polish crisis by opposing Germany, which was the strongest European power, for the Polish Government would have submitted to the German demands had it not been for the British. 'The conclusion was clear that England was responsible for the present war.'

The implication of this remark was that Hitler had never intended to go to war against Britain, that he had not expected the British to declare war, and that British intransigence in rejecting Hitler's peace offers had led to escalation.

154

When in May last year, Great Britain started bombing Germany, Herr Hitler had believed that this was a momentary aberration; and with exemplary patience, he had waited, partly so as to spare the world the horrors of unrestricted air warfare, and partly out of a sentimental regard for English culture and English monuments. It was only with the greatest reluctance that after many weeks of waiting, he had given the order to bomb England.

The bombing of civilians in English cities was in his view a necessary expedient in order to make the British plead for peace. And as the British remained stubborn, Hitler had no alternative but to 'pursue the struggle to its logical conclusion'.

Hess then proceeded to explain why Germany was going to win the war. Germany was producing enormous numbers of aircraft and Britain could never reduce the lead which the Luftwaffe had over the R.A.F. As for naval warfare, a vastly increased number of submarines would be operating with the Luftwaffe against British convoys and shipping, and would have a deadly effect. Germany had obtained plenty of raw materials in German-occupied Europe and was self-sufficient. 'There is not the slightest hope of bringing about a revolution in Germany. Hitler possesses the blindest confidence of the German masses.'

Hess now turned to the most important part of his talk, dealing with peace proposals. He had been horrified at the idea of so much unnecessary killing, and had come without Hitler's permission in order to 'convince responsible persons that since England could not win the war, the wisest course was to make peace now'.

From a long and intimate knowledge of the Fuehrer which had begun eighteen years ago in the fortress of Landsberg, he could give us his word of honour that the Fuehrer had never entertained any designs against the British Empire. Nor had he ever aspired to world domination. He believed that Germany's sphere of interest was in Europe and that any dissipation of Germany's strength beyond Europe's frontiers would be a weakness and would carry with it the seeds of Germany's destruction. Only as recently as May 3, after his Reichstag speech, Hitler had declared to him that he had no oppressive demands to make on England.

The solution was that England should give Germany a free hand in Europe, and Germany give England a completely free hand in the Empire, with the sole reservation that we should return Germany's ex-colonies which she required as a source of raw materials.

Furthermore it might be a mistake to keep Hitler waiting, for he could be impatient, even if he was a 'tenderhearted man'. Kirkpatrick tried to draw Hess on Hitler's plans towards Russia, and asked Hess whether he regarded Russia as being in Europe or in Asia.

He [Hess] replied 'In Asia'. I [Kirkpatrick] then retorted that under the terms of his proposal, since Germany would only have a free hand in Europe, she would not be at liberty to attack Russia. Herr Hess reacted quickly by remarking that Germany had certain demands to make of Russia which would have to be satisfied, either by negotiation or as the result of a war. He added however that there was no foundation for the rumours now being spread that Hitler was contemplating an early attack on Russia.

Kirkpatrick wrote in his memoirs, 'I got the impression that Hess was so much out of things that he really did not know'. Hamilton, on the other hand, thought that Hess looked as though he had over-reached himself when he mentioned the possibility of war against Russia, and that he tried to recover his balance by denying that Hitler was thinking of an early attack.

Finally as we were leaving the room Herr Hess delivered a parting shot. He had forgotten, he declared, to emphasise that the proposal could only be considered on the understanding that it was negotiated by Germany with an English Government other than the present British Government. Mr Churchill, who had planned the war since 1938, and his colleagues who had lent themselves to his war policy, were not persons with whom the Fuehrer could negotiate.

Kirkpatrick admitted that his patience was exhausted long before the end of the interview, which had lasted two and a quarter hours, and he ended his report with these words:

But in general, I allowed even the most outrageous remarks to pass unanswered, since I realised that argument would be quite fruitless and would certainly have deprived us of our breakfast.

On the next day, Wednesday 14 May, the Foreign Secretary instructed Kirkpatrick and Hamilton to pursue their conversations with Hess. On his return to the prisoner's room Kirkpatrick noticed that Hess was surprised that nothing had been done to meet his demand for negotiations. Kirkpatrick later recorded that Hess still seemed to have some faith in the ability of Dukes to deliver the goods.

The interview which followed was not as important as the one which had preceded it. Hess requested the loan of certain books, including *Three Men in a Boat*, the return of his medicines and a piece of his aeroplane as a souvenir. He next described his flight and the extreme difficulty in parachuting out of a plane which was flying upside down.

He then said that Germany had one or two additional demands. For example Germany could not leave Rashid Ali and the Iraqis 'in the lurch'. Britain would have to evacuate Iraq. Also there would have to be reciprocal indemnification of those Britons and Germans whose property had been requisitioned on account of the war. Taken as a whole (he added) his proposals were more than fair. If by any chance Britain continued the war, there would be a completely effective blockade, and if Britain capitulated, but tried to wage war from the Empire, it was Hitler's intention to continue the blockade so that the population of Britain would be deliberately starved to death. Kirkpatrick was beginning to find such interviews very irritating, but on Thursday 15 May he was instructed to interview Hess yet again, this time by himself, as Hamilton had been told to return to London in case he might be needed.

The chief interest of this conversation between Hess and Kirkpatrick lay in the fact that Hess tried to make Kirkpatrick's 'flesh creep' by suggesting that the Americans wanted to take over the British Empire. Hess also reverted to his old theme that if Hitler's terms were rejected Britain would be subjugated. As Kirkpatrick recorded:

I then threw a fly over him about Ireland. He said that in all his talks with Hitler, the subject of Ireland had never been mentioned except incidentally. Ireland had done nothing for Germany in this war and it was therefore to be supposed that Hitler would not concern himself 'in Anglo–Irish relations'. We had some little conversation about the difficulty of reconciling the wishes of the south and north and from this we passed to American interest in Ireland, and so to America.

On the subject of America, Hess took the following line. The Germans reckoned with American intervention and were not afraid of it. They knew all about American aircraft production and the quality of the aircraft. Germany could outbuild England and America combined.

Germany had no designs on America. The so-called German peril was a ludicrous figment of the imagination. Hitler's interests were European.

156

If we made peace now America would be furious. America really wanted to inherit the British Empire.

Hess concluded by saying that Hitler really wanted a permanent understanding with us on a basis which preserved the Empire intact. His own flight was intended to give us a chance of opening conversations without loss of prestige. If we rejected this chance it would be clear proof that we desired no understanding with Germany and Hitler would be entitled, in fact it would be his duty to destroy us utterly, and keep us after the war in a state of permanent subjection.

After this interview Kirkpatrick was permitted to return to London. Hess remained in Drymen, where he repeated many times to Captain Cummack, an officer of the Royal Army Medical Corps in attendance, that Russia was the greatest enemy of Europe. Meanwhile Kirkpatrick reported to the Prime Minister. Hess's flight had not impressed Churchill, who was in bad humour in case it might appear that peace negotiations were taking place. He told Kirkpatrick, 'If Hess had come a year ago and told us what the Germans would do to us, we should have been very frightened, and rightly, so why should we be frightened now?'

One of the most interesting questions arising out of Hess's mission is how a person like Hess, whose loyalty to Hitler had always been unquestioned, could have acted so indiscreetly. The answer must be that Hess was loyal to Hitler's innermost thoughts in a way which Hitler himself was not, for Hitler, contrary to all that he had said and written for many years, was seriously contemplating a war on two fronts.

There were two essential matters which Hess with his over-simplified Nazi outlook on the world did not understand. First, the British were not prepared to contemplate peace with Hitler or the Nazis. Hitler and the leaders of the Third Reich had broken too many treaties, lied too often, and killed too many people. In any case, the British would not have considered a peace proposal even from a non-Nazi German Government unless it had been coupled with a German withdrawal from all occupied territories. Hess did not understand this. He relied for his information primarily on Hitler and on Albrecht Haushofer, and he was unwise enough to believe that it was Hitler rather than Albrecht Haushofer who understood Britain best.

Secondly, Hess did not fully comprehend that Hitler had come to believe in his own infallibility, as sometimes happens with men who succeed against great odds. As Alan Bullock wrote, 'No man ever more surely destroyed himself by coming to believe in the image which he had himself created than Adolf Hitler'. The turning point in Hitler's case came on 22 June 1941, six weeks after Hess's flight, with the attack upon Russia, while a bitter war against Britain was still being waged in the West. Hitler based his gamble on the premise that he could knock out Russia with a lightning blow and then return to settle the old score with Britain and seize such parts of the British Empire as he desired. Hess, on the other hand, believed that Hitler should not break the cardinal rule laid down in *Mein Kampf*, never to conduct a war on two fronts, and could not understand that Hitler was no longer worried about the British resolve to fight.

As Kirkpatrick wrote, 'The Hess episode was one of the oddest in history, and the oddest thing about it was that it was not in character.' It was not in character for one reason and one reason alone. Hitler was a master of deceit and a liar *par excellence*, while Hess was an arrogant fool who was only too anxious to reveal all the cards in his hand. It was not until he had been in Britain for some time that he realised that he had never held any cards, and that the British were not interested in a Nazi peace offer. Then in despair he tried to take his own life, but even in that was frustrated.

157

Hess's secret mission, involving unconventional means, is easily understood in the light of what he himself said. Might he not make peace with Britain and return to Germany to be acclaimed a popular hero, second to none but the Fuehrer? Was there not a chance that before long the whole might and fury of the 'Third Reich' would be turned on Russia alone?

NOTE
1. In a later interview with Lord Simon, Hess said that the English historian Farrar laid the main guilt for the Great War on the policies of Edward VII, so it appears that in this passage he was referring to Farrar.

EIGHT

The Silence of the British Government: 1941

On 14 May the Prime Minister issued an instruction that it would be more convenient to treat Hess as a prisoner of war, with special guardians, under the jurisdiction of the War Office, 'as one against whom grave political charges may be preferred. This man is potentially a war criminal, and he and his confederates may well be declared outlaws at the close of the war.' But whilst the war lasted Hess was to be isolated, and every attempt should be made to get information from him. In short 'he should be treated with dignity as if he were an important General who had fallen into our hands'.

That was the nature of the Prime Minister's ruling on the treatment for Hess, but although it was always the policy of Churchill to tell the British public the truth, however unpalatable, the British Government did not at any stage make a statement as to why Hess had come to Britain, nor was any information given as to what had been extracted from him. This led to wild guessing in the Press, and A. P. Herbert on 18 May 1941 gave a summary of the speculations which followed in the wake of Hess's flight, in a rhyme which he entitled *Hess*:

> He is insane. He is the Dove of Peace.
> He is Messiah. He is Hitler's niece.
> He is the one clean honest man they've got.
> He is the worst assassin of the lot.
> He has a mission to preserve mankind.
> He's non-alcoholic. He was a 'blind'.
> He has been dotty since the age of ten,
> But all the time was top of Hitler's men.
> (Indeed from all the tales he had to tell,
> Joe Goebbels must be slightly touched as well.)
> He is to pave the way to Britain's end.
> He is – as dear old Lindbergh was – a 'friend'.
> He's fond of flying. He was racked with fear.
> He had an itch to meet a British Peer.
> He thought that Russia was a crashing bore.
> He simply can't stand Hitler any more.

> In such rich fancies I am not engrossed
> For this is what appears to matter most –
> He came unasked, an enemy, a Hun;
> And nobody was ready with a gun.

Very few people understood why Hess had come, and the incident remained as a question mark in the mind of the British public. Eden in his memoirs told part of the inside story, starting on Monday 12 May. During dinner that day he heard the German wireless communiqué that Hess had disappeared. Churchill telephoned 'immensely excited', and wanted the Government to make an announcement quickly. The B.B.C. were instructed to announce Hess's presence in Britain later that night. Eden then went round to see Churchill, and together they concocted a statement although they found it a problem as to how much should be said about Hess's 'confused obsessions'.

On Tuesday 13 May Kirkpatrick telephoned the Foreign Office at 8.30 a.m., in

15 May 1941. A cartoon by David Low, expressing a popular British reaction to Hess's flight
(The Source/Solo)

order to give a brief account of his interrogation of Hess. He was told 'that the British Government were embarrassed by the whole affair and did not know exactly how to handle it'. Later in the day the Prime Minister told the House of Commons 'I have nothing to add at present to the statement issued last night by His Majesty's Government', which had been an official recognition of the fact that Hess had arrived in Britain. Churchill went on, 'but obviously a further statement will be made in the near future concerning the flight to this country of this very high and important Nazi leader'. In answer to the suggestion that the Minister of Information should handle the news with skill and imagination, the Prime Minister replied, 'I think this is one of these cases where imagination is somewhat baffled by the facts as they present themselves.'

However, Churchill had made no final decision, and on Wednesday 14 May Harold Nicolson, Parliamentary Secretary to the Ministry of Information, was included in a lunch party given by the Prime Minister. Nicolson tried to get directives on Hess and was merely told by Churchill that 'we must not make a hero out of him'. That night Churchill rang Eden with a text of the statement which he wanted to make in the House of Commons about Hess on Thursday 15 May, quoting the trend of Hess's statements. Eden objected on the grounds that the Germans must be left guessing as to what Hess had said. Churchill then demanded an alternative draft and Eden 'struggled out of bed', drew up a statement and telephoned it to Churchill. A few minutes later Churchill telephoned back saying that Eden's statement had been approved by Lord Beaverbrook, Minister of Air Production, but had upset Duff Cooper, Minister of Information, and was not to his own liking. Churchill said that he was either going to make his own statement or no statement, and which was it to be? Eden replied, 'No statement', whereupon Churchill answered angrily, 'All right, no statement', and the 'telephone was crashed down'; the time being 1.30 a.m.

Accordingly no statement was made, and for once Churchill acted rather indecisively. Nicolson records in his diary that Duff Cooper persuaded Churchill that a directive must be put out as to the British attitude towards Hess. Churchill replied, 'We must think this over. Come back at midnight and we shall discuss it again.' When Duff Cooper arrived he found Lord Beaverbrook with the Prime Minister, seeking to persuade him that a statement must not be made.

Churchill was wavering and he brought up the subject again. Eden wrote: 'The Prime Minister reverted to his projected statement about Hess, this time at the Cabinet, but nobody liked it so that nothing came of it. Lord Beaverbrook told me afterwards that we might have to "strangle the infant" a third time, but fortunately it was not reborn.' Eden and Beaverbrook had got their way.

Eden was no doubt opposed to making a full statement on the grounds that it would be best to keep the Germans guessing, while the German propaganda machine was floundering, and Beaverbrook probably thought this as well. Churchill himself finally decided to play down the whole episode and to remain silent.

As could be expected when the Government lapsed into a mysterious silence, there was speculation. Harold Nicolson related, 'This is bad, since the belief will get around that we are hiding something and we shall be blamed in this Ministry', namely the Ministry of Information. As it happened Duff Cooper had already issued inaccurate information to the B.B.C. which later had to be withdrawn. He told the B.B.C. that the Duke of Hamilton had met Hess at the Olympic Games at Berlin in 1936, and that Hess had written a letter which Hamilton had placed in the hands of the authorities.

Hamilton had never met Hess before May 1941. The British M.P. who had interviewed Hess had been Kenneth Lindsay, M.P., and after Hess's flight in May 1941 he suggested to several M.P.s that Hamilton might have seen Hess, as he did. Chips Channon, M.P., who had also been to the Olympic Games, was under a similar erroneous impression. Thus it was that a rumour of the vaguest description came to be accepted uncritically.

As to the belief that Hess had written a letter to Hamilton which had been handed over to the authorities, in fact it was Albrecht Haushofer who, with Hess's knowledge, had written the letter to Hamilton, which had been intercepted by the British censor. It was not until Hess's flight that the light dawned upon the British Secret Service, the Intelligence Branch of the Air Ministry and on Hamilton, that Albrecht Haushofer was the *eminence grise* behind Rudolf Hess.

Neither the British Press nor the British public knew about the existence of Albrecht Haushofer and certainly nobody in Britain would have guessed that on 12 May 1941 Albrecht had been taken to Hitler's residence in Berchtesgaden, a summons which he most certainly did not enjoy. Instead, the British Press, armed with Duff Cooper's inaccurate information, went speeding off along the wrong scent, imagining that all Rudolf Hess's ideas about the British emanated from conversations at the Olympic Games in 1936.

Hamilton had returned to London on Thursday 15 May, as the Prime Minister wished him to be available, and during the afternoon went to see Duff Cooper in order to emphasise that he had never met Hess before May 1941. Duff Cooper was very apologetic and offered to put out any statement which Hamilton wished to give him. Hamilton pointed out that the Prime Minister had sworn him to secrecy, and that no information of any consequence was to be divulged, so the matter was left in the air.

On Friday 16 May, Hess was transported late at night in great secrecy to the Tower of London. On the same day Hamilton had been asked to lunch with the King at Windsor. George VI was very curious to know what had happened, so Hamilton put him in the picture, and a few days later sent him the report on Hess which had been submitted to the Prime Minister, along with a covering letter:

> It is clear that Hess is still an unrepentant Nazi who repeats *ad nauseam* the usual Nazi 'claptrap'. While his action seems unlikely to affect the course of the war, his arrival here uninvited has been of considerable advantage to us, if only in the difficulties and discredit in which it has involved the German propaganda machine.
>
> I heard yesterday from Kirkpatrick that Hess had told him that he thought of flying to see Vansittart but gave up the idea when he learned of the *Black Record*. It is indeed extraordinary how little the Nazis understand us. . . .

It is of interest to read what it was that Lord Vansittart had written which had disturbed Hess. It was a book entitled *Black Record: Germans Past and Present*, and if ever a book captured the feelings of the British towards Nazi Germany early in 1941 it was this book. What Vansittart wrote explained all too well that Hess had made a fundamental miscalculation about the atmosphere in Britain, and the determination of the British to fight on whatever the consequences. Typical passages ran:

> But don't think Hitler was, or is, an exception. As early as the Franco-Prussian War of 1870 the King of Prussia was continually thanking God in letters to his wife for the number of fellow-men whom he had killed. Even to our Victorian ancestors this seemed insufferable, and I think it was Punch that published a parody of the correspondence:
>
> > 'Thanks to the Lord, my dear Augusta,
> > We've hit the French an awful buster.
> > Ten thousand Frenchmen sent below!
> > Praise God from whom all blessings flow.'

162

By the grace of God and for the salvation of man we shall rescue the earth from Germany and Germany from herself.

When Hamilton returned to London, he found that he was not required by the Prime Minister, who on Tuesday 20 May had become preoccupied with the invasion of Crete. He was fitted in for a ten-minute interview while Churchill travelled from 10 Downing Street to Buckingham Palace. Hamilton mentioned that he was being pestered by the Press, and put it to him: 'What do you tell your wife if a prostitute throws her arms around your neck?' Churchill roared with laughter, and said that whatever happened the Press were not to be told a word. Nonetheless the point was taken. On Thursday 22 May Sir Archibald Sinclair, Secretary of State for Air, made a statement about the Duke of Hamilton's position in relation to Hess's arrival, in answer to a question by the M.P. Major Lloyd.

When Deputy Fuehrer Hess came down with his aeroplane in Scotland on 10th May, he gave a false name and asked to see the Duke of Hamilton. The Duke being apprised by the authorities, visited the German prisoner in hospital. Hess then revealed for the first time his true identity, saying that he had seen the Duke when he was at the Olympic Games at Berlin in 1936. The Duke did not recognise the prisoner and had never met the Deputy Fuehrer. He had, however, visited Germany for the Olympic Games in 1936, and during that time had attended more than one large public function, at which German Ministers were present. It is, therefore, quite possible that the Deputy Fuehrer may have seen him on one such occasion. As soon as the interview was over, Wing Commander the Duke of Hamilton flew to England and gave a full report of what had passed to the Prime Minister, who sent for him. Contrary to reports which have appeared in some newspapers, the Duke has never been in correspondence with the Deputy Fuehrer. None of the Duke's three brothers, who are, like him, serving in the Royal Air Force, has either met Hess or has had correspondence with him. It will be seen that the conduct of the Duke of Hamilton has been in every respect honourable and proper.

Yet the question as to why Duff Cooper had given inaccurate information to the B.B.C. still remained unanswered. On the same day Sir Archibald Sinclair, on behalf of the Air Ministry, wrote a formal letter of complaint to Duff Cooper, who was in charge of the Ministry of Information:

I am shocked to hear through a telephone conversation between my Private Secretary and Sir Walter Monckton that the story which was published in some newspapers, that the Duke of Hamilton has been in correspondence with Hess, was actually inspired by your Department.

There is no truth whatever in the story. The Duke has assured me personally that he has never received a letter from Hess. I feel surprised that your Department should have given currency to a story that affects the reputation of a serving officer in the Royal Air Force without consulting me. I feel sure I can rely on you to give instructions which will prevent such a thing ever happening again.

The Ministry of Information immediately took steps to rectify their mistake.

Harold Nicolson, on Tuesday 27 May, was asked by the M.P. Major Adams how it was that the B.B.C. incorrectly broadcast that Hamilton had received a communication from Hess. Nicolson replied:

The statement broadcast by the B.B.C. was based on information supplied by the Ministry of Information to the B.B.C. and the Press, which has since been found to be erroneous. The true facts are those stated in the reply given on 22nd May by my Right Honourable Friend the Secretary of State for Air to the Honourable and gallant Member for Renfrew [Major Lloyd] . . .

Hamilton had returned to Scotland on 30 May to take up a Group Captain's command. Mrs Pyne wrote:

I do remember very well the pleasure we felt in H.Q. when he came in with the insignia of a Group Captain on his sleeves and cap. Obviously whatever may have been said in the corridors of power did not adversely affect him. In fact the 'Waafery' decided we should throw a party for him – we did and he had a jolly good time I remember. He was able to relax by then. The station returned to normal after that, and the whole Hess affair was no longer spoken of. We knew that he [Hess] was in the Tower – so what?

Although it was unknown to Hamilton, a further attempt to contact him was made by the Nazis. On the early morning of Monday 19 May, near Luton Hoo, while the Luftwaffe was engaged in bombing, the searchlights picked out two parachutists descending. They were S.S. men in plain clothes, who had a map in their possession with circles drawn around certain places, one of which was Hamilton's home in Lanarkshire. Clearly they wished to make contact with certain persons in Britain in order to find out where Hess was confined. It is not known whether they were sent by Himmler, Schellenberg or Heydrich. All that is known is that the British Secret Service picked them up, and drove them to a secret establishment, where they were identified, interrogated and executed. Such were the rules of war: Rudolf Hess had at least arrived in uniform.

Even so, his presence in Britain was never explained by the British Government, and as no statement was made he could not be exploited for propaganda purposes. Sefton Delmer, who was working for the Directorate of Psychological Warfare, wrote that he found it frustrating that the psychological warfare agencies and the deception experts were not permitted to use the incident in order to confuse and distress the Germans. However, Churchill was now adamant that no useful purpose could be served by telling the British people that a Nazi leader had made a serious peace initiative and that was the end of the matter. Churchill was quite content to leave the Germans weltering in their own embarrassment.

Sefton Delmer remained dissatisfied; and he was not alone. Dr Kurt Hahn believed that he, too, could see an opportunity in Hess's flight. Hahn was a patriotic German of Jewish origin and had been imprisoned by the Nazis in 1933 for his outspoken opposition to Nazism. After the British Premier Ramsay Macdonald interceded on his behalf Hahn was released; and he came to Britain, where he founded Gordonstoun School. During the war he worked for the British Foreign Office translating German news cuttings, and on 20 May 1941 he submitted a report on Hess's flight, suggesting that the Haushofers were behind it. His theme was that Hess's action indicated that 'there was a great longing for peace in Germany of which Hess had become the unconscious and silent ambassador. Now was the moment to encourage the German Resistance and to make it clear to the German people that the British would never make peace with Hitler, but that a cleansed and liberated Germany had nothing to fear from Britain.'

The blunt answer to Hahn's suggestions was that by May 1941 Churchill and the Cabinet believed that Nazism was too deeply rooted in the German people and too firmly embedded in the German mind for it to be removed by placing faith in a possible German Resistance to Hitler. Churchill and the Cabinet were thinking in terms of carrying the battle on to German soil at the first available opportunity, so that Nazism would be wiped off the map of Europe. There was a resolve that never again would Britain be tricked into an Armistice as in 1918, and that this time Germany would be crushed and occupied.

In the meantime the Foreign Office had given further consideration to a statement which could be made to Parliament. Con O'Neil of the Foreign Office drafted a memorandum dated 22 June with a draft statement saying that 'the undiluted truth about the Hess case does not make good propaganda'.

The draft statement and notes with it brought out the Haushofer involvement by stating that:

> Hess brought with him what he called terms of peace. These terms he was anxious to communicate to the Duke of Hamilton who, because of his slight acquaintance with the Haushofer family, Hess had singled out as a likely contact. It was a bad choice, but I do not know where in this country he could have made a good one.

There is an interesting note that Hess was confirmed in his plan by the dream of General Karl Haushofer and by Albrecht Haushofer's reference to the Duke of Hamilton. In this dream, Karl Haushofer had seen Hess walking along tapestried corridors of British castles seeking to bring peace to the two warring nations. Hess believed in the 'prophetic vision of (Karl) Haushofer and looked upon this incident as divine guidance and confirmation that he was to carry out his plan or, as he prefers to call it, his vision'.

The Foreign Secretary, Anthony Eden, was unwilling to make a statement that was 'wide of the truth' and the Government decided to say nothing, so as to keep the Germans guessing as to what revelations Hess might be making in Britain.

Various proposals from Richard Crossman, later Labour Secretary of State for Education, and others as to how to make propaganda out of the Hess case were put forward, including a suggestion to broadcast statements from Hess, concocted from recordings of his conversations. One suggestion in particular, emanating from Dr Kurt Hahn, was that the younger brother of the Duke of Hamilton, should broadcast on the B.B.C. German Service in German, which he spoke fluently but with a Tyrolean accent. The purpose of this talk would have been to separate the German people from Hitler and the Nazi leaders by asking some devastating questions:

> I would put these questions to Hess. Where was your conscience when, on February 28th 1933, the Reichstag was burned? Where was your conscience when, on June 30th 1934, at least 700 Germans were murdered in cold blood, some of them, according to their lights, great patriots? Where was your conscience when, on July 25th 1934, Dolfuss was murdered, and when, in 1938, a memorial was set up in honour of his murderers? Where was your conscience when on March 3rd 1938 Niemoller, acquitted in a German court, was seized as he left it and taken to the concentration camp where he still is today? Where was your conscience on November 9th 1938 (the night of the Kristallnacht)? Where was your conscience when on September 1st 1939, as the war he had schemed for was breaking out, Hitler lied to the German people and told them that Britain and Poland had rejected the compromise of the so-called 16 points, which in fact had never been submitted to them?
>
> These are the questions I would ask Hess and Hess's friends in Germany today. I would ask them where their consciences were when Warsaw, Rotterdam and Belgrade were destroyed by the German Air Force without mercy and – as an airman I can allow myself this much contempt – without opposition.
>
> What has been achieved by the conscience of Hess and those like him? Nothing at all: for their consciences are futile, ineffective and – I am obliged to say it – cowardly . . .

Dr Kurt Hahn, Headmaster of Gordonstoun and of German origin, urged the British Government to utilise Hess's flight for propaganda purposes (Hulton-Deutsch)

This is what my generation, the fighting men of England, feel. No peace with the murder gang. No peace with the murderer who murders his enemies and tortures them before he murders them; who murders every nation which blocks his way. And Hess, whatever he may be now, was a member of the murder gang and shares the guilt of all its crimes . . .

No action was taken on these proposals. David Douglas-Hamilton never knew that Kurt Hahn had put forward his name in this way. After commanding a Spitfire squadron during the height of the Blitz in Malta, he was killed after his Mosquito was hit by anti-aircraft fire when carrying out photo-reconnaissance operations on German military installations on 2 August 1944.

Kurt Hahn was not the only person to be disgruntled. The whole of the Enemy Propaganda Department was 'very disappointed' as regards the ruling that 'silence was what will keep the Germans guessing'. Richard Crossman believed it was impossible to keep the Germans guessing with a policy of silence.[1]

Years later, Jock Colville told the author that Churchill and Eden had not trusted the experts not to get it wrong. In any case, shortly after Hess's flight, Crete had been invaded and the *Hood* and the *Bismarck* had been sunk, all of which caused the presence of Hess in Britain to fade into the background.

Thus secrecy was maintained and the Hess affair remained an enigma. Still, Churchill had at an earlier stage made use of the statement which he had proposed for the House of Commons. He had asked Sir Alexander Cadogan to adapt it, so that it could be sent to President Roosevelt. His letter is worth quoting in full, because it shows in broad outline how Churchill would have described the episode to the British people, if his Cabinet had deemed it expedient for him to make a lengthy statement:

Former Naval Person to President Roosevelt. 17th May 1941.

Foreign Office Representative has had three interviews with Hess. At first interview on night of May 11–12,[2] Hess was extremely voluble, and made a long statement with the aid of notes. First part recapitulated Anglo-German relations during past thirty years or so, and was designed to show that Germany had always been in the right and England in the wrong. Second part emphasised certainty of German victory, due to development in combination of submarine and air weapons, steadiness of German morale, and complete unity of German people behind Hitler. Third part outlined proposals for settlement. Hess said that the Fuehrer had never entertained any designs against the British Empire, which would be left intact save for the return of former German colonies, in exchange for a free hand for him in Europe. But condition was attached that Hitler would not negotiate with present Government in England. This is the old invitation to us to desert all our friends in order to save temporarily the greater part of our skin.

Foreign Office Representative asked him whether when he spoke of Hitler having a free hand in Europe he included Russia in Europe or in Asia. He replied, 'In Asia.' He added however that Germany had certain demands to make of Russia which would have to be satisfied, but denied that attack on Russia was being planned.

Impression created by Hess was that he had made up his mind that Germany must win the war, but saw that it would last a long time and involve much loss of life and destruction. He seemed to feel that if he could persuade people in this country that there was a basis for a settlement, that might bring the war to an end and avert unnecessary suffering.

At second interview, on May 14, Hess made two further points:

1. In any peace settlement Germany would have to support Rashid Ali and secure eviction of British from Iraq.
2. U-boat war with air-co-operation would be carried on till all supplies to these islands were cut off. Even if these islands capitulated and the Empire continued the fight, the blockade of Britain would continue, even if that meant that the last inhabitant of Britain died of starvation.

At third interview, on May 15, nothing much emerged save incidentally some rather disparaging remarks about your country and the degree of assistance that you will be able to furnish us. I am afraid in particular, he is not sufficiently impressed by what he thinks he knows of your aircraft types and production.

Hess seems in good health and not excited, and no ordinary signs of insanity can be detected. He declares that this escapade is his own idea and that Hitler was unaware of it beforehand. If he is to be believed, he expected to contact members of a 'peace movement' in England, which he would help to oust the present Government. If he is honest and if he is sane this is an encouraging sign of ineptitude of German Intelligence Service. He will not be ill-treated, but it is desirable that the Press should not romanticise him and his adventure. We must not forget that he shares responsibility for all Hitler's crimes and is a potential war criminal whose fate must ultimately depend upon the decision of the Allied Governments.

Mr President, all the above is for your own information. Here we think it best to let the Press have a good run for a bit and keep the Germans guessing. The German officer prisoners of war here were greatly perturbed by the news, and I cannot doubt that there will be deep misgivings in the German armed forces about what he may say.

There is no doubt that Roosevelt did not accept this explanation as being the whole story. Robert Sherwood refers to a conversation which he had at dinner with Roosevelt, Harry Hopkins and Sumner Welles about ten days after Hess's flight. Knowing that Welles had met Hess in Berlin in 1940, Roosevelt asked him what he was like. Welles gave a picture of a stupid man possessed of a fanatical and mystical devotion to Hitler. After listening to this account Roosevelt was silent for a moment and then said, 'I wonder what is really behind this story.'

Welles did not know and Sherwood learnt that Roosevelt was asking the same question as countless others in the U.S.A. Sherwood believed that Roosevelt and Hopkins imagined that there remained 'a small but potentially powerful minority' in Britain who were not averse to peace talks. The British Ambassador in Washington, Lord Halifax, also telegraphed to Eden saying that the latter's speeches had received a good press in the U.S.A., which would be 'useful in counteracting rumours circulating that our silence about Hess connotes peace talks through him'. Eden's comment in his memoirs was to the point: 'So little was our temper understood even by our best friends'.

NOTES

1. Public Record Office F01093/7–F01093/10.
2. In fact this first interview with Kirkpatrick took place on the night of May 12–13.

NINE

A Prisoner of War and Russian Suspicions

In the summer of 1941 the Cabinet invited Lord Simon, who was a Minister, but not a member of the War Cabinet, to interview Hess. Lord Simon was sent because if Hess was an emissary from Hitler something of interest might be discovered, although the British had not the slightest intention of negotiating with him. Simon had already met Hess in Berlin when he and Eden were there in March 1935. Now, together with Kirkpatrick, he saw Hess again at Mychett Place near Aldershot on 10 June 1941. It was considered vital that no one should know that a Minister had seen Hess so that there should be no rumours about peace negotiations. Simon and Kirkpatrick assumed the pseudonyms of Doctors Guthrie and Mackenzie respectively and Hess was referred to in the transcript as Jonathan.

The interview lasted for more than two hours and it can be split into three parts. First, Hess explained the reasons for his mission; secondly, he maintained that Germany had to reverse the Versailles Dictat and was in any case winning the war; and thirdly he declared that while he had come without Hitler's knowledge, he had been repeatedly told by Hitler the four indispensable conditions for the conclusion of an Anglo–German understanding. Many of his statements were a straight repetition of what he had said earlier to Kirkpatrick, but he did bring up additional points during this interview.

One such point was that the idea of making a peace overture had first occurred to Hess in 1940, during the German campaign against the French, while Hess was visiting Hitler. Convinced that Germany was in the process of conquering England, Hess had expressed the opinion to Hitler that Germany must demand from England the restitution of goods – such as the equivalent of the German merchant fleet, which had been confiscated from Germany under the Versailles Treaty. Hitler contradicted Hess.

Hitler thought that the war could possibly provide an occasion for coming to terms with England, something he had tried to accomplish ever since he had been politically active. Hitler told him that severe conditions should not be imposed on a country with which one hoped to come to an arrangement. This put the idea into Hess's mind that if the English knew Hitler's thoughts they might be ready to come to a suitable agreement. Hess believed that the refusal of Hitler's peace offer by the British after the French campaign stemmed from a reluctance to lose prestige by a peace agreement. He said:

> I had to realise my plan, because if I were over in England she would be able to cultivate negotiations with Germany without loss of prestige.

169

Lord Simon, the Lord Chancellor, interviewed Rudolf Hess on 10 June 1941 (Hulton-Deutsch)

I was of the opinion that, apart from the question of terms for an agreement, there would still be in England a certain general distrust to overcome. I must confess that I faced a very critical decision, the most critical in my life, of course, and I believed I was aided by continuously keeping before my inner vision the picture of an endless row of children's coffins with the mothers crying behind them on the German side as well as on the English side, and vice versa, the coffins of mothers with the children behind them. . . .

Whilst making these observations Hess never expressed concern at the thought of an endless row of children's coffins in relation to the Poles, the Jews or the Russians, peoples whom he had always regarded with the greatest disdain. He next turned to the Versailles Settlement, saying that this treaty was 'not only a frightful calamity for Germany but also for the whole world'. He explained that if the war, for which Britain was responsible, continued, the Fuehrer would have to act according to the rule of conduct of Admiral Lord Fisher. 'Moderation in war is folly. If you strike, strike hard and wherever you can.' Hitler had no alternative although 'it pained him deeply'. Hess listed all the terrible things which the Germans would do to Britain if the British remained stubborn. Britain would be doomed to total destruction at the hands of the Luftwaffe and would be starved into submission by U-boat warfare.

Hess admitted that he had come entirely without the knowledge of Hitler, but claimed that he knew the four conditions required by the Fuehrer prior to any peace agreement:

1. In order to prevent future wars between the Axis and England, the limits of the spheres of interest must be defined. The sphere of interest of the Axis is Europe, and England's sphere of interest is the Empire.
2. Return of German colonies.
3. Indemnification of German citizens who before or during the war had their residence within the British Empire, and who suffered damage to life and property through measures of a Government of the Empire or as a result of pillage, riot etc; indemnification of British subjects by Germany on the same basis.
4. Armistice and peace to be concluded with Italy at the same time.

Hess went on to say that during their conversation, Hitler repeatedly put forward these points to him as the basis for an understanding with England. These remarks of Hess had their effect on Lord Simon. Instead of listening to Hess with the silent contempt which had been characteristic of Kirkpatrick, Simon forgot his Intelligence mission, and, as Sefton Delmer wrote, fell into 'the role of the heroic British statesmen refusing to capitulate before a tyrannical enemy'. Simon made the angry retort, 'There is a good deal of courage in this country and we are not very fond of threats.' In fairness to him, Hess's offer that the British must submit to an agreement or be destroyed could not have been couched in more offensive terms. Still, Simon felt a certain amount of contemptuous pity for Hess, and wrote in his memoirs, 'Nobody could see him as I did at Aldershot without feeling some sympathy for a man who had made such a frightful miscalculation. His ignorance of the British temper was colossal.'

Lord Simon also passed judgment on Hess's state of mind:

He is certainly a hypochrondriac and mentally unstable and not all in a condition where he could keep up a 'bluff' of acting independently when really acting on instructions.

He was certain that Hess acted without Hitler's knowledge. As the most senior Government Minister to see Hess, Lord Simon reported to Churchill:

Hess has come on his own initiative. When he contemplates the failure of his mission he becomes emotionally dejected and fears he has made a fool of himself. He imagined there was a strong peace party in this country and that he would have the opportunity of getting in touch with leading politicians who wanted the war to end now. . . . There is nothing whatever in his mental bearing to suggest the cool mentality of a clever agent.[1]

Churchill read the transcripts of Lord Simon's interview and wrote in a memorandum that Hess's remarks seemed to him to be 'the outpourings of a disordered mind. They are bits of conversation with a mentally defective child who has been guilty of murder or arson'. He stated that it might be as well to send them by air 'in a sure hand' to President Roosevelt, but he was not prepared to accept Lord Simon's assumption that Hess in fact reflected Hitler's inner mind, and he saw no need for a public statement on Hess at that moment in time.

Hess must have known that his mission had totally failed; and the Nazi leaders hated failure. Five days later, at Mytchett Place, he dived over the banisters into the basement three floors below in a suicide bid, but merely broke his leg and pelvis. It might have been a very serious matter since, if he had succeeded in taking his own life, Hitler might well have used his death as an excuse for the murder of thousands of British prisoners of war, as he had used the death of von Rath as an excuse to murder the Jews. Consequently, after 15 June Hess was watched more closely.

On 22 June 1941 Germany attacked Russia, and Churchill and the Cabinet became a great deal less interested in Hess. Yet Hess did have one more interesting interview in Britain. It took place on 9 September 1941 when Lord Beaverbrook conversed with him for one hour. His talk with Hess centred around the topic of Germany's invasion of Russia which was dear to Hess's heart.

Hess completely changed the story he had given to Hamilton, Kirkpatrick and Simon. He now said that the purpose of his coming had been to make peace between Britain and Germany 'on any terms', provided that Britain would join Germany in an attack on Russia. Hess's line was that the British were mistaken if they believed that Operation Barbarossa would so weaken Germany and Russia that Britain's nineteenth-century position in Europe would be restored.

> A victory for England as the ally of the Russians will be a victory for the Bolsheviks. And a Bolshevik victory will sooner or later mean Russian occupation of Germany and the rest of Europe. England will be just as incapable of preventing this as any other nation. I am convinced that world domination awaits the Soviet Union in the future, if her power is not broken now.

One naturally wonders why it was that Hess told a completely different story to Lord Beaverbrook. However, on close examination both stories fit into one pattern. It would appear that Hess wished to split his mission into two parts. First, he would have to make peace with the British through the use of an unselfish and sporting gesture. If all went well, as he hoped, he would go on to discuss the possibility of Anglo–German co-operation against Russia, in whatever form that might take.

As Beaverbrook told Churchill, Hess was not insane. In spite of his supposedly self-sacrificing act Hess's proposals would have suited Hitler and the Nazis perfectly. It was one of the most cynical peace tenders of all time, and as far as the Russians were concerned it could with justice have been described as a mission of war.

The Russians never regarded Hess as a madman. On 12–13 November 1940, Molotov, Russia's Foreign Minister, had visited Berlin for talks with Hess and the other Nazi leaders. At that time Molotov had not noticed any signs of insanity in Hess, and when Hess made his appearance in Scotland five months later Stalin was not prepared to accept the explanation from the German Ambassador in Moscow that Hess was crazy. The news of Hess's arrival in Britain gave rise to the gravest anxiety in Russia, and there were fears that the British and Germans might be negotiating behind the scenes at Russia's expense.

They need not have feared, as Britain's commitment to eliminate Nazism was total. In April 1941 Churchill warned Stalin that Germany was about to invade Russia, and when the German armed forces attacked on 22 June Churchill made one of his greatest speeches in support of the Russians. This support was welcome to the Soviet Government, but they still remained suspicious.

The person in charge of the Russian army's Intelligence Division was General Golikov, who knew very well that Stalin preferred to believe that Hitler was not going to attack Russia. Therefore Golikov had classified reports warning that the Germans were about to attack as 'doubtful'. After the war it was confirmed by Gnedish, who handed the reports to Stalin, that the latter deliberately chose to ignore warnings that Hitler was going to attack.[2]

Churchill later wrote in his history of the Second World War that 'so far as strategy, policy, foresight, competence are arbiters Stalin and his commissars showed themselves at this moment the most completely outwitted bunglers of the Second World War'.[3]

Later on in the war, Churchill reminded Stalin of his warning of April 1941, as recorded in *The Hinge of Fate*:

Stalin shrugged his shoulders. 'I remember it. I did not heed any warnings. I knew war would come, but I thought I might gain another six months or so.' In the common cause I refrained from asking what would have happened to us all if we had gone down for ever while he was giving Hitler so much valuable material, time and aid.[4]

After Hess's flight, Russian suspicions were very considerable. Khrushchev voiced to Stalin what he believed to be the view of the whole of the Politburo, that Hess had flown to Britain for the purpose of making a peace settlement with Britain and obtaining her support for an onslaught on Russia or at the very least the neutrality of Britain.

Stalin answered in the affirmative. He had no doubt been influenced by the first report on Hess by Philby that Hess had arrived in Britain with peace proposals, and that

Eden with Maisky, the Russian Ambassador. But the Soviet Union remained suspicious about Hess's presence in Britain (Hulton-Deutsch)

Hamilton had become a friend of Hess as a result of their common participation in aviation competitions in 1933. He also alleged that Hamilton was a member of 'the so-called Cliveden clique'.[5]

The only one of these allegations which was correct was that Hess had brought peace proposals. Hamilton had never participated in the same aviation competitions as Hess and had never met Hess before May 1941, nor did he have any connections with the Cliveden Set.

Of greater importance was the later report, dated 24 October 1942, which was put before Stalin. This memorandum was based on information from Colonel František Moravetz, Chief of the Czech Military Intelligence Service, and it was passed by Lavrenti Beria, the head of the K.G.B., to Stalin who clearly believed it. The report, signed by Beria, read:

> The disseminated opinion that Hess arrived in England unexpectedly is not correct. Long before his flight Hess had discussed his mission with the Duke of Hamilton. The correspondence covered in detail all the questions involved with organisation of this flight. But Hamilton himself did not participate personally in the correspondence. All Hess's letters did not get to their addressee but were intercepted by the intelligence service where the answers to Hess were also elaborated in the name of *Hamilton*. In this way the Britons managed to lure Hess to come to England.
>
> Colonel Moravetz also declared he personally saw this correspondence between Hess and *Hamilton*. Moravetz also declared that the letters of Hess clearly represented the objectives of the German Government, were linked with the plans of their attack on the Soviet Union.
>
> The same letters argued the necessity of stopping war between Britain and Germany.
>
> In his conclusion Colonel Moravetz declared that the English therefore possess written proofs of the culpability of Hess and other Nazi leaders in preparing this attack on the Soviet Union.[6]

Interestingly enough, Colonel Moravetz's service as an intelligence agent was discontinued by the Communist Party after the war and his memoirs contained no mention of these false allegations.

There had never been any correspondence on the part of Hess to Hamilton, a fact which both of them confirmed. The letter sent by Albrecht Haushofer on 23 September 1940 had not been answered, as both Hess and Albrecht Haushofer would confirm, a fact which was well within the knowledge of Hamilton, R.A.F. Intelligence, MI5 and Churchill.

Years later Hess told Colonel Bird in Spandau Prison:

> We had waited a long time for a reply to the letter sent by Albrecht Haushofer. Months went by and the reply did not come. I suspected but did not know until I read it recently, that the British Secret Service had intercepted the letter and retained it. I did not suddenly make up my mind. I thought a lot about it.[7]

The Russian reaction may have been triggered off by the libel action initiated by Group Captain the Duke of Hamilton against prominent Communists, including Harry Pollitt and Ted Bramley, arising out of a pamphlet which had been distributed to the effect that Hamilton had been a friend of Hess. The British Government had been concerned in this matter, in case Hess might be called as a witness, as there was no knowing what kind of propaganda he might utter, and the Secretary of State for War was determined that he should receive no opportunity.

He hoped that Hamilton would drop the case, but the Secretary of State for Air recognised Hamilton's point that failure to proceed with the action would reflect discreditably on the R.A.F. Besides Churchill saw no reason why the Duke should not defend his honour. The libel action settled when the defendants declared in a statement which appeared in *The Times* on 19th February 1942:

(1) That the statements complained of were directed solely against Hess and the political tendency to welcome Hess and against any proposals which Hess may have brought which were bound to be contrary to the best interests of this country.

(2) That they had no intention whatever of impugning the character or loyalty of the plaintiff (Hamilton), and unreservedly accept the plaintiff's assurance that he had no sympathy with the Nazis or the Government in Germany; that he had never met Hess; and that he has never received any letter from Hess at any time. The defendants therefore regret and unreservedly apologise for any of the statements made by them which could be interpreted as reflecting personally on the plaintiff.

On a very different level the British Government were to fare less well with the Soviet Government. Indeed in October 1942 the Russian media attacked the British Government for failing to try Hess as a war criminal and for having allowed Britain to be converted into 'a haven for criminals and gangsters'. The British Foreign Secretary, Eden, noted these remarks with 'astonishment and keen displeasure'.

At a meeting of the War Cabinet on 20 October 1942 it was resolved not to respond to the Soviet demand to bring Hess to trial immediately, but rather to give Hess 'the same treatment that was being laid down and elaborated for war criminals generally'. But Russian suspicion remained so intense that on 26 October the War Cabinet decided that the Russians should be given the full facts. Sir Stafford Cripps was asked to arrange for a full dossier of papers relating to the Hess affair to be circulated to the War Cabinet, which was done on 29 October.

On that day Eden expressed the thought that Britain's attitude to recent articles in the Russian Press should be made clear. Churchill sent a robust note to Eden:

I am sure it would be a great mistake to run after the Russians in their present mood. . . . By all means let the Lord Privy Seal focus and refresh in our minds the Hess story. When it is ready, the Cabinet can consider whether the facts should be imparted to the Russian Government. I assure you the only thing that will do any good is fighting hard and winning victories. . . .

Meanwhile I should treat the Russians coolly, not getting excited about the lies they tell, but going steadily on with our task. You must remember the Bolsheviks have undermined so many powerful Governments by lying, machine-made propaganda, and they probably think they make some impression on us by these methods.

We must let events speak – Words do not count now as much as they do in time of peace. What matters is action.

Accordingly, on 4 November 1942 Eden was authorised to despatch a Memorandum entitled 'The facts about Rudolf Hess', together with a note giving particulars of Hess's medical condition to the Soviet Government. This was done, and undoubtedly it had an effect on Stalin.

In his speech of 6 November Stalin said that the Germans, as was obvious from Hess's mission, had intended that Britain and the U.S.A. should join them in a war against Russia, or at least give Germany a free hand in the East. Hess had failed, he added, because Britain, the U.S.A., and the Soviet Union were in one camp.

Years later Stalin asked Churchill about the Hess mission and Churchill wrote:

I had the feeling that he believed there had been some deep negotiation or plot for Germany and Britain to act together in the invasion of Russia, which had miscarried. Remembering what a wise man he is, I was surprised to find him silly on this point. When the interpreter made it plain that he did not believe what I said, I replied through my interpreter, 'When I make a statement of facts within my knowledge I expect it to be accepted'. Stalin received this somewhat abrupt response with a genial grin. 'There are lots of things that happen even here in Russia, which our Secret Service do not necessarily tell me about'. I let it go at that.

Stalin's reactions caused Churchill some anxiety, and in April 1945 Hamilton indicated that he wished to go to the U.S.A. on business, and if pressed, to speak to a prepared statement on Hess cleared by the Foreign Office.

When the matter was brought to the Prime Minister's attention, Churchill drafted a Personal Minute for the Foreign Secretary, Minister for Information, and Secretary of State for Air:

The Russians are very suspicious of the Hess episode, and I had a lengthy argument with Marshal Stalin about it at Moscow in October, he steadfastly maintaining that Hess had been invited over by our Secret Service. It is not in the public interest that the whole of this affair should be stirred at the present moment. I desire therefore that the Duke should not, repeat not, undertake this task.

Thus Hamilton was told he should not go, and for the duration of the war the British part of the story remained secret.

Early in November 1942 Stalin had been given an accurate appraisal of the position, and he might have been amused if he had known about the treatment Hess was receiving in Britain. Hess, under armed guard, had been turned over for examination to the British medical authorities, and had become the guinea-pig of British psychiatrists under Brigadier Rees. In Rees's book *The Case of Rudolf Hess* it emerged that far from regarding Hess as a war criminal and as a man who would willingly kill anyone who stood in Hitler's way, they thought of him as a patient, and as a poor lost wayward brother who had strayed into the company of strange men. Even so they agreed that Hess was not insane medically or legally, and that he was mentally alert.

The psychiatrists tried to explain Hess in medical terms. They argued that he was suffering from hysterical amnesia, paranoid schizophrenia, psychogenic disturbances, hypochondria, delusions of persecution, and last but hardly least, an inferiority complex. It is of relevance that the psychiatrist Douglas Kelley described Hitler as a psychoneurotic of the obsessive and hysterical type with pathological deviations and an inferiority complex. While these views may be sound in medicine, they are not of much assistance to the historian, because at virtually all times Hess and Hitler were physically and mentally able to form and carry out their intentions. If there was a difference between Hess and other Nazi leaders it was not that he was mentally sick, since all Nazi leaders were mentally sick in varying degrees. Hess differed from the other members of the Nazi High Command because he was more loyal and less intelligent.

His flight had been a product of his fanatical devotion and of his steady decline. Indeed his uncritical devotion to Hitler had contributed to his decline, because he had allowed his will to be completely subordinated to that of Hitler. On 21 May 1941 Major Sheppard wrote down his impressions on Hess which were later included with the Prime

176

Minister's papers: 'I believe by the very nature of his make-up, which reflects cruelty, bestiality, deceit, conceit, arrogance and a yellow streak, that he has lost his soul and has willingly permitted himself to become plastic in the hands of a more powerful and compelling personality. My personal view is that he has lost favour and in order to rehabilitate himself he has cunningly conceived the idea of appearing as a Peace Envoy to enable him to justify his action, both here and in Germany.'

As Major Sheppard suspected Hess had not possessed the ingenuity necessary for fitting into the role of a triumphant Nazi war leader. Besides, he genuinely disliked the thought of two Nordic peoples, the Germans and the British, killing each other although he never allowed himself to be burdened with such ideas about Russians, Poles or Jews. He had supported Hitler in word, thought and deed, and he gave himself away even to the psychiatrists, as can be seen in his attitude towards Russia, towards the Jews and towards Hitler.

When he was told about the invasion of the Soviet Union by Germany on 22 June 1941, he said, 'So they have started after all'. He made out that very soon Germany would be victorious, and that she would then turn her attentions to the conquest of Britain. He still believed, however, that there was a possibility that Britain might come to a settlement with Germany, once Russia had been overrun. He later 'expressed satisfaction over the war with Russia, because he now felt that England would be more sympathetic towards Germany in her war against Communism'.

As time passed, even Hess realised that Britain was not interested in Nazi peace offers. He made it clear that he regarded the Jews as being responsible for Britain's intransigence and for his present treatment. Indeed it appears that his hatred of Jews was so great that, if he had been given the opportunity, he would have supported Hitler and Himmler in their policy of genocide. In June 1942 he wrote: 'It had not been one of my duties to decide the treatment of Jews. However if this had been the case I would have done everything to protect my people from these criminals, and I wouldn't have had a bad conscience about it.'

Never at any time did he outwardly waver in his loyalty to his Fuehrer and, prior to attempting to commit suicide, he wrote a letter to Hitler. This letter records clearly that Hess was an archetypal Nazi German who made Hitler possible: an anti-semitic thug who gloried in all the awful violence, and one who also believed that Nazi Germany must not make the mistake again of fighting on two fronts.

My Fuehrer. My last greeting is for you who have made my life meaningful for two decades. You made my life worth living after the collapse of 1918. For you and therefore for Germany I have been able to achieve and serve.

Can it ever have been given to people to serve such a man and his cause with so much success as under you? Please accept my thanks from all my heart for everything that you have given me and for what you have done for me.

I write these lines in clear recognition of the fact that I have no other way out, as difficult as this end is for me. I commend my relatives my old parents to your care.

You, my Fuehrer, I greet with Greater Germany, which is headed for a size nobody dreamed of. I die in the conviction that my last mission, even though it ends in my death, will somehow bear fruit.

Heil, mein Fuehrer, your loyal Rudolf Hess.[8]

It was apparent from the terms of his letter to Hitler that he wholeheartedly supported the onward expansion of the Third Reich by military means. He had also written, on 19 May, an unbalanced and incoherent letter to Hamilton:

My dear Duke,

I feel it necessary that you should know the following facts:

In the letter that I left behind for the Fuehrer, I wrote that it was possible that there might be news from England of my death. At the same time some cause of death would be announced – as, for example, suicide or during a dispute – and even if there were reason to suspect that my death was brought about by elements in England opposed to peace, they, in Germany, should on no account allow themselves thereby to continue the war. It is *only right*, even if my death should have occurred in such peculiar circumstances, to make peace with those who want peace. This was to be, as it were, my last wish. Probably my death would on the whole even be helpful to the whole affair; for only after the conclusion of peace could the English themselves settle accounts with those people, who would probably also be responsible for my death. My death would play a great part in this from a propaganda point of view.

I am sure that the Fuehrer fully understands this train of thought and would fulfil my wish.

I have, moreover, given the Fuehrer my word that I will not on any account commit suicide. He knows that I will keep my word. So that in any case is ruled out. If the opponents of peace try to make trouble, it will certainly be of no avail.

With best wishes, Rudolf Hess.

P.S. Please treat this letter as meant only for you personally and for someone reliable to translate. R.H.

The letter never reached Hamilton. He never knew of its existence and he would not have liked it. He had not met Hess before the war and did not know him. This point was confirmed unequivocally by Hess in conversation with Colonel Eugene Bird in Spandau Prison.[9]

Thus Hamilton would have undoubtedly replied that the handling of Hess as a prisoner of war was not a matter for him, as an R.A.F. operational commander who was involved in the effective and successful prosecution of the war against the Nazi Regime. In these circumstances the minute of Alexander Cadogan, head of the Foreign Office, to the Foreign Secretary was entirely correct: 'It is not right that Hess should correspond with the Duke – and possibly embarrassing for the latter. I shall hold the letter.' Anthony Eden endorsed this course of action by initialling the minute.

As for Hess, within weeks of saying he would *not* commit suicide, he tried to take his own life by throwing himself down the stairwell on 16 June, thereby fracturing his leg. After expert attention he recovered.

He had been moved from the Tower to Mytchett Place, near Farnborough and Aldershot, where he was guarded by 135 soldiers, and where some of the most revealing reports on his state of mind were made by Dr Gibson Graham.

On 28 May Hess was told about the sinking of the *Bismarck*. His reaction was immediate: 'Hess suddenly looked ill and very upset. He asked for a glass of water and went to bed complaining of a severe backache.' The invincibility of the Third Reich was more in doubt for Hess than he had been prepared to realise, until confronted with reality.

Some time after the Nazi onslaught on Russia, Hess wrote on 23 October 1941 to Lord Beaverbrook, whom he had met. He wrote, 'The Fuehrer could do no more than he has done, i.e. stretched out his hand over and over again. And I staked everything as far as I was personally concerned.' Hess produced various written statements to Lord Beaverbrook and others supporting Anglo–German co-operation against a Bolshevik enemy, becoming 'the world power of the future'.

Dr H. V. Dicks, Graham's successor, wrote in one report about Hess's total infatuation with Hitler:

To preserve intact the facade of this unswerving loyalty for reasons of his own mental stability, he has to delude himself that he is doing the work of the Fuehrer ... At most therefore, at least consciously reject the bad and aggressive qualities in his idol. I believe, however, that his flight was impelled by a deep doubt of Hitler, a feeling he could never voice. The conflict became too great. His feelings of guilt at the aggression of the Fuehrer is reinforced by guilt at being disloyal to him. He could save his mental integration only by some dramatic act of 'redemption' which at the same time had the effect of removing him from the fateful spell his idol had cast over him.

With information becoming available of slave labour, genocide and mass murder, Hess's mind from time to time took refuge in unreality.

Early in 1941 he sent a letter to the King complaining about the treatment given to him by the doctors. Sir Alexander Hardinge at Buckingham Palace noted that Hess had evidently got persecution mania and that he supposed there was not anything to be done about it.

Hess asked the Swiss minister, who he met, to appeal on his behalf for a transfer to a prisoner of war camp, but the request was refused. Churchill had instructed that he be treated like a senior German general who had fallen into our hands.

In July 1941 the Intelligence Service, investigating rumours, discovered a plot by Polish soldiers to kidnap Hess or to break into the camp and beat up the prisoner, and precautions were taken. Alexander Cadogan readily recognised this: 'We have in this country many people from the countries he and the Fuehrer have ravaged, whose greatest desire is to tear him to bits.'

In June 1943 he was removed to Abergavenny in South Wales. The Government remained concerned that Hess should not be certified as insane, as he would then have had to be returned to Germany under the terms of the Geneva Convention. Therefore under no circumstances could any doctor be allowed to establish that Hess was mad. Had he been a civilian, according to Brigadier Rees, Consultant Psychiatrist to the Army, he would certainly have been certified, on account of his suicidal tendencies.

Towards the end of the war, Rees gave his assessment that Hess was sane, a view accepted by the Allied Governments. He wrote:

Hess is understandably a constitutionally unstable man – a constitutional psychopath – He has probably for many years had a paranoid or delusional tendency . . . He is in fact suffering from a paranoid psychosis.

At the same time he has, I think, at all relevant times so far as is possible to judge, been responsible for his actions. He certainly is at the present time and he also is at the moment able to plead in a Court of Law.

As a result on 10 October 1945 he would be flown to Nuremberg to stand trial as a war criminal with nineteen other Nazi leaders.[10]

Possibly the most accurate expression of Hess's motives was given by his secretary, Ingeborg Sperr, who wrote of Hess that 'in his fanatic love for the Fatherland, he wanted to make the greatest sacrifice of which he was capable to Adolf Hitler and the German people, namely, to leave nothing undone to bring the German people the dearly desired peace with England, and thereby to risk his life, his family, his freedom and his honourable name'.

The evidence indicates that what mattered about Hess's secret mission was not the neuroses which afflicted him after his lack of success. The fact of importance is that he knew what he was doing, why he was doing it, and had only one regret: that he failed.

179

He wrote letters home to his wife and family and sent a tactless letter to his Adjutant thanking him for keeping the secret of his flight, a fact which had caused Pintsch to be arrested. Hess penned letters, not to Albrecht Haushofer but to his father, General Professor Karl Haushofer, his friendship being primarily with the latter. In one of them he wrote that his efforts to bring about peace between Nazi Germany and Britain had failed. Karl Haushofer did not reply.

One theme which came repeatedly out of his letters was that he had acted entirely without Hitler's knowledge. In a letter of 9 September 1942 he wrote about his flight and his relations with the Luftwaffe General Udet:

He did not let me fly the ME (Messerschmitt) when I wanted to fly for pleasure near Berlin. The poor fellow insisted on the Fuehrer's permission. I might just as well have had myself taken into custody right away. But it was fortunate that nothing came of the flying near Berlin. I could not have hidden my activities and the Fuehrer would have heard about them sooner or later. My plan would have been stopped and I should have blamed myself for carelessness.[11]

This explains why he flew from Augsburg in southern Germany, a very much longer flight. He was allowed to read books including *Three Men in a Boat* and to go for walks. He was closely guarded to make certain that there was no possibility of escape, nor of rescue by parachutists. In his letters home he wondered what life would be like after the war, when he returned to his family. So little did he know what his fate would be.

By the end of May 1941 the war was over for Rudolf Hess, but for Albrecht Haushofer back in Germany the crisis of his life was about to unfold. He had known nothing of Hess's plans to fly to Scotland. On 12 March 1941, however, Hassell wrote in his diary that he had met Albrecht Haushofer at Popitz's home and Haushofer had spoken about 'a desire for peace in high quarters', although he agreed with Popitz and Hassell that owing to the 'distrust and abomination in which the world holds Hitler', the existence of the Nazi regime constituted an insuperable barrier to any peace talks.

Hassell asked Albrecht to make use of his connections in Switzerland, so that a guarantee might be extracted from Britain that there would be peace negotiations once the Nazi Government had been removed. Hassell's wife Ilse made preparations for Albrecht's journey to the Swiss neutral Carl Burckhardt, who lived in Geneva and was Vice-President of the International Red Cross. She told Burckhardt in advance that 'Haushofer was coming with two faces'. (Ostensibly for Hess, but actually for the resistance movement.)

Hess's authority gave Albrecht the opportunity to travel abroad as his agent, and by doing this Albrecht was pursuing his own objectives for the Resistance. With Hess's approval he met Carl Burckhardt on 29 April 1941, and asked Burckhardt to get in touch with certain persons in Britain. Burckhardt told him that Britain wanted peace on a 'rational basis', but not with the Nazi regime and time was possibly running short. Hassell knew that Albrecht was playing a tricky and delicate game, and he said of him:

I have a profound regard for him; he is a highly talented man and not for nothing do we jokingly call him 'Cassandra'. It is a pity that among young German politicians we have so few of his talent. But perhaps he is already too clever by half.

When the news of Hess's flight to Scotland came through Albrecht was beside himself with anxiety. Rainer Hildebrandt wrote after seeing him on Sunday 11 May 1941:

I found Haushofer, whom I had always known as being completely collected, in utter despair and helplessness. He said 'This motorised Parsifal wants to bring peace to Hitler, and he imagines that he could get round the Churchill government and could sit down at the negotiating table with the King.'

Haushofer had calculated all possibilities. The most improbable and unusual developments were included in his reckoning, but here something had happened which brought his whole edifice of thought crashing down, Haushofer walked about like a wounded animal not knowing what to do with himself.

Ever since 1933 it was as though Albrecht had been standing with a noose around his neck on account of his Jewish ancestry, and the chair upon which he had been standing was Rudolf Hess. He was now in the unhappy position of learning that this chair had been swept from under his feet. His protector had literally flown away. A few hours later two Gestapo agents came for him. Hitler wanted an account of his recent activities at the Obersalzberg, Berchtesgaden. Albrecht was under arrest.

NOTES

1. Public Record Office: F01093/1–5.
2. Bullock, *Hitler and Stalin: Parallel Lives*, pages 792–3.
3. Churchill, W. S. *Second World War Vol III*, page 216.
4. Churchill, W. S. *Second World War Vol IV*, page 443.
5. Extract from K.G.B. archives as made available to European media.
6. Extract from K.G.B. archives as made available to European media.
7. Eugene Bird. *The Loneliest Man in the World*, page 250.
8. Public Record Office: F01093/1–5.
9. See Part One, Chapter Five.
10. Public Record Office: F01093/6–F01093/19.
11. Public Record Office: F01093/1–5.

Part Three

THE FATE OF
ALBRECHT HAUSHOFER

'And if my Fuehrer, this project . . . ends in failure. . . . Simply say I was crazy.'
Rudolf Hess's letter to Hitler, 10 May 1941

'I know exactly that at present I am a small beetle which has been turned on its back by an unexpected and unforeseeable gust of wind, and which realises that it cannot rise to its feet by its own strength. . . .'

Albrecht Haushofer's letter to his parents from the
Prince Albrecht Strasse Gestapo Prison, 7 July 1941

'There are times when madness rules the land
It is then that the best are hanged.'
Albrecht Haushofer, No. 21 Sonnets of Moabit

ONE

Turmoil at the Dictator's Court: 11 May 1941

Early on the morning of Sunday 11 May 1941 Hess's adjutant Pintsch arrived at Berchtesgaden and was told that Hitler was interviewing Todt, the Minister for Armaments, and that he was preparing a reception for Admiral Darlan of Vichy France after lunch. Pintsch pressed his attentions, and when he handed Hess's letter to Hitler, the latter was 'overcome by a tremendous agitation'. Speer, who was also present, heard an 'inarticulate almost animal shout'. The letter which had given rise to Hitler's trepidation and fury began with these words:

> My Fuehrer, when you receive this letter I shall be in England. You can imagine that the decision to take this step was not easy for me, since a man of 40 has other ties with life than one of 20. . . .

It went on to give a lengthy description of the technical requirements necessary for such a flight, which had been attempted more than once. Hess underlined that he was not motivated by 'cowardice or weakness', and that his flight should not be regarded as an escape since undertaking a hazardous mission of this kind required more courage than it would to remain in Germany.

His aim was to make contact between England and Germany by getting in touch with certain distinguished men in England. He felt that the interests of both England and Germany dictated that a serious attempt should be made to effect a peace settlement through negotiation. He reminded Hitler that he had recently asked him 'a point blank question' on his policy towards England, and was convinced the answer was that Hitler still wanted an Anglo-German accommodation. He had not revealed to Hitler his plans to fly to Britain, because he knew that he would not have been allowed to go.

Nonetheless Hess wrote that he considered himself to be especially well qualified for this mission since he had been brought up in Alexandria, Egypt, which was an English environment. Naturally he would tell the British that his mission must not be construed as an indication of 'German weakness'. He would emphasise on the contrary that Germany was militarily invincible and 'did not have to ask for peace'. Hess's letter ended significantly with these words:

> And if, my Fuehrer, this project – which I admit has but very small chance of success – ends in failure and the fates decide against me, this can have no detrimental results either for you or for Germany: it will always be possible for you to deny all responsibility. Simply say I was crazy.

Hitler at once asked Pintsch what time Hess had disappeared from Germany, and Pintsch confirmed that at about 6.10 p.m. on the previous evening Hess had flown from Augsburg to Scotland. Hitler promptly called Martin Bormann, who was ordered to telephone Ribbentrop, Goering, Goebbels and Himmler, the first two of whom were summoned. Hitler asked the Luftwaffe General Ernst Udet, who happened to be at hand, what chance there was of Hess reaching Britain and Udet expressed the belief that with the limited range of an Me 110 Hess would come down in the sea.

Yet Hitler remained uncertain and shaken; his anger accumulated as the hours passed. His interpreter Schmidt wrote that it was 'as though a bomb had hit the Berghof'. Meanwhile all personnel on Hess's staff, including his adjutants, Pintsch and Leitgen, who were thought to have withheld information from Hitler, were locked up. SS Gruppenführer Muller, head of the Gestapo, made many arrests among personnel at Augsburg Airport, and when the reports of Heydrich's SD revealed that Hess had been associating with astrologers, nature therapists and anthroposophists, a large number of these individuals were imprisoned. Organisations which Hess had supported, such as the Rudolf Steiner schools, were closed down.

Karl Haushofer was temporarily placed under guard while his house was searched. Amongst the documents found were Hess's letter to him, Albrecht Haushofer's memorandum of the possibilities of a German-English peace, and also Albrecht's letter to Hamilton sent at Hess's instigation. The Gestapo took these papers. It emerged from the confiscated manuscripts and from other enquiries that Hess's action had been one of personal initiative.

Albert Speer, Hitler's architect, later wrote:

> At the time it appeared to me that Bormann's ambition had driven Hess to this desperate act. Hess, also highly ambitious, could plainly see himself being excluded from access to and influence over Hitler. . . By his flight to England Hess was probably trying, after so many years of being kept in the background, to win prestige and some success.
>
> Hitler put the blame for Hess's flight on the corrupting influence of Professor (Karl) Haushofer . . . If I judge correctly Hitler never got over this 'disloyalty' on the part of his deputy. Some while after the assassination attempt of 20 July 1944, he mentioned in the course of one of his fantastic misreadings of the real situation that among his conditions was the extraction of the 'traitor' – Hess would have to be hanged, he said.[1]

Everyone in the proximity of Hitler at this time, when asked about it later, confirmed that never in his wildest moments had Hitler imagined that his Deputy Fuehrer would deliberately fly into enemy hands. It was true that Hitler had given Hess permission to make cautious enquiries through Albrecht Haushofer, but Hess's action infinitely exceeded the authority which Hitler had given him. As General Halder noted, Hitler told his army commanders that Hess's flight had taken him completely by surprise, and General Keitel saw Hitler on Sunday 11 May pacing restlessly up and down in his study, trying to frame as plausible an explanation as was possible for the German people.

He was extremely concerned about Hess's flight on three accounts. First, he believed that once the German people learnt that his Deputy had flown to Britain on a peace mission, the German soldiers at the front would fight less hard. Secondly, he feared that Hess's action might result in the complete disintegration of the Anti-Comintern Pact between Germany, Italy and Japan, and that Mussolini, not to be outdone, would hasten to make his own peace terms with Britain. And, lastly, Hitler was afraid that Hess would reveal the Nazi plans to attack Russia. He kept muttering that a fool could cause unimaginable harm, and that the British might drug Hess and drag him before a radio, forcing him to make a statement. In these circumstances, Hitler felt that he had to make an explanation to the German people, and to Mussolini, and to confirm the date for the attack on Russia.

To make matters worse, he had no idea whether Hess had reached Britain and, if he had, what his reception had been. Whatever happened, Hitler could never bear being associated with failure. He was not getting much support from Goebbels, the Reichsminster for Propaganda, who had disappeared to his country residence and had refused to give any directive to his Ministry, saying, 'There are situations which even the best propagandist in the world cannot cope with.' Goebbels confided to his subordinate, Rudolf Semmler, that he regarded the Hess episode as being more serious than the desertion of an army corps.

The responsibility for issuing the first communiqué was left to Dr Otto Dietrich, the Reich press chief who, along with Hitler, Goering and Ribbentrop, prepared a deliberately vague statement. In order to cover themselves in the event of the expected failure of Hess's mission, they took Hess's advice and attempted to suggest that he had suddenly and inexplicably gone off his head. The communiqué was redrafted many times and the final product, which was broadcast on the evening of Monday 12 May, ran:

> The Party authorities state – Party Member Hess, who had been expressly forbidden by the Fuehrer to use an aeroplane because of a disease which has been becoming worse for years, was, in contradiction of this order, able to get hold of a plane recently.
>
> Hess started on Saturday 10 May, at about 18.00 hours from Augsburg on a flight from which he has not yet returned. A letter which he left behind unfortunately showed traces of a mental disturbance which justifies the fear that Hess was the victim of hallucinations.
>
> The Fuehrer at once ordered the arrest of Hess's adjutants, who alone knew of his flights, and who in contradiction to the Fuehrer's ban, of which they were aware, did not prevent the flight nor report it at once. The National Socialist Movement has unfortunately, in these circumstances, to assume that Party Comrade Hess has crashed or met with a similar accident.

This communiqué caused consternation and bewilderment in Germany. It was regarded as a serious and tragic matter that Hess had fled, especially as no signs of mental disturbance had been previously noted. The news that Hitler's Deputy had for a considerable time been to all intents and purposes insane made many Germans wonder whether others of their leaders might not be in a similar condition. Hitler's interpreter Schmidt was asked by an old gardener, 'Didn't you already know that we are governed by madmen?' Messerschmitt too expressed discontent when he was taken to task by Goering for lending Hess an aeroplane. Goering said, 'I see that anybody can fly at your airfield despite the Regulations.' Messerschmitt replied, 'This is not so. Hess is not anybody; he is one of the most important ministers in Germany.' Goering then said, 'Well, you knew that Hess was crazy.' Messerschmitt's answer to this was, 'How would you expect me to know that? That was for you to determine.' He asked how on earth he could have been expected to know that one so senior as Hitler's Deputy was crazy, and why, if that had really been the case, his resignation had not been secured. Hitler's first communiqué was clearly inadequate.

Late on Monday 12 May, at about 11.20 p.m., a British announcement was put out from 10 Downing Street to the effect that Rudolf Hess had arrived in Britain. This announcement was accompanied by a total silence on the reasons for his arrival. Fritz Hesse, who worked for Ribbentrop, was asked by Himmler whether there was any possibility of peace negotiations with Britain arising out of Hess's flight, as this was the only matter that interested the Fuehrer. Fritz Hesse told him there was none, and Ribbentrop gave his opinion that the entire business was as stupid a piece of tomfoolery as could be imagined. According to Ribbentrop, Hitler had thought that Hess might have been successful and now that he no longer thought so members of Hess's staff would be victimised. It was imperative that another explanation should be given to the German public and the following communiqué was published on 13 May 1941:

> On the basis of a preliminary examination of the papers which Hess left behind him, it would appear that Hess was living under the hallucination that by undertaking a personal step in connection with the Englishmen with whom he was formerly acquainted it might be possible to bring about an understanding between Germany and Britain. As has since been confirmed by a report from London, Hess parachuted from his plane and landed near the place in Scotland which he had selected as his destination; there he was found apparently in an injured condition.
>
> As is well known in Party circles, Hess has undergone severe physical suffering for some years. Recently he had sought relief to an increasing extent in various methods practised by mesmerists and astrologers, etc. An attempt is also being made to determine to what extent these persons are responsible for bringing about the condition of mental distraction which led him to take this step. It is also conceivable that Hess was deliberately lured into a trap by a British party. The whole manner of his action, however, confirms the fact, stated in the first announcement, that he was suffering under hallucinations.
>
> Hess was better acquainted than anyone else with the peace proposals which the Fuehrer has made with such sincerity. Apparently he had deluded himself into thinking that, by some personal sacrifice, he could prevent developments which, in his eyes, could only end with the complete destruction of the British Empire.
>
> Judging by his own papers, Hess, whose sphere of activities was confined to the Party, as is generally known, had no idea how to carry out such a step or what result it would have.
>
> The National Socialist Party regrets that this idealist fell a prey to tragic hallucinations. The continuation of the war, which Britain forced on the German people, will not be affected at all. As the Fuehrer declared in his last speech, it will be carried on until the men in power in Britain have been overthrown or are ready to make peace.

This statement did not clarify the confused picture in the mind of the German populace. Hess was still mad, but it was the madness of an idealist rather than of a lunatic. Weizsaecker, Secretary of State at the Foreign Office, touched on the crux of the matter when he wrote:

> To hold office meant, in fact, to be above criticism. That is why the fall of Hitler's Deputy, Rudolf Hess, in May 1941 seemed so fantastic; yesterday he had been a demigod and today he was nothing but a pitiful idiot. . . . I was sorry when his old friends attributed to him defects other than defects of intelligence.

On 18 May Ulrich von Hassell wrote in his diary what must have been thought by many:

> The effect of Hess's flight . . . was indescribable, but immeasurably increased by the stupidity of the official communiqué, which could clearly be traced to Hitler's personal explosions of wrath. The first one especially, which implied that for months, even for years, he had presented to the people a half or even entirely insane 'Deputy' as heir-apparent of the Fuehrer. . . .

The background of Hess's flight is not yet clear. The official explanations are, to say the least, incomplete. Hess's sporting and technical performance alone showed that he could not be called crazy.

Nonetheless, Hitler's explanation had been given and on Tuesday 13 May all Reichsleiters and Gauleiters were summoned to Berchtesgaden. They were instructed that the official interpretation to be laid on this tragic case was that Hess, that everlasting idealist and sick man, had suffered from Messianic delusions and had tried to save the British Empire from the terrible destruction that awaited it. Whilst there, Goebbels had an interview with Hitler, whom he later reported as looking ten years older and in tears.

On the same day Ribbentrop met Mussolini and Ciano in Rome. The official German record of the conversations signed by Schmidt relates that Ribbentrop had been sent to give information about Hess's disappearance. Hitler had been 'completely taken aback by Hess's action', which 'had been the action of a lunatic', although Hess 'had acted only from idealistic motives. His being unfaithful to the Fuehrer was utterly out of the question.' He had written to the Fuehrer 'a long and confused letter', explaining that he had flown in order to persuade the British that further resistance was hopeless, and he had confronted everyone with a *fait accompli*. 'When this letter reached the Fuehrer, Hess was already in England. It was hoped in Germany that he would perhaps have an accident on the way, but he was now really in England and had tried to contact the former Marquis of Clydesdale, the present Duke of Hamilton. Hess quite wrongly considered him to be a great friend of Germany and had flown to the neighbourhood of his castle in Scotland.' Ciano entered in his diary on 13 May that Mussolini and himself were not very impressed with Ribbentrop's visit:

> Von Ribbentrop arrives in Rome unexpectedly. He is discouraged and nervous. He wants to confer with the Duce and me for various reasons, but there is only one real reason: he wants to inform us about the Hess affair. . . .
> The official version is that Hess, sick in body and mind, was a victim of his pacifist hallucinations, and went to England in the hope of facilitating the beginning of peace negotiations. Hence, he is not a traitor; hence he will not talk; hence, whatever else is said or printed in his name, is false. Ribbentrop's conversation is a beautiful feat of patching things up. The Germans want to cover themselves before Hess speaks and reveals things that might make a great impression in Italy.
> Mussolini comforted von Ribbentrop, but afterwards told me that he considers the Hess affair a tremendous blow to the Nazi regime. He added that he was glad of it, because this will have the effect of bringing down German stock, even with the Italians.

Hitler's main concern had been that Hess would reveal his plans to attack Russia, but this was a matter about which he could do nothing and Hess's flight in no way altered his plans. On 12 May Hitler reaffirmed the decision to attack Russia on 22 June. As it happened, Hess did not give away Hitler's planned operation against Russia, and the British interrogator Kirkpatrick had such intellectual contempt for him that he jumped to the incorrect conclusion that Hess did not know. But this oversight made no difference. The British already knew about the impending onslaught in the east, for they had broken the Luftwaffe code, and Churchill had warned Stalin.

The only apparent effect of Hess's flight was the obliteration of his name from all public places. His photograph was to be removed from salerooms, shop windows, streets and public buildings. New books on the N.S.D.A.P. were to be published without pictures or information about him and eventually his name was erased from the Reich's Card Index and from the list of members of the Reich's Leadership Section. Hitler gave orders that he was to be shot if he returned. On 29 May 1941 Hess's office of Deputy Fuehrer ceased to exist and its functions were absorbed by the Party Chancellery under the leadership of Martin Bormann.

Only a few days before, Hess had been a powerful Nazi but now that he was in disgrace there was a flood of derogatory criticism. Bormann, far from regretting the absence of his former superior, wrote to Himmler that Hess's flight was due to the fact that he had an inferiority complex, that he had been treated for impotence even when his son was born, and that he wanted to prove his virility to himself and his wife, to his party and to his people.

Goebbels too was not reluctant to pour scorn on Hess and with great glee and pettiness declared that Hess had become impotent for reasons that were psychological, that he had visited astrologers and mystics with Frau Hess and that they had drunk mixtures before the child was born. After the birth of his son, Hess danced in a manner similar to the birth celebrations of South American Indians. Every Gauleiter was required to send a receptacle enclosing Germanic earth from each Gau to Hess, and the soil was put under a cradle so that the Deputy Fuehrer's son would begin to live on Germanic soil in a symbolic sense. Goebbels himself being Gauleiter of Berlin nearly sent a Berlin paving stone, but in the end decided to send some of the manure from his garden in an official container.

Goebbels's diaries are particularly interesting in relation to Hess's disappearance. On 13 May he regarded the news as appalling, doing incalculable harm, as well as an almost unbearable blow. In Goebbels's words Hess 'had become too remote from the day-to-day struggle and had turned soft'. He believed that Professor Karl Haushofer had been an 'evil genius' in this affair, while Hitler's view was that 'one can be prepared for anything, except the aberrations of a lunatic'.

Goebbels was upset since he knew the Germans were asking how someone capable of such enormous stupidity and folly could be Hitler's Deputy and the most important man in the Nazi Party after the Fuehrer. What Goebbels particularly disliked were the number of Berlin jokes going around directly concerned with Hess's disappearance – for example mimics imitating the B.B.C. saying that on Sunday no further German Cabinet Ministers arrived by plane, and there had been a German High Command communiqué that Goering and Goebbels were still firmly in German hands.

A further joke was that the 1,000-year-old Reich had become the 100-year Reich as one zero had gone. It was also suggested that when Churchill had put it to Hess that he was a madman, Hess replied, 'Only his deputy'.

The basic point which kept on coming up was that for the first time the Nazi Government admitted one of its leaders was mad. All the jokes along these lines were a colossal embarrassment to Hitler and extremely worrying for Goebbels.[2]

To Goebbels's intense relief the British had not put out statements in Hess's name, without his knowledge, which is what he would have done if a senior British statesman had been captured by the Germans. His comment on British propaganda was 'we are dealing with dumb amateurs over there'.

On 17 May he noted that the Duke of Hamilton had spoken to Hess and had described him as crazy, but that nonetheless the Hess affair was 'running out of steam'. He also expressed the view that Duff Cooper was 'uniquely stupid'. 'What I would have made of the case! But England's ruling class is ripe for a fall!' By the end of the day he believed the Hess affair to be at an end.

On 19 May he expressed the view that, so far as the German public were concerned, the affair was played out and that London had missed a big chance. Also he considered that world opinion was of the view that the Nazis had won the propaganda battle over Hess.

In fairness to Churchill, Eden and the British, it should be pointed out that Hess's flight took place against the background of a strong intensification of the war between Britain and Germany. The night Hess arrived the House of Commons was bombed and it was remembered as the Great London Raid. It was followed in quick succession by the German invasion of Crete, during which the British and Commonwealth troops killed enormous numbers of German parachutists before succumbing to the devastating bombing by the Luftwaffe. The naval battles involving the blowing up of the *Hood* and the subsequent sinking of the *Bismarck* followed a few days later.

The British Government were primarily interested in winning the war and to them actions counted far more than words. If there had been less military activity by land and air, the Government might have concentrated more on propaganda. However, even as it was, the Hess episode remained an overall embarrassment to the Third Reich, something which Hitler and Goebbels would have very much preferred not to have happened.

Goebbels later recognised that Hess's flight had gone down extremely badly with the German Wehrmacht after fighting at the front, but that with no mention of the subject it would die a natural death. This was a theme to which Hitler returned on 22 June.

Hitler despised Hess for harming the Party tremendously, especially in its relations with the Wehrmacht, the effect on the soldiers being very negative. Hitler emphasised, 'If the man was not mad he would deserve to be shot'.

It was not only Hess who was in disgrace. On 1 July Goebbels recorded that General

Hess's flight was followed by the invasion of Crete by German parachutists on 20 May 1941
(Hulton-Deutsch)

Professor Karl Haushofer and Albrecht Haushofer had been drummed out of public life. He blamed both of them for the Hess affair and alleged that they had peddled 'mystic rubbish' to Hess.

This may have been a reference to Karl Haushofer's dream imparted to Hess in which he had seen Hess walking the corridors of castles in Britain beside walls with tapestries, in an attempt to bring peace between Britain and Germany. However, not even Goebbels accused Karl and Albrecht Haushofer of having advance knowledge of his flight, but he did think correctly that they had encouraged him to think in terms of putting out a peace feeler to Britain through neutral countries. Apart from the disfavour into which the Haushofer family had fallen by 1 July, Goebbels had helped to ensure that Hess's name had been forgotten by the media in Germany.[3]

If most Nazi leaders were glad to see Hess go, Hitler was sorry. Goebbels had seen Hitler in tears shortly after Hess's departure, and a few weeks later Mussolini told Ciano that in a conversation he had had with Hitler the latter had spoken about Hess and wept.

There was an atmosphere of black comedy about the whole episode. His secret mission had astonished the British, bewildered the Americans, horrified the Germans, and struck fear into the Russians. It was remarkable to see how a man quite as unintelligent as Hess could make so many clever people run around in circles, as though he was a Trojan horse to all concerned.

But if Hess's flight appeared to many as a comedy, to Albrecht Haushofer it was a fearful tragedy. When the first news of Hess's escapade was reported, Hitler had said darkly that this venture was due to the subversive influence of Professor Haushofer. On Hitler's orders Albrecht was placed under close arrest and brought to Berchtesgaden. Since 1933 he had been sheltering under the protecting hand of Rudolf Hess, and he was now left with nothing. He knew that when giving an account of his activities to Hitler his life would hang in the balance.

NOTES

1. Albert Speer. *Inside the Third Reich*. London, 1970, pages 174–176.
2. *The Berlin Diaries*, by Marie 'Missie' Vassiltchikov, pages 50 and 51.
3. *The Goebbels Diaries 1939–41*, pages 363–375, 424 and 440.

TWO

Hitler and Albrecht Haushofer: 12 May 1941

On arrival at the Obersalzberg, Berchtesgaden, on 12 May 1941, Albrecht Haushofer was not even admitted into Hitler's presence. Instead, he was given a pen and paper, under armed guard, and was ordered to make a report for Hitler entitled *English Connections and the Possibility of Utilising Them*. He knew that Hitler had a fair idea as to why Hess had disappeared, and well appreciated that he was writing for his life.

Consequently Albrecht's report was a plausible and convincing mixture of truths, half-truths and camouflage, designed not to implicate any of his friends in the Resistance. In his writings he used phrases and expressions in harmony with Hitler's prejudices for the purpose of clearing himself in Hitler's eyes and of reducing any suspicion. What he wrote did not represent his real belief, which was that Britain would never consider peace talks of any description with Nazi Germany. Nonetheless Albrecht hoped to convince Hitler that in any possible further negotiations with Britain he would be indispensable on account of his numerous English connections:

> The circle of English individuals whom I have known very well for years, and whose utilisation on behalf of a German-English understanding in the years from 1934 to 1938 was the core of my activity in England, comprises the following groups and persons:
> 1. A leading group of younger Conservatives (many of them Scotsmen). Among them are: the Duke of Hamilton – up to the date of his father's death, Lord Clydesdale – Conservative Member of Parliament; the Parliamentary Private Secretary of Neville Chamberlain, Lord Dunglass; the present Under Secretary of State in the Air Ministry, Balfour; the present Under Secretary of State in the Ministry of Education, Lindsay (National Labour); the present Under Secretary of State in the Ministry for Scotland, Wedderburn.
> Close ties link this circle with the Court. The younger brother of the Duke of Hamilton is closely related to the present Queen through his wife; the mother-in-law of the Duke of Hamilton, the Duchess of Northumberland, is the Mistress of the Robes; her brother-in-law, Lord Eustace Percy, was several times a member of the Cabinet and is still today an influential member of the Conservative Party (especially close to former Prime Minister Baldwin). There are close connections between this circle and important groups of the older Conservatives, as for example the Stanley family (Lord Derby, Oliver Stanley) and Astor (the last is owner of *The Times*). The young Astor, likewise a Member of Parliament, was Parliamentary Private Secretary to the former Foreign and Interior Minister, Sir Samuel Hoare, at present English Ambassador in Madrid.
> I have known almost all of the persons mentioned for years and from close personal contact.

The present Under Secretary of State of the Foreign Office, Butler, also belongs here; in spite of many of his public utterances he is not a follower of Churchill or Eden. Numerous connections lead from most of those named to Lord Halifax, to whom I likewise had personal access.

2. The so-called 'Round Table' circle of younger imperialists (particularly colonial and Empire politicians), whose most important personage was Lord Lothian.

3. A group of the 'Ministerialdirektoren' in the Foreign Office. The most important of these were Strang, the chief of the Central European Department, and O'Malley, the chief of the South Eastern Department and afterwards Minister in Budapest.

There was hardly one of those named who was not at least occasionally in favour of a German-English understanding.

This last statement was a fair point for Albrecht Haushofer to make, in that the persons mentioned wanted to avoid a Second World War, but, contrary to what Albrecht was writing, after the invasion of Poland none of these men would have considered peace talks with the Nazi regime. The report elaborated:

Although most of them in 1939 finally considered that war was inevitable, it was nevertheless reasonable to think of these persons if one thought the moment had come for investigating the possibility of an inclination to make peace. Therefore when the Deputy of the Fuehrer, Reich Minister Hess, asked me in the autumn of 1940 about possibilities of gaining access to possibly reasonable Englishmen, I suggested two concrete possibilities for establishing contacts. It seemed to me that the following could be considered for this:
A. Personal contact with Lothian, Hoare, or O'Malley, all three of whom were accessible in neutral countries.
B. Contact by letter with one of my friends in England. For this purpose the Duke of Hamilton was considered in the first place, since my connection with him was so firm and personal that I could suppose he would understand a letter addressed to him even if it were formulated in very veiled language.
Reich Minister Hess decided in favour of the second possibility; I wrote a letter to the Duke of Hamilton at the end of September 1940 and its despatch to Lisbon was arranged by the Deputy Fuehrer. I did not learn whether the letter reached the addressee. The possibilities of its being lost *en route* from Lisbon to England are not small, after all.

Albrecht now came to the second peace feeler which he had attempted to put out through Professor Carl Burckhardt:

Then in April 1941 I received greetings from Switzerland from Carl Burckhardt, the former League of Nations Commissioner in Danzig and now Vice President of the International Red Cross, whom I had also known well for years. He sent the message that he had greetings to pass on to me from someone in my old circle of English friends. I should please visit him some time in Geneva. Since the possibility existed that these greetings were in connection with my letter of last autumn, I thought I should again submit the matter to the Deputy of the Fuehrer, though with the reservation (as already last autumn) that the chances of a serious peace feeler seemed to me to be extremely slight. Reich Minister Hess decided that I should go to Geneva.

Carl Burckhardt read this report after the war and said that he did not know any of Albrecht Haushofer's friends. He explained that he had seen Lord Halifax in London in October 1939 and that he had often seen the British Consul General in Geneva, mostly in

On 27 May, after blowing up HMS Hood, *the* Bismarck *was sunk, these battles leading to an intensification of the war (Hulton-Deutsch)*

relation to the treatment of prisoners of war. However, Burckhardt denied that he had summarised the opinions of any British group in the manner stated by Albrecht Haushofer. Albrecht's report continued:

> In Geneva I had a long conversation with Burckhardt on 28 April. I found him in something of a quandary between his desire to support the possibilities of a European peace and the greatest concern lest his name might somehow be involved with publicity: he expressly asked that what went on be kept strictly secret. In consideration of the discretion enjoined upon him he could only tell me the following.
>
> A few weeks ago a person well known and respected in London, who was close to the leading Conservative and city circles, had called on him in Geneva. This person, whose name he could not give, though he could vouch for his earnestness, had in a rather long conversation expressed the wish of important English circles for an examination of the possibilities for peace; in search for possible channels my name had been mentioned.
>
> I for my part informed Professor Burckhardt that I had to expect the same discretion with regard to my name. Should his informant in London be willing to come to Switzerland once more and should he further be willing to have his name communicated to me in Berlin through confidential channels, so that the earnestness of both person and mission could be investigated in Germany, then I thought that I, too, could agree to taking another trip to Geneva. Professor Burckhardt stated that he was willing to act as go-between in this manner: it would simply be communicated to England through an entirely safe channel that there was a prospect for a trusted representative from London, after he himself had given his name, to

meet in Geneva a German also well known in England, who was in a position to bring such communications as there might be to the attention of the competent German authorities.

My own conversation with Professor Burckhardt furnished a number of important points regarding the substantive part of possible peace talks. (Burckhardt has not only been in England during the war – for example, he had a long and detailed conversation with Halifax – but he also has frequent contact with the English observer in Geneva, Consul General Livingston, who likewise is one of those Englishmen whom the war does not please.) Burckhardt's general impression of the opinions of the more moderate groups in England can be summarised as follows:

1. The substantive English interest in the areas of eastern and south-eastern Europe (with the exception of Greece) is nominal.

2. No English Government that is still capable of action will be able to renounce (the aim of) a restoration of the western European system of states.

3. The colonial question will not present any overwhelming difficulties if the German demand is limited to the old German possessions and if the Italian appetite can be curbed.

All of this, however – and this fact could not be stressed seriously enough – under the assumption, which overshadowed everything else, that a basis of personal confidence could be found between Berlin and London; and this would be as difficult to find as during the Crusades or in the Thirty Years War.

As matters stood, the contest with 'Hitlerism' was being considered by the masses of the English people, too, to be a religious war with all the fanatical psychological consequences of such an attitude. If anyone in London was inclined toward peace, then it was the indigenous portion of the plutocracy, which was able to calculate when it, along with the indigenous British tradition, would be destroyed, whereas the indigenous, mainly Jewish element, had already in large part completed the jump to America and the overseas dominions. It was Burckhardt's own and deepest concern that if the war continued for a considerable length of time every possibility that the reasonable forces in England would force Churchill to make peace would disappear, since by that time the whole power of decision regarding the overseas assets of the Empire would be taken over by the Americans. Once the remainder of the indigenous English upper class had been eliminated, however, it would be impossible to talk sense to Roosevelt and his circle.

Burckhardt, writing to Albrecht Haushofer's assistant, Walter Stubbe, after the war, emphasised that this report misrepresented what he had said, but he omitted to mention what had passed between himself and Albrecht Haushofer. It may be that Burckhardt did not wish to reveal the precise extent to which he was prepared to act as an intermediary between the Nazi regime and the British.

Hitler read Albrecht's report when he was still uncertain as to how Hess was being received in Britain, and he had no means of checking its truthfulness or accuracy. He thus decided to take no hasty and irrevocable action. Instead he merely gave orders that Haushofer was to be sent to the Prince Albrecht Strasse Gestapo Prison in Berlin, so that he could be interrogated by SS Gruppenführer Mueller.

In the Gestapo prison Albrecht was relatively well treated. His father, who had been arrested and then released after a short time, was allowed to visit him. The most unpleasant aspect of his imprisonment was the interrogations by Mueller. Haushofer had nothing in common with the head of the Gestapo. The latter was a coarse, ruthless and brutal man who had an instinctive distrust for a man like Albrecht Haushofer with his finely tuned intellectual mind. Mueller continually accused him of sending Hess to Britain, but was not intelligent enough to unravel the web of Albrecht's subtle activities. In no way was he able to incriminate Albrecht, although he regarded him with loathing and suspicion.[1]

There were other Nazi leaders interested in Albrecht and on 15 May 1941 Heydrich sent the following telegram to Himmler, after discussions with Albrecht's old enemy, Gauleiter Bohle, of the Nazi Ausland Organisation:

1. After today's conversation with Gauleiter Bohle, the result of which I am transmitting to you today by courier within the next few hours, I have the profound impression that Rudolf Hess was in a particular measure under the influence of both Haushofer senior and Haushofer junior. Gauleiter Bohle thinks that Haushofer junior in particular influenced Rudolf Hess in his evaluation of British neutrality. He [Bohle] is also convinced that Haushofer junior is well able to supply possibly valuable information. I share this view and I would ask your permission to have Haushofer junior thoroughly interrogated about his knowledge of the matter. In the meantime I shall have his flat and office watched, so that, according to the result of the interrogation, any material found there can be seized. I shall of course once again ask for your views.

The postal and telephone surveillance ordered a few days ago will be carried out. . . .

As regards Item 1. I shall be glad of an early decision.

This telegram reached Himmler at a time when he was displeased with Heydrich. For some time Heydrich had been coveting Himmler's position at the head of the S.S. and on Monday 12 May he grilled Himmler's doctor, Kersten, about his treatment of Hess and only released him when Himmler intervened. Heydrich knew that Himmler was interested in astrology and particularly enjoyed helping to imprison astrologers in accordance with Hitler's orders, in order to spite his senior. Nevertheless it appears that Himmler gave Heydrich permission to interrogate Albrecht. One day Heydrich appeared in Albrecht's cell without warning and asked many questions, which resulted in Albrecht giving a long talk on the incompetence, inability and stupidity of Ribbentrop. He may well have convinced Heydrich that Ribbentrop was a disastrous Foreign Minister. That would not have been too difficult. However, Heydrich also believed that Albrecht was a potential traitor. Ribbentrop, who had been described in such disparaging terms to Hess and Heydrich by Albrecht, was smouldering with hostility. He sacked Albrecht from his position in the Foreign Office on 28 May and tried to get him suspended from his professorship, but without success, as Himmler refused to let him be removed. And Himmler had his reasons.

Two months before, Himmler had told his higher S.S. leaders that the Slav population of Europe would have to be reduced by thirty million. He was not lacking in enthusiasm for the war against Russia, but he had a clear sense of self-preservation. He wished to make peace with Britain, as he did not want to fight a war on two fronts. He wanted to keep alive anyone who might help him to make such a peace behind Hitler's back, as he knew that the British would not contemplate peace talks with Hitler. And he knew about Albrecht Haushofer. He knew about him through Volksdeutsch work, through reading his reports after his missions to Czechoslovakia and Japan and his memorandum on the possibilities of a German-English peace, and through examining the recent report which Albrecht had written about the utilisation of his English acquaintances. So when Lorenz of the S.S. recommended to Himmler after Hess's flight that it was the right moment to finish off all the Haushofers, Himmler replied that he did not think it would be necessary yet. For the time being Himmler abstained from having Albrecht shot, in case he might prove potentially useful.

Nobody understood the position better than Albrecht, who wrote to his parents from the Gestapo prison on 7 July 1941:

. . . I know exactly that at present I am a small beetle which has been turned on its back by an unexpected and unforeseeable gust of wind, and which realises that it cannot rise to its feet by its own strength – and now, with some knowledge of two-legged creatures, does not entertain great illusions regarding its future. . . .

I suppose you are now going to the Alpine pasture. My regards to the mountains! Sometime I shall, no doubt, see them again – and, if I am lucky, I shall be able to conclude my existence as a hermit on the Partnachalm. . . .

While in prison Albrecht had been writing, with a sense of impending doom, a play called *The Macedonians*, in which the dictator Alexander was cast as a person with the characteristics of Hitler. He put these words into the mouth of Alexander's old teacher Aristotle:

Albrecht Haushofer, haggard and harassed after repeated interrogation by the Gestapo (Martin Haushofer)

198

When Alexander exceeded all norms I knew that he would destroy himself and not only himself. . . . They will all thirst; they will fight, go berserk; they will think they are doing it for the Empire, for glory and power. But all that has passed is only a chase for the souls lost in the intoxication of Alexander's dreams. . . .

By the end of May 1941 Albrecht had no more dilemmas as to what he should do. There was only one problem, and that was how to survive. Heydrich and Mueller had sent reports on him to Hitler which proved nothing against him, but which recommended that he should be kept in prison. For a month Hitler hesitated and then decided that he should be released. The war against Russia had been launched, and no doubt Hitler intended to keep Albrecht alive for possible future dealings with Britain, once Russia had been overrun.

At any rate, in July 1941, after eight weeks' imprisonment, Albrecht was released; an individual under the suspicious watch of the Gestapo. It had become clear to the entire Nazi High Command, to Mueller and Heydrich in particular, that Albrecht Haushofer was not a good Nazi. He had English friends; he hated the war; he had written that the British regarded Ribbentrop as being in large part responsible for it and they thought of Hitler as 'Satan's representative on earth'. Albrecht had written these things with too much enthusiasm, as though he believed what the British had been saying.

Heydrich and Mueller were determined to liquidate Albrecht Haushofer sooner or later. If they could not get him for being a traitor they would get him for being partly Jewish. Albrecht's life was hanging by a thread.

NOTE

1. The Gestapo were hoping to discredit Albrecht, and one of their questions was whether he could be a homosexual since he was unmarried, an allegation which Albrecht totally rejected. Clearly he was not, as his brother Heinz confirmed to the author. His girlfriend had died tragically when young, and had been buried in the Engadin in Switzerland.

THREE

The Peace Memorandum:
November 1941

It had been hoped by the members of the Resistance in the Wednesday Society that Albrecht could soon go back and see Burckhardt in Switzerland, but after Hess's flight Hassell wrote that all possibility of advancing their cause through Haushofer was now gone. Albrecht had emerged from the Gestapo prison in Berlin as a man in too vulnerable a position; in Nazi circles he had become a subject of the utmost suspicion. Previously Hess's authority had enabled him to travel abroad, but with Hess's disappearance any possibility of being despatched on foreign missions, or of escaping from Germany had disappeared. All that Albrecht had left to him was his post as Professor at the University of Berlin.

His father was unable to help him because he himself was out of favour with the Nazi regime after Hess's flight. This fact was emphasised by Martin Bormann in a letter dated 17 June 1942 from the Fuehrer's Headquarters to Rosenberg.

> I have been informed that Professor Dr Karl Haushofer was very prominently featured in the last number of the National Socialist Monthly magazine. It was on the occasion of a book review of his work on war geopolitics, in which the reviewer came to the conclusion that this book must by no means be overlooked.
>
> I am of the opinion that Professor Karl Haushofer and his son, Professor Albrecht Haushofer, should no longer be given any publicity and I would be thankful if you, too, would join in this decision. I would request information as to your position and conclusion in this matter.

After Hess's flight Albrecht knew that he owed his survival to the fact that Hitler and Himmler had no wish for the time being to destroy an expert who might be able to formulate peace plans with Britain. Consequently Albrecht wrote *Thoughts on a Peace Plan* for Hitler's consumption in November 1941, which was submitted to Weizsaecker, the Secretary of State of the Ministry for Foreign Affairs, who was a friend of his. It can safely be assumed that Weizsaecker ensured that the document reached Hitler without it being seen or blocked by Foreign Minister Ribbentrop, who had become Albrecht's dedicated enemy.

The document, as one would expect, was not a model of social democratic thought. The writing can hardly be taken to represent what Albrecht really believed, which was that Germany should have predominance only in Central Europe, where there were large enclaves of Germans or of German-speaking citizens. It was his desire that all other regions then occupied by German armed forces should have autonomy, and that German armed forces should withdraw. It was impossible, however, to change Hitler's belief that all Nazi gains should be held, that the conquered peoples should be exploited and those who were no longer useful should perish. Albrecht knew that if he wrote expressing his personal views he would soon face a firing squad. In September 1940 he had written documents highly critical of the official Nazi line and had got away with it. After his imprisonment he had to try to blend more closely with his surroundings.

Even so his peace memorandum had more in common with Resistance peace plans than with the Nazi line. By late 1941, when he was writing, German troops had penetrated deep into Russia, had occupied Norway, the Baltic States, the Low Countries, France, Greece, east and south-eastern Europe including all the countries of the Danube Basin. Even the Eastern Mediterranean and large parts of North Africa were under German control. Albrecht, far from maintaining that Germany could hold on to these gains, was making proposals which would have involved withdrawal and the establishment of a German hegemony only in Central and East Europe. His suggestions were only slightly more ambitious than the Resistance peace plans of Ulrich von Hassell, written in February 1940, and of Goerdeler, written in May 1941. Like Hassell and Goerdeler, Albrecht was of the view that Germany's 1914 frontiers should be accepted as the blueprint for further frontier revisions.

Albrecht's memorandum was based on the premise that a future world peace would have to be negotiated and that the war could not be totally won by either side. He therefore put forward his four basic ideas: first, that the British-American alliance was economically and militarily unassailable; second, that Japan could not successfully monopolise control over Greater East Asia; third, that Russia with its nucleus on the Volga or in the Urals could not be forcibly subjugated any more than China could be; and fourth, that Germany's forces were sufficient to prevent military defeat on European soil and perhaps on Near Asian and North African soil, so that the naval powers of Britain and the U.S.A. would have to recognise Germany's preferential continental position.

His proposals advocated that Austria and the Sudetenland should remain within the Reich, while Germany's western frontiers were to be settled by negotiation. In the east he desired the creation of buffer states and suggested that the western frontiers of Russia should be under German control. Lastly he recommended that there should be an all-European responsibility for African colonisation and that Germany should acquire colonies, so that she might obtain raw materials and assist in economic development.

His very lengthy document had no effect on practical politics, because it contained suggestions which were as unacceptable to Hitler as they were to everybody else. Nonetheless, it did help to keep him alive for a considerable period, as Hitler took a decided interest.

It appears that Hitler had not only read Albrecht's peace memorandum, but was receiving information about him from S.S. Gruppenführer Mueller and Heydrich. One of Albrecht's students, Frau Irmegard Schnuhr, had married a high-ranking S.S. man and came into contact with Nazi circles before she separated from her husband. She had come to detest the Nazi regime and became Albrecht's assistant. One day Mueller saw her and asked her to report on Haushofer's acquaintances, as well as on what he had said about the Hess case and his English friends. She was asked to make monthly reports on him. Frau Schnuhr accepted and told Albrecht, who saw to it that she gave carefully worded answers to the Gestapo. She said that she performed this job in the belief that, had she refused, someone else less sympathetic to Albrecht would have continued to keep watch on him. Being under surveillance, Albrecht acted very cautiously and was therefore of little practical use to the Resistance. As Frau Schnuhr said of him, 'Finding himself in opposition he acted too timidly to have any real effect. At every point he would have preferred a compromise if that had been possible.'

In December 1941 she was summoned by Hitler not long after the U.S.A. had declared war on Germany. Hitler wanted to know who Albrecht's acquaintances were and said that he had a 'special interest' in Albrecht and was interested to learn whether he thought there was a possibility of making peace with Britain. In February 1942 she was again called before Hitler and was asked the same questions. She told him that Albrecht's views were that to the best of his knowledge neither Britain nor Germany had any intention of putting out a peace feeler. However, even if Hitler did desire to negotiate with Britain, the very fact that the German Foreign Minister was Ribbentrop would make it impossible for any negotiations to get off the ground. Hitler told her that Albrecht Haushofer was not as clever as he thought he was, and that it would be easy to sack Ribbentrop if the British first sacked their Foreign Minister, Anthony Eden.

Frau Schnuhr asked Hitler whether he wanted to see Albrecht Haushofer and Hitler replied that he would not dream of it, the outcome of the war was going to be settled on the battlefield, and he indicated that Albrecht Haushofer was only a *mischling*, a halfbreed. Frau Schnuhr had the impression that Hitler, whilst being fundamentally suspicious of Albrecht, wished to keep him available should peace negotiations with Britain ever become a possibility. Such thoughts almost certainly evaporated as the months passed, and by the time of the crushing German defeats at Stalingrad and El Alamein Hitler may well have had no further use for Albrecht Haushofer.

However, Albrecht had learnt that Himmler, of all people, also had a decided interest in keeping him alive. Professor Rolf Italiaander wrote:

> Superficial knowledge of Albrecht Haushofer may lead to the assumption that he was a cold, even icy, calculating intellectual. However, each intensive discussion soon made it clear that he was endowed with a deep kindness of heart and warmheartedness. These qualities combined with much melancholy were so strong that, in order to avoid becoming a victim of sentimentality, he had to clothe himself, in his political tasks, in ice-cold sarcasm. Had he not done so, he would have been eliminated much sooner by his protagonist Himmler, whom he hated passionately.

It was not only Hitler and Hess who wanted to make peace with Britain. Himmler, the Reichsführer S.S., had taken up the idea of making peace overtures precisely where Hess had left off, the difference being that Himmler, unlike Hess, had no affection for Hitler. Himmler realised that the British would not make peace with Hitler in any circumstances, and he was therefore ready to enter into treacherous negotiations behind Hitler's back. Himmler's vanity was such that he thought that the British might regard him as being preferable to Hitler.

One of Himmler's neighbours on the Tegernsee, outside Munich, was Carl Langbehn, a friendly acquaintance of Albrecht Haushofer, a man who had gained entry to Admiral Canaris's Abwehr which made it easy for him to travel abroad. Himmler thought that Langbehn might be useful to him in trying to open up a channel to the British. Following Hess's example of sending Albrecht Haushofer to Switzerland, Himmler also sent Langbehn to Professor Burckhardt.

Langbehn was a curious character and like Albrecht Haushofer had been playing a double game, working for the Resistance and also for Himmler. On Sunday 17 August 1941, Langbehn, representing Himmler or the Resistance and quite possibly both, saw Professor Burckhardt in Geneva. As Gerald Reitlinger expressed it, Langbehn explored the possibilities of Britain making peace with a Hitlerless but not Himmlerless Germany.

Himmler apparently hated having to fight a war on two fronts especially after the entry of the U.S.A. into the war. On 9 April 1942, Ciano recorded in his diary that Himmler wanted a compromise peace, and it seemed that Himmler's plans for expansion into Russia were based on his hope of coming to an understanding with the West.

All this had its importance for Albrecht Haushofer, who knew that for the time being Himmler and the S.S. might leave him alone if he was really cautious. Although he was under surveillance he was still collaborating with three important circles of the Resistance. He often attended the Wednesday Society, and there continued to meet with such members of the Resistance as General Beck, Popitz, Hassell and Jessen. They had contact with the generals in the Resistance including Witzleben, Hoepner, Olbricht and Wagner. Yet these military plotters remained hesitant.

Albrecht also had contact with the Kreisau Circle. In the autumn of 1941, he lectured to those who surrounded Count Helmuth von Moltke, Count Peter Yorck von Wartenburg, Adam von Trott zu Solz and Stauffenberg on Moltke's estate at Kreisau. The Kreisau Circle had feelers of Resistance in the churches, in the Abwehr, in the military, and it was assisted by planners such as Albrecht Haushofer and Count Fritz Schulenburg, the Deputy Police President of Berlin.

Fritz Schulenburg also worked in the Reich Office for Space Research, with Albrecht as geographical expert, and occasionally with Popitz. The three of them co-operated in the preparation of drafts for the internal reorganisation of Germany, which was to be of use to a non-Nazi German government, once Hitler had been destroyed. In those drafts Albrecht envisaged Germany's 1914 frontiers as a basis for the Reich once Nazism had gone.

Strangely enough, Albrecht, who has been described as the 'darkest horse' of the German Resistance to Hitler, also had loose connections with the Rote Kapelle or Red Orchestra, a Communist Resistance movement in Germany. This organisation, through the use of more than a hundred short-wave transmitters, was supplying secret information to Russia. Its leader was Harro Schulze-Boysen, a grandson of Admiral von Tirpitz, who had through family influence got himself installed in an important position in the Luftwaffe Intelligence Service under Goering. One of the Schulze-Boysen's most loyal adherents was Horst Heilman who had been a promising student of Albrecht's at the University of Berlin. Albrecht had met Schulze-Boysen through Rainer Hildebrandt and Horst Heilman, and they struck up a friendly relationship. The two men were representatives of different Resistance movements. Schulze-Boysen was working for the military defeat and economic collapse of Germany, whilst Albrecht was hoping to stir the hesitating generals to action against Hitler. Schulze-Boysen's friends were mostly of Communist persuasion, Albrecht's patriotic Germans.

Both Albrecht and Schulze-Boysen agreed that Hitler had removed the inferiority complexes which had overcome the German nation after the First World War, by appealing to their most primitive traits, and they both expected that the Russians would have advanced into the heart of Europe by the end of the war. But while Schulze-Boysen hoped for German-Russian co-operation, Albrecht expected the Russians to be hostile to a European standard of life which was higher than their own.

Although Albrecht had talks with Schulze-Boysen he was in no way involved in the latter's actions. But he did wish to know about the activities of his militant students such as Horst Heilman, so that if their activities were discovered he would not be implicated. He felt he was in far too vulnerable a position to take risks, and as his brother Heinz said of him, Albrecht's attitude of self-defence was very necessary to him as he did not possess the brute courage of a soldier. Accordingly Albrecht warned Schulze-Boysen and Horst Heilman that security and discretion were vital as there were thousands of Gestapo agents

The student Rainer Hildebrandt with Albrecht Haushofer during a peaceful moment (Martin Haushofer)

about, whose activities were not to be disregarded. Notwithstanding this advice, in August 1942 more than a hundred persons connected with the Rote Kapelle were arrested on the instructions of Himmler, who found it convenient to humiliate Goering by arresting a nest of conspirators in the Air Ministry. Schulze-Boysen and Horst Heilman were hanged as well as an unknown number of others.

It was a depressing time for Albrecht. Three of his favourite students, Wolfgang Hoffman, Moser and Kinzler had been killed at the front. Another student, Paul Meller, was poisoned in a concentration camp, and Albrecht's girlfriend, who had parted from him some years previously and with whom he had never lost touch, had died in the Engadine, Switzerland. He was always under surveillance by the Gestapo. Albrecht, with his part-Jewish ancestry and his fingers in a number of anti-Hitler pies, was an obvious candidate for one of Himmler's extermination lists. But his name was omitted, part-Jewish or not, since Himmler kept anybody alive who might be of possible use to him.

Heydrich and Mueller had no such feelings about him. Heydrich was just as brutal as Mueller but he was more shrewd. He correctly guessed that Albrecht's assistant, Frau Schnuhr, was being of more assistance to Albrecht than to Mueller and Hitler. On one occasion Heydrich summoned her, and told her, with menaces, that he saw through her game and that she was not performing her duties as Hitler would have wished. No doubt he passed on his suspicions to Mueller.

Mueller summoned Albrecht into the grim surroundings of the Gestapo Head-quarters on one occasion. He merely wished to tell Albrecht how often he might write and lecture for the public. After this interview Albrecht found that his map briefcase, left in the anteroom, had in the interval been filled with communist pamphlets by some malicious person. Knowing that it might cost him his life to be found with them, he rapidly discarded them to learn that the precaution had not been in vain. He was unsuccessfully searched on his way out of the Gestapo Headquarters. It had been Mueller's way of playing a little joke.

Hildebrandt wrote that the activities of Heydrich and Mueller were constantly present in Albrecht's mind, like a recurring nightmare which a man would long to forget. Whenever the telephone rang, whenever he went out, whenever he saw a friend the thought of Heydrich and Mueller was never far away. He loathed being a shadowed man.

In April 1942 Albrecht heard from Frau Schnuhr that an S.S. man called Wilke had told her that Heydrich's staff was making plans for taking over Himmler's command forcibly. Armed with this knowledge Albrecht decided to do Heydrich a bad turn. He told Langbehn to report the matter to Himmler, which was done, and Himmler thanked Langbehn. Himmler had been instrumental in recommending to Hitler that Heydrich should be appointed as Deputy Protector of Bohemia and Moravia, and it may be taken for granted that he took every precaution to ensure that Heydrich's presence remained as far removed from his own as possible. On 29 May 1942 Jan Kubiš and Josef Gabcik of the Free Czechoslovak Forces saw to it that Heydrich was blown up in his car by a bomb. At the end of the first week in June Heydrich died from his wounds, and shortly afterwards the S.S. murdered virtually the entire population of the small Czech village of Lidice.

Heydrich was dead but even so this fresh example of Nazi brutality can hardly have done anything to quieten Albrecht's apprehensions about his own future.

FOUR

Himmler's Treachery and the July Plot: 1943–4

In 1943, the military plotters in the Resistance had still made no headway with their plans to remove Hitler. Albrecht was certain that the formula of unconditional surrender propounded by the Allies in January 1943 had acted as a dampening influence on the activities of the wavering Resistance generals. In the summer he wrote a note to a friend, 'It is now either too late or too early for a successful action. What I could achieve is being ignored by those who seem to be able to do everything much better. Thus I sit in my home mountains and wait. I wait, in contrast to most of my coevals and contemporaries, but with the same helplessness in the face of the stream of events.' Yet one of his acquaintances, whose thoughts were developing along a dangerous track, did not want to wait. This man was Langbehn, and Langbehn argued that there could be no *coup d'état* carried out against Himmler and the S.S.

Langbehn had told Popitz and Albrecht Haushofer that in November 1941, after the failure before Moscow, Himmler and some senior S.S. officers had sensed defeat, had thought that Himmler could manage matters better than Hitler and had entertained the idea of forcibly changing the system. After the German defeats at Stalingrad and El Alamein Langbehn encouraged S.S. General Karl Wolff (Himmler's A.D.C.) to believe that Hitler would have to be 'written off' so that Himmler could save the Third Reich. Wolff thought that Himmler and the Waffen S.S. might be amenable to the idea of making a putsch in co-operation with army units under Himmler's control.

Langbehn saw in this planned putsch a possibility of dispensing with Hitler and Himmler one by one. First, with Himmler's co-operation, the Resistance would destroy Hitler, and then, as soon as the army had reorganised, the Resistance would doublecross Himmler, kill him, take over the S.S. and disband it. Thereafter peace negotiatons would be instituted with the Allies. Thus it was that a desperate plan was concocted.

In principle Albrecht Haushofer was not against this stratagem. He told his assistant, Walter Stubbe, that Germany could only be freed by an act of violence carried out by the army. The war was being lost, and in order to prevent a repetition of the 'stab in the back' legend, it was important that the blame for any putsch should be laid on Himmler and the S.S. Naturally he hoped that Hitler and Himmler would be knocked down like ninepins, but he did not expect matters to take such a course. Yet, according to Rainer Hildebrandt and H. W. Stahmer, Albrecht actively encouraged Popitz to negotiate with Himmler through the medium of Langebhn, Himmler's solicitor.

Langbehn considered himself in a good tactical position to engage in this risky game. With the approval of Himmler and the S.D., Langbehn had in December 1942 met a

British official in Zurich and Professor Bruce Hopper of the O.S.S. (U.S. Secret Service) in Stockholm, in order to explore the chances of peace negotiations. He was periodically in touch with Himmler, and in May 1943 he informed the military leaders of the Resistance that Himmler was psychologically ready to be approached by those in the opposition who wanted to play off Himmler and the S.S. against the Hitler-Bormann clique.

There were a considerable number of people in the Resistance who liked this plan, including General Beck, General Olbricht, Field Marshal Witzleben and General von Tresckow, as well as Langbehn, Popitz, Albrecht Haushofer, Jessen and Planck. The head of the Berlin Police, Count Helldorf, and the head of the Criminal Police, General Nebe, who were both in the S.S. and had dubious Resistance records, were also in favour of the idea. Hassell and Goerdeler were in on the secret and apparently did not oppose it, although they had misgivings. In May 1943 Langbehn tried to arrange a Himmler-Popitz meeting through S.S. General Karl Wolff. Langbehn explained to Wolff that with Hitler the war could not be won, that a tolerable peace could be obtained for Germany, however, with a Reich government of reliable persons such as Himmler and Popitz, and that Hitler would be given an 'honourable position in retirement'. Wolff said that a reply from Himmler would be forthcoming.

Shortly afterwards Popitz and Langbehn heard from Field Marshal von Bock's army group in Russia, through General von Tresckow, that Bock was prepared to participate in a revolt if the putsch had Himmler's support. Tresckow encouraged Popitz and told Langbehn to 'swallow the bitter pill and go into the lion's den'. On 21 August Langbehn was informed by Wolff that Himmler would see Popitz in his office on 26 August.

Himmler knew exactly why Langbehn was trying to arrange such a meeting, as he revealed a year later at Posen on 3 August 1944, in his speech before Bormann, Goebbels and the Gauleiters on the antecedents of the July Plot.

> Now there was another clue. An unusual man, a State Minister, Popitz, tried for some months to get into touch with me. He let it be known through a middleman that he wanted an urgent interview with me. We let this middleman chatter, we let him talk, and this is more or less what he said. Yes, it was of course necessary that the war should end, we must make terms of peace with England – just as the opinion is today – and the first requisite was that the Fuehrer must be removed at once and relegated by the opposition to an honorary president's post. His group was quite certain that this plan could not be carrried out against the S.S. They therefore hoped, since I was an understanding and responsible German, that I would not interfere – only for Germany, of course, and in God's name no self-seeking matter.
>
> As soon as I was informed of the plot I went to the Fuehrer and said, 'I will kill the rascal! Such an unblushing thing to put an idea of his kind into my head, of all people's!' But the Fuehrer laughed and said: 'Oh no, if this is what he really intends you will not kill him, you will listen to him. Let him come and see you. It might be interesting, and if he says the same thing as at the first interview then you can arrest him. . . .'

However, Himmler had given an entirely different impression to Popitz on 26 August 1943 at the Reich Ministry of the Interior, where he and Popitz had a serious discussion while Langbehn and Wolff waited in the anteroom outside. Popitz declared that the war situation was critical and that the Fuehrer, for his own sake, should be relieved of the many heavy responsibilities which he carried. The western allies would never negotiate peace with Hitler and there could be no more appropriate person to supersede him than Himmler who could take firm action to save the Reich. Himmler listened and was very interested. Popitz was given to understand that, far from showing disapproval, Himmler was not against the proposals and found them somewhat appealing.

Afterwards Popitz was informed by Wolff that the discussions were to be continued and that Langbehn and Field Marshal Witzleben were also to take part. A few days later Popitz told a friend that he had said things to Himmler which might cost him his head – if Himmler wanted it. But at present Himmler did not want to arrest Popitz, nor did he wish to be too closely involved with the plan of the Resistance generals to destroy Hitler. Himmler liked to encircle his victims and render them defenceless before he struck them down, and Hitler was not defenceless. Himmler was content to wait in the hope that the Resistance would do his dirty work for him. Once done, he could thrust Bormann and Goering to one side, become Fuehrer, and take the credit with the German people for killing off those in the Resistance who could not be used. He was willing to play a double game until he saw which turn events were going to take.

Albrecht Haushofer must have watched these machinations with dread, because the Resistance was operating from a position of extreme weakness. If Himmler chose to, he could take action against them at any time, and he was not such an easy man to outwit as Hess. Albrecht may well have feared that Langbehn and Popitz had insufficiently appreciated that in the art of playing off one group against another, in the doublecross and double doublecross of power politics, Himmler was equalled only by Hitler.

Hitler had advised Himmler to see Popitz for a second time, but the second interview did not materialise because Himmler's double dealing was very nearly discovered by Hitler. Himmler had been dubious about his own acceptability to the western allies as a peace negotiator in the event of Hitler's liquidation; like Hess before him, however, he hoped that the British could be brought round to his way of thinking and to this end he sent Langbehn to Switzerland yet again to make enquiries. Langbehn made contact with British and American Intelligence officers in Berne, and a certain allied agency sent a telegram to London to the effect that Himmler's lawyer had arrived to make a peace initiative. This telegram was decoded by the Abwehr and the S.D., and it is thought that it was Mueller who forwarded the telegram to Bormann and Hitler.

As soon as he learnt that Hitler knew about Langbehn's trip to Swtizerland, Himmler had Langbehn arrested for the sake of his own skin. When he was summoned to Hitler and asked what the telegram meant, Himmler naturally lied and denied all knowledge of peace negotiations, saying that the telegram must have been sent behind his back. Hitler was so dependent on Himmler that he accepted this 'unblushing' explanation, but from then on Himmler was forced to sit tight and watch carefully so as to avoid falling under suspicion.

Langbehn was sent to Sachsenhausen Concentration Camp, but no efforts were made to bring him to trial: that would not have been in Himmler's interests. Instead he was subjected to endless interrogations by Leo Lange of the Gestapo who admitted in June 1944 that, strictly speaking, Popitz ought to have been interviewed as well, but it was much too difficult. By this he meant that he was not going to risk being liquidated by Himmler, simply by asking too many questions. In time Himmler discovered that Langbehn had sought to doublecross him on behalf of the Resistance, and he first tortured and then executed him.

Himmler had been keeping his options open. He had a good reason for wanting to keep Albrecht Haushofer alive, although he was having him watched. If the Resistance were to eliminate Hitler and thereby destroy an obvious obstacle to peace negotiations, resisters like Albrecht Haushofer and Dohnanyi, the senior Abwehr official who were believed to have connections in Britain and the U.S.A. could be utilised as middlemen in a bid for peace with Britain. The only times that Himmler acted against the Resistance, prior to the July Plot, were when he suspected that Hitler had learnt about its activities from other sources. He took good care to keep up his pretence of loyalty.

By late 1943 Haushofer had lost all hope of a successful *coup d'état*. The plan to play off Himmler against Hitler had not worked to any satisfactory extent, and he believed it was now too late to eliminate Hitler. He felt that Nazism must burn itself out, and that there was no sense in the Resistance destroying Hitler only to be held responsible for Hitler's war. By 1944 he was opposed to any attempt on Hitler's life, because with or without Hitler Germany no longer had a card to offer her enemies in peace negotiations, as she had had in 1942. He probably appreciated that if the Resistance did kill Hitler it would not be the Stauffenbergs and Haushofers who would gain, but the Himmlers and Muellers. Himmler was chief of the S.S., of the S.D., of Kripo (the Criminal Police) and Schupo (the Traffic Police), of the Ministry of the Interior, and had about 500,000 or more S.S. men under his personal command who were ready to obey him unconditionally at any time, while Mueller's Gestapo, being subordinate to Himmler, had spread its tentacles into every town. Even if the Resistance did kill Hitler it was inconceivable that it could have withstood the savage counter-attack from Himmler's S.S. and Mueller's Gestapo, which were poised to strike.

Most members of the Resistance, like Albrecht Haushofer, were spending much of their time in trying to stay alive. Albrecht wrote to Prince Hohenlohe on 14 July 1944 saying that he was 'preparing for a change of occupation and perhaps even residence'. This was a guarded allusion to what would happen six days later, on 20 July.

When the bomb planted by Stauffenberg exploded at Rastenburg, there was not a single member of the Resistance who was prepared to check on whether Hitler was dead. Later that day Albrecht Haushofer was in Popitz's study; together they heard Hitler's grating voice over the radio saying that an attempt had been made on his life, and that an accounting would be given such as National Socialists were wont to give. Popitz was arrested the following day and Himmler, newly appointed by Hitler as Commander-in-Chief of the replacement army, took ruthless measures to arrest all those circles of the Resistance about which he had previously known so much. It is reasonable to assume that Himmler was most disappointed that Stauffenberg's bomb had failed to do its work.

Albrecht knew that he was in imminent danger of arrest, partly because he knew about Himmler's treacherous dealings with Popitz and Langbehn, and partly because Himmler wanted to have an expert who could write and speak perfect English and was adept at drafting peace plans. In any case Albrecht's connections with the Resistance were being rapidly discovered.

Kaltenbrunner, who had taken over Heydrich's command at the head of the S.D., investigated the Wednesday Society's resistance activities, and Albrecht's name was mentioned in his reports of 25 July and 1 August 1944. The Resistance plan for the reorganisation of the Reich, which had been written by Albrecht Haushofer and Fritz Schulenburg, also fell into Himmler's hands, and he is said to have been much impressed.

Fearing the worst, Albrecht went into hiding, and on 25 July 1944 left Berlin, travelling to his father's alpine hut at Partnachalm in Bavaria. He suspected that Himmler had already sent the Gestapo after him, and arrived only to discover that the Gestapo had arrested his father a few hours earlier, and had taken him to Dachau Concentration Camp. He found to his relief that his mother was still free. After a brief stay with her he fled again, this time to the house of his brother Heinz on the Ammersee. Heinz met him for a hurried discussion and told him that the Gestapo had been searching everywhere. There was little time to waste, and Albrecht continued his flight.

He was sheltered by the sisters of a convent for a night and then was sent on to stay with a doctor. The Gestapo were following close on his heels. They arrested his brother Heinz on his return to his job as an agriculturist in Vienna, and also Albrecht's sister-in-law and nephew, and the Mother Superior of the convent. They reached the doctor's

Count Klaus Schenk von Stauffenberg who tried to blow up Hitler with a
bomb on 20 July 1944 (Hulton-Deutsch)

house and Albrecht escaped into the woods with only seconds to spare. The doctor, his father and his wife were arrested. Albrecht was free, but his world was rapidly collapsing around him.

FIVE

Hunted by the Gestapo:
Moabit Prison 1944–5

One day early in September 1944 Frau Zahler, who lived in a mountain chalet near Partenkirchen in the Bavarian Alps, heard a knock at the door. She had been a friend of the Haushofer family, and was surprised to find a dusty, tired and bearded man, whom she recognised as Albrecht Haushofer. She agreed to hide him. Her guest had hardly eaten for two days, had narrowly escaped being captured by the Gestapo in the forest, and was greatly relieved to be given shelter. That night he and Frau Zahler listened to the English radio, and heard that thousands of Germans were being sought by the Gestapo as a result of the July Plot, and that within weeks they would be freed by the Western Allied advance. Albrecht considered the possibility of trying to escape to Switzerland across the strictly guarded border, but in the end decided to lie low as he expected the British or American Armed Forces to arrive during the autumn of 1944.

However, the British and Americans did not come: the Gestapo came instead. On 7 December Frau Zahler answered the door, and three Gestapo agents who were searching for Albrecht entered. They could find no one and were about to depart, when one of them decided to make a final examination before leaving. He climbed the ladder into the hayloft and gazed around. It was a cold winter's day and suddenly he noticed a column of vapour rising from the hay. He called the other Gestapo agents, and they burrowed down and found Albrecht buried beneath. Frau Zahler saw them bring him down from the hayloft with an expression of despair written all over his face. They took him and Frau Zahler to Munich Prison; Albrecht was particularly unhappy that she had been arrested as well. He told her that nothing would happen to her, a statement which turned out to be correct.

Late on the evening of 9 December the Gestapo drove their newly acquired prisoner all the way from Munich to Moabit Prison in the Lehrterstrasse, Berlin. It was a star-shaped building with several wings, containing in all some 550 cells joined together by a control tower, and supervised by the S.S. Sonderkommando. After the July Plot the R.S.H.A. (the Reich Security Main Office) under the overall charge of Himmler, had established the Sondercommission on 20 July under Mueller, so that detailed investigations into the conspiracy could be made. Himmler and Mueller were working hand in glove, and as the Prince Albrechtstrasse Prison was not large enough to hold all resistance suspects, the Lehrterstrasse Prison of Moabit situated one mile and a half away was used as an annex.

Immediately after his arrival at the Lehrterstrasse Prison on 10 December Haushofer was taken to the Gestapo Headquarters at the Prince Albrechtstrasse Prison. There he was seen, quite by chance, by another prisoner, Prince Ernst August, who had been arrested on the Russian front under suspicion of having collaborated with the Resistance. Ernst August was sitting in the office of the Gestapo interrogator, when another Gestapo officer burst into the room with the exclamation, 'We have got him'. He said that they had driven all night from Munich and that the prisoner was in the next room. Both Gestapo agents went to look through the door at their prisoner, and when their backs were turned Prince Ernst August had time to raise himself from his seat and take a quick look at the written report which had been laid on the desk. It was entitled *Albrecht Haushofer*.

Prince Ernst August, grandson of the Kaiser, saw Albrecht Haushofer at Gestapo Headquarters (Duke of Hanover)

After a while Ernst August was taken into the next room and left there in the presence of a secretary. On entering he saw a man in a most dejected state. Slumped on a bench was a bowed figure, dressed in an old green hunting coat, with hair down to his shoulders and flowing beard, his elbows resting on his knees and his hands, which were manacled, hanging towards the ground. Written on the name card hanging around his neck were the words 'Albrecht Haushofer'.

The Gestapo guard who led Ernst August away told him, 'You have seen nothing – remember that. If anybody asks you, you saw nobody at all.' Ernst August replied, 'But I think I know that man. I have heard that he is a great friend of Ribbentrop.' He had a faint hope that he might be able to say something to help the drawn and bedraggled prisoner whom he had just seen. The Gestapo guard answered, 'No, he is one of the most dangerous traitors and criminals alive. Remember you did not see anyone.' Evidently the Gestapo were treating Albrecht as a very important prisoner.

During the following days and months Albrecht was interrogated constantly. His connections with the Resistance were established beyond doubt. Dr Goerdeler had broken down under torture and had disclosed the nature of the close association between Albrecht, Popitz and Langbehn, and whatever Albrecht might say there was no adequate excuse to be given for his flight from Berlin after the July Plot. When Albrecht saw his brother Heinz after an interrogation he gave him the thumbs down sign.

It was amazing that the Gestapo did not bring him to trial before the Nazi judge Freisler, and have him executed without delay. As always the Gestapo had their reasons,

Dr Carl Goerdeler, civilian leader of the German Resistance to Hitler, for whom Albrecht Haushofer wrote peace plans prior to his execution (Hulton-Deutsch)

213

which gradually became evident to Albrecht's fellow prisoners. Albrecht remarked to them that he had been taken to the Prince Albrechtstrasse Prison to state his views on the possibility of a quick armistice, and that he had taken this opportunity of telling his interrogators about the disastrous mistakes of Ribbentrop. One Gestapo agent had said to him, 'What a pity they did not listen to you', and Albrecht said to his fellow prisoners in the air raid shelter of Moabit Prison, 'I would like to risk one more stake – and I can'. He was almost certainly trying to present himself as an indispensable peace negotiator with the Western Allies on account of his connections with Britain.

Albrecht once bitterly told the other prisoners that he had two fears, that of the Rollcommando or Extermination Squad, and that of being compelled to become Hitler's last Foreign Minister. It is of interest that in Albrecht's play *Sulla* the dictator orders the Greek sage Zosias to assume office, and even under threat of death Zosias refuses. Perhaps Albrecht pictured himself in a role similar to that of Zosias. If so it appears that Albrecht was given a misleading impression, for the one man amongst the Nazi leadership who was keeping him available for possible use was Himmler rather than Hitler.

Himmler knew that he would have to tread warily before making any peace overtures to the west through imprisoned members of the Resistance, in case Hitler might find out. He well knew that it was Hitler's policy to execute everyone connected with the Resistance. So Himmler ensured that when the Gestapo caught Albrecht Haushofer they would be suitably discreet, and for this reason Prince Ernst August had been ordered to keep quiet about what he had or had not seen. It was convenient for Himmler to have Albrecht Haushofer within his clutches, because less was known about him than about Langbehn and Popitz (the last of whom was under sentence of death). Besides, Himmler felt that he could trust a man when he was surrounded by armed S.S. men and could be taken out and shot if there were the slightest signs of non-co-operation.

In despair Albrecht wrote a poem *On the Threshold* indicating that even suicide might be preferable to his present existence, though he did not allow himself to entertain such thoughts for long:

> The means for leaving this existence
> I have tested them by eye and hand
> A sudden blow and no prison wall
> Is strong enough to touch my soul
> Ere the guard watching this door
> Puts in the heavy iron bar
> A sudden blow and my soul
> Would shoot into the night
> The belief, desire and hope
> That keeps others
> Is dead in me.
> Life, like a play of shadows
> Looks senseless to me, aimless
> What keeps me; the door is open.
> But we are forbidden to steal away
> Be it God or Devil who torments us.

Albrecht was not the only prisoner in the Lehrterstrasse prison who was being kept alive temporarily by Himmler. Gerhard Ritter wrote that in March 1945 Himmler seemed to have hopes of Haushofer and of Dohnanyi. The theologian the Reverend Eberhard Bethge, also in Moabit Prison, noticed that Albrecht had certain privileges, such as books

214

Moabit Prison where Albrecht Haushofer was incarcerated (Landesbildstelle)

to read as well as newspapers, pencils and writing paper. This was because Albrecht had been ordered to write an account of his political views for Himmler and to advise Himmler how he should comport himself in order to get a reasonable peace with the Western Allies. As Bethge wrote:

> I was a co-prisoner and as such for some time an attendant in the prison passages, where I helped in the distribution of food, and on such occasions was able to speak to one or other of the prisoners; thus I was able on several occasions to have short talks with Haushofer. In this way I had an opportunity to see that Haushofer had objects in his cell which he could not have had there in the beginning. He also mentioned some very friendly interrogations when he was requested to write down things for Himmler. . . .
>
> At any rate, in those days we watched with interest the change in Haushofer's treatment, and derived some measure of hope from it for all of us. We believed that it was the intention to make use of Haushofer at a later date.

What Albrecht wrote for his captors we do not know. As he himself understood, peace plans for Himmler would not have been worth the paper on which they were written. He was using his time and energies in writing his last work *The Sonnets of Moabit*. In the course of his life he had written a number of plays, in all of which there was a political slant directed against tyranny, but it was the *Sonnets of Moabit*, written in the Lehrterstrasse Prison, which later made him known throughout Germany. They were desperate poems

215

21 April 1945. S.S. Gruppenführer Mueller gave orders for the murder of Albrecht Haushofer and the last remnants of the German Resistance to Hitler in Moabit Prison

216

set down by a man who keenly felt the destruction of his country, and knew that his days were almost certainly numbered.

By March 1945 Himmler's interest in Albrecht Haushofer was beginning to slacken because he had found a more suitable intermediary to take messages to the Western Allies. In February he met Count Folke Bernadotte of the Swedish Red Cross and in April he despatched the Swedish Count with an offer to capitulate to the Western Allies but not to the Russians. Churchill and Truman rejected this offer on 25 April. While the Himmler-Bernadotte talks were in progress (they have been described in Bernadotte's book *The Fall of the Curtain*) Himmler was scarcely in Berlin at all. On 19 April his chief inquisitor Kaltenbrunner left the Lehrterstrasse Prison. By this time Himmler no longer cared whether the last remnants of the Resistance in Moabit Prison lived or died and he was content to leave Albrecht Haushofer and his companions to the care of the head of the Gestapo. This was not welcome news for Albrecht as it was not the first time that he had come under the auspices of S.S. Gruppenführer Mueller.

It was clear that if only he could hang on for a few more days, the Russians would liberate him and his fellow prisoners in Moabit prison; for by the middle of April the bombardment of Berlin had begun, and between 16–21 April the Russians came much closer. On 21 April the Lehrterstrasse Prison, which had already suffered bomb damage, was hit by shellfire from Russian artillery. The prisoners were moved down into the cellars, and there Albrecht shared a cell with Herbert Kosney, a young Communist. They struck up a friendly relationship, both men being equally helpless.

On 20 and 21 April many prisoners, with the exception of the political ones were released or made to serve with the army. When this came to the ears of Goebbels, the Gauleiter of Berlin, he sent a telegram threatening that anybody who attempted to free other prisoners would be executed. The remaining captives in Moabit suspected that Mueller would send the S.S. Rollkommando. Some of the prisoners determined to attempt a rising; however, when they heard that other prisoners had definitely been freed they decided to postpone their revolt. It was a fatal decision.

They were not to know that on 21 April 1945 Mueller had called a meeting at the Reich Security Main Office to discuss the future of the last prisoners in Moabit. It was attended by the leaders of the S.S. Sonderkommando and by the Commandant of Moabit Prison, S.S. Untersturmführer Albrecht. It was at that meeting that Mueller gave his orders.

217

SIX

The End:
1.05 a.m. 23 April 1945

In Moabit Prison a great change came over Albrecht Haushofer, a change reflected in *The Sonnets of Moabit*. Unlike his letters to his mother these poems were expressed with great simplicity. In 1930 he had written to his mother that poems were 'better when one is very desperate', and during those last weeks he was deeply despondent. From his sonnets emerges the picture of a tormented man watching through prison bars the glow of Berlin burning, as a result of the war which he had sought to prevent.

The Reverend Edmund Walsh of the U.S. armed forces wrote that in the shadow of anticipated death Albrecht recaptured a whole lifetime of memories – his travels in Tibet, his colleagues Yorck and Moltke, Schulenburg and Schwerin, his mother, the scenes of happiness at Partnachalm, the voice of dead years and the ruins that now disfigured his devastated Fatherland and haunted soul. The Sonnets became for him the means through which he could finally resolve his inner conflicts, and he chose poetry as the medium for expressing his feelings. He described his loneliness in a poem called *In Fetters*:

> For him who nightly sleeps in it
> The cell is bleak but its walls
> Are full of life. Guilt and Fate are
> Veiled in grey in its vaults
> Of all the grief filling its frame
> There is below masonry and bars
> A breath alive, a secret flutter
> Revealing the deep pains of other souls.
> I am not the first in this room
> Whose wrists are cut by fetters
> And in whose grief alien wills rejoice
> Sleep turns to awakening
> Awakening to dream
> I listen and feel through walls
> The tremble of many brotherly hands.

His words sprang out of the knowledge that all that he and his friends in the Resistance had attempted would be swept away amidst the ruins of Berlin. 'For a short while among dead walls sorrowful humanity will endure: thereafter all will be covered with

218

ivy. . . . We are the last. Our thoughts tomorrow will be empty chaff, blown by the wind and without value where young morning dawns.'

> When today I was lost in dreams
> I saw the whole host passing,
> Yorck and Moltke, Schulenburg, Schwerin
> Hassell, Popitz, Helfferich and Planck
> Not one with thoughts of gain
> Not one of them forgetting
> In pomp and circumstance, in mortal danger,
> The nation's desperate needs.
> My long despairing glance for them
> Who all had mind and rank and name
> And shared these cells with me
> And for them all the rope is waiting
> There are times when madness rules the land
> It is then that the best are hanged.

Albrecht's thoughts were dwelling on the past. He remembered his girlfriend as in a dream, and she stood over him and asked whether he had yet come to terms with himself. 'Now you test me in my dream that had neither pain nor sorrow. You nod and you ask me: "Are you recovered now?" I lie still, slowly beats my heart. What has remained is gratitude that travels to your grave in Engadin.' He thought of his brother Heinz who had been arrested for helping him to escape from the Gestapo. He very much hoped that his brother would survive, for he saw Heinz as the anchor which would hold the remnants of his family together.

Albrecht had been reproached for not escaping from Germany after his flight from Berlin, and he explained in the sonnet *Home* that it had not been his wish to run away from his country. If he had decided to leave he would have done so long before. It was a source of great comfort to him that the beauty of the mountains of southern Bavaria would remain untouched by the war; mountains which had become for him a symbol of indestructibility:

> They asked me about my escape
> Why did I miss the way to the Rhine
> To nearby Switzerland, swimming away
> Before the chase for me began in earnest.
> I would not leave my homeland
> That had given such good shelter
> Then she could hide me no more
> And I shall not see her again
> I am glad to know that its wall of mountains
> Hides our Alm and hut
> Though I must miss the mountain's beauty
> The walls of silver grey will endure
> Whether man climbs them or flees
> Until fresh ice encircles their peaks.

He likened the war to the launching of a vast avalanche, started by 'criminals and madmen', which had led to 'a push, a flurry, then a deadly cold'. He wrote in *The Rats* that German soldiers in their hordes had followed a Pied Piper who had wilfully led them to destruction:

219

A host of grey rats eats the land
Approaching the stream in wild array
In front a piper who with crazy sound
Binds them in maddened twitches
They leave full granaries abandoned
Waverers are grimly pushed along
Objectors cruelly chewed to death
Thus they speed towards the stream

The French church in Berlin hit by one of countless bombs dropped during Allied raids (Hulton-Deutsch)

Leaving ransacked fields behind
They smell blood and flesh in the turmoil
Shriller and harsher grows the sound
Now they storm into the abyss
A shrill whistle, a yelling screech
The crazy noise drowns into the stream
All rats are dead swept into the sea.

Albrecht now acknowledged that as early as the Olympic Games in 1936 he had foreseen that the magic of international co-operation and friendship had been illusory, and that Germany's rulers were abusing the Games for their own warlike purposes. In *Arena* he recaptured the memory of a conversation with Lord Vansittart, head of the British Foreign Office at the time of the Olympiad, and Albrecht wrote that Vansittart had said to him:

'Now they celebrate victory with flags
Soon they'll scream for blood
Then they will be authentic'
Vansittart finished;
I shut up too
His Lordship is right.

In their separate countries Vansittart and Haushofer occupied roles which were in certain respects similar. In Britain Vansittart continually gave warnings about the dangers inherent in Nazism, and implored the Government of Neville Chamberlain to rearm rapidly, but his warnings went unheeded. He had told Chamberlain facts which Chamberlain had not wanted to hear, and consequently Vansittart had been relegated to a minor role in the British Foreign Office. In Germany too Albrecht Haushofer had given his warnings:

They called me Cassandra in the office
Since, like the seer of Troy,
I had through bitter years
Foreseen the whole agony of death
Of people and country.
Though they praised my deep knowledge
They ignored all my warnings.
They were angry when I dared to interfere
When I adjuringly pointed to the future.
They drove the boat full-sail
In tempest on to the rocks
With shouts of early victory
Now they are shipwrecked and so are we.
An attempt in final distress to grasp the rudder has failed.
We now wait for the sea to engulf us.

In June 1938 Albrecht had told Ribbentrop and Hitler in the clearest possible terms, both verbally and in writing, that if Germany launched a military invasion into eastern Europe, Great Britain would fight in earnest together with France, and Britain would receive the full support of the U.S.A., the end result being an incalculable Russian

221

expansion into the heart of Europe. He had done everything within his power by non-violent means to prevent the outbreak of war. The broad outline of what he had said and written had been correct, and he could have given no better advice, but his warnings were discarded. Hitler thought that the British would at most only put up a token gesture of opposition, and, as always, Hitler was sure that he knew best.

In April 1945 it was manifest to everyone that the war was lost. The Russians were fighting within the outskirts of Berlin, slowly and determinedly burning their way towards the Unter den Linden and Kurfürstendamm, shattering virtually every house in their path.

Albrecht wrote in *Toward the End* that the war could not end until no corporals and generals dare say that it had not been lost. In his last poems he wrote that time had lost its value for him. He felt he knew how a man would feel in a boat without steering being swept towards the world's largest waterfalls. But Hitler even at this hour was not a man to acknowledge that he had been mistaken. He believed that a dead man would tell no tales. Mueller saw Hitler on most days and would almost certainly have drawn his attention to the fact that the last remnants of the Resistance were in Moabit Prison. The precise instructions which passed between them during those last days will probably never be known, because between 20 and 22 April the Gestapo and R.S.H.A. destroyed all their files, including the records of Albrecht Haushofer's interrogations. Mueller was covering all his tracks before he disappeared from Berlin without trace.

Even if the details of Hitler's instructions are not available for scrutiny, his policy was quite clear. Hitler had said, 'I'm beginning to doubt whether the German people is worthy of my great ideals', and it was his aim to kill any German who might be considered as a candidate for an alternative government to Nazism. If he could not rule, then as far as he was concerned nobody else would rule, and he would destroy as much as he could. That was Hitler's policy, and Mueller took measures to put that policy into effect on 21 April 1945.

Back in Moabit Prison during the afternoon of the next day, 22 April, twenty-one men had been freed, raising the hopes of those who remained. Late that night two groups of eight men were summoned from the cellars to receive their personal effects, so that the release of all prisoners should not be delayed.

In the first group were Professor Albrecht Haushofer; Max Jennewein, a mechanical engineer; Herbert Kosney, a Communist; Carlos Moll, a German Argentinian; Lieutenant-Colonel Ernst Munzinger of the O.K.H., Armed Forces High Command; Major Count Hans Victor Salviati, the Olympic athlete who had been Field Marshal von Rundstedt's adjutant from 1941 to 1943, and was the brother-in-law of Prince Friedrich Wilhelm of Prussia; Sosimoff, the Russian prisoner of war, whom the Gestapo had considered to be very important, and through whom Himmler may have wished to open peace negotiations with the Russians, and Colonel Wilhelm Staehle, who had been a member of the Abwehr and Commandant of the Invalidenhaus, Berlin.

In the second group were Klaus Bonhoeffer, a barrister and legal adviser to Lufthansa and brother of the theologian Dietrich Bonhoeffer; Hans John, a lawyer and assistant of Rudiger Schleicher; Richard Kuenzer, a Counsellor of Legation in the Foreign Office; Karl Marcks, a merchant; Wilhelm zür Nieden, an industrialist, Dr Friedrich Justus Perels, the legal adviser to the Confessional Church; Professor Dr Rudiger Schleicher, Chief of the Institute for Aviation Law at Berlin University and brother-in-law of Dietrich Bonhoeffer, and Hans Ludwig Sierks, a former Councillor of State.

They were a distinguished and varied group of men. They returned to their cells to pack what little clothing they had with them. Herbert Kosney helped his cell companion

Albrecht Haushofer with his packing. Among his belongings was a loaf of pumpernickel which he gave to Herbert.

Later that night the sixteen men were marched up the cellar steps to the prison yard, where they received the rest of their valuables such as pencils, cigarette lighters, watches, rings and wallets. They signed receipts and were asked to complete forms stating that they had been released, which they did. They were told by the prison commandant that they would be immediately released. One S.S. man mentioned to Herbert Kosney that he would see his wife soon.

Even Albrecht Haushofer may have been momentarily filled with hope. How can one describe all the pent-up emotions of a man at such a moment when he desperately wants to live? He walked with the other prisoners towards the prison's entrance, through a narrow hallway, when suddenly a flashlight was switched on, and they saw on both sides of the passage about thirty-five S.S. Sonder commando armed with machine pistols. Many of the faces under the steel helmets of the S.S. were those of youths. Albrecht had been promised his freedom; he had signed documents confirming that he had been freed, but when he saw the S.S. it must have been too much to hope for, too much to believe.

They went out on to the street outside the prison, surrounded by the S.S. who outnumbered them by more than two to one, and they were told by the S.S. Obersturmbannführer that they were going to be transferred to another prison and would be shot if they tried to escape. The sixteen prisoners were marched down the Lehrterstrasse towards the Invalidenstrasse where they were halted. They were asked to surrender any valuables which they might have, such as their watches which had just been given to them and for which they had signed receipts a few minutes before. Herbert Kosney noticed that it was 1.00 a.m. and Jennewein remarked that there were some marks in his pocket book; and the S.S. sergeant told him that the matter would be examined on the train.

The S.S. men turned towards the bombed-out Ulap Exhibition site. All the prisoners knew that this was not the way to the Potsdam station, even if the S.S. sergeant said that they were taking a short-cut. The prisoners marched through the rubble and debris pitted with bomb-holes and craters and entered the ruins of the once-massive building; there the S.S. stopped. Albrecht Haushofer's group was marched to the left and the rest were taken to the right. On the left Munzinger went first, followed by Herbert Kosney, Albrecht Haushofer and the others.

The prisoners were made to face the wall of the building. Then everything happened very quickly. Herbert Kosney heard shots nearby, and found himself staring at Albrecht Haushofer, who was standing absolutely still. Then they were mown down by a volley of shots in the back of the neck.

But one man was not dead: Herbert Kosney. He had turned his head, and felt himself struck a terrible blow from behind. The bullet had entered the back of his neck and had come out under his eye. Herbert lay on the ground still conscious and saw the S.S. Obersturmbannführer walk up to Colonel Munzinger's body, shine a torch at him, and fire his revolver into Munzinger's face. He saw him walk down the row of prostrate forms, putting a bullet through each man's head.

When he came to Herbert's body, Herbert heard him say that this pig had had enough, and that they would have to hurry, as they had more work to do. He put his boot into Herbert's face, and thereafter the still-conscious Herbert heard the sound of moaning and more shots, until all sounds ceased. Then he heard footsteps fading away and felt an uncanny stillness.

At last slowly and painfully he dragged himself towards his home, as he himself described it, like a hunted and wounded animal. At about 3.15 a.m. he crept up to his house in the Hagenauer Strasse, and it was some time before his wife realised that the battered figure covered in blood, collapsing in front of her, was her husband.

When he recovered consciousness several days later in a public hospital he found in his pockets a bloody piece of bread – the bread which had been given to him by Albrecht Haushofer, and the only tangible memory he had of the man who had been murdered at his side. Through Herbert the news leaked out and Heinz Haushofer, after being freed by the Russians, set out to search for his brother.

On 12 May Heinz found Albrecht where he had been shot. Clutched in the dead man's hand were scraps of paper with poems written out in longhand entitled *The Sonnets of Moabit*. The thirty-eighth sonnet was called 'Guilt':

> I lightly carry what the judge calls my guilt
> Guilt in planning and caring
> I would feel guilty had I not from inner duty
> Planned for the people's future
> But I am guilty other than you think:
> I should have sooner seen my duty
> I should have sharper condemned evil
> I have too long delayed my judgment.
> I now accuse myself
> I have long betrayed my conscience
> I have lied to myself and to others.
> I soon foresaw the evil's frightful path;
> I have warned,
> But my warnings were too feeble.
> I know today wherein lies my guilt.

Epilogue

After the July Plot Karl Haushofer had been imprisoned in Dachau Concentration Camp for a short period, but even that experience had not shaken his loyalty to the German State. To the old General patriotism meant everything, and the maxim 'My country right or wrong' had been one of the first articles of his political creed. He had always considered obedience to authority to be a moral necessity. His son Albrecht, on the other hand, did not shrink from the recognition that as an individual he had full responsibility for his own actions. Opposition might become a duty, and the plea of 'obedience to a superior authority' was never a valid excuse in his eyes where a moral issue was involved.

The German language contains two words for treason, *Hochverrat* and *Landesverrat*, and in all his activities with the opposition Albrecht attempted to draw a clear line between the two. The first word covers activities subversive to a particular system or regime and Albrecht had been prepared to engage in such activities. The second term is used for actions which are directed against the interests of the country itself, and he deliberately did not participate in such actions, as he was anxious to avoid the stigma of being called a traitor. His aim had not been to deliver Germany to her enemies but to secure a change of government which would enable Germany to negotiate a peace settlement, in which her interests as he saw them might be safeguarded.

For Karl Haushofer there was no such distinction; treason was treason and any German who worked against the State was a traitor. After the July Plot he learnt that Albrecht had been engaged in writing plans for the Resistance, that he was being sought everywhere by the Gestapo, and that he had gone into hiding. The old General thought that the disappearance of his son Albrecht would result in the persecution of the rest of the family. While he was sent to Dachau Concentration Camp – before his old friend General Ritter von Epp helped to secure his release – his other son Heinz was sent to Moabit Prison. Both Karl and Heinz Haushofer feared that the Gestapo might remove to a concentration camp Karl's wife Martha and Heinz's children, if accurate information as to Albrecht's whereabouts was not given. As it was Heinz's wife had been imprisoned in the Gestapo Prison in Munich for several months.

However, neither Karl nor Heinz knew where Albrecht was hiding, and in this case, because the Gestapo believed them, no irrevocable action was taken against the other members of the Haushofer family. Nonetheless Karl Haushofer was bitter with Albrecht for having endangered the rest of his family by running away from the Gestapo. Towards the end of the war he heard that Albrecht had been captured and interned in Moabit Prison. Frau Schnuhr approached him saying that something must be done to get legal aid

225

for his son, and he replied, 'Why should I do that? He has betrayed his country and his people and deserves no help from me.' At length he consented, but only for the 'honour of the family'.

After the unconditional surrender, Karl Haushofer was a broken man. He understood that all his teachings had been in vain, saw his country in ruins and was well aware that the Third Reich, which he had always supported, had murdered his own son. Throughout the years of Nazism he had supported Nazi propaganda, had written that Hitler was 'a God-given leader' and that the German people must direct their course with that of the Fuehrer. He now said in explanation that his teachings had been misused by the Nazis, and that for the last seven years – especially since Hess had left for England – he had lived under the fear that his half-Jewish wife would be taken to Theresienstadt or Auschwitz. He was a nineteenth-century imperialist similar in thinking to the British imperialist Cecil Rhodes, and he had supported the Third Reich, only because he would have supported any German state.

He wrote in his *Last Defence of German Geopolitics* that he had interceded with Hitler on 8 November 1938 because he had hoped that Hitler would be satisfied with the solution reached at Munich, and he called the period from 1938 onwards 'The Way of Sorrow for German Geopolitics'. Yet it had always been his belief that 'war was the highest test for human virtues such as could not be experienced in times of peace', and his teaching of geopolitics had amounted in practice to little more than the study of how Germany might annexe, colonise and dominate other nations by stealth, cunning and covert aggression. Considerations of abstract morality never played a large part in his thinking.

He had hoped that Albrecht would be the heir to his intellectual work, but Albrecht at the end of his life had wanted nothing to do with his father's teachings. He felt no bitterness, but he firmly believed that an obsession with geopolitics had made his father close his mind to the results of a desire for domination and a lust for war. He wrote in his poem *Acheron*, the River of Sorrow:

> Father was dazzled blind by dreams of power.
> I knew all mystery ahead of time;
> Destruction, fire, hunger, wounding, death
> The total horror of a devil's night.
>
> I have often taken conscious leave
> From all good things in life;
> Home, work, love, wine, bread.
>
> Now darkness rolls over me;
> Life is distant . . . Acheron near
> A tired eye searches after a star.

No prosecution was made against Karl Haushofer at Nuremberg because the American prosecuting team regarded his role as being academic and advisory. He was taken to Nuremberg merely to see Hess who was alleged to be suffering from amnesia and who refused to recognise him. He was also asked to prepare a last statement on German geopolitics, which he agreed to do. On his way back to his lodgings, Karl Haushofer said that Hess was completely sincere in his fanatical support of Hitler, that his flight to Britain was characteristic of him, and that at no other time had Hess concealed his plans from him. Whilst being driven back he could see the ruins of the bombed city and he was dismayed.

He had always been in favour of setting aside the Versailles Treaty; now he saw Germany occupied and with far less territory than she had had under the Treaty of

Versailles. He did not want to live in a Germany which had been defeated for the second time in a world war. In 1943 he had quarrelled with Albrecht and had told him that if the war was lost as Albrecht thought, he would kill himself, and his mind kept reverting to this theme.

Only the presence of his family kept him from putting his threat into action. At the end of 1945 after the return of his son Heinz, although his health was deteriorating, he did not wish to escape a confrontation regarding his life's work. Once he had completed his last defence of German geopolitics in which he claimed that his teachings had been misunderstood, and once he had discovered that Hess's counsel did not require him as a defence witness at the Nuremberg war trials he felt freed from all obligations. He told Heinz, 'You no longer need me' and again emphasised the right of the stoic to put an end to his life, once he had fulfilled all his duties.

He had been bitterly disillusioned, and harder than anything for him was the denunciation by his murdered son. It had only been because of the General's friendship with Hess, and because of his influence and encouragement that Albrecht had worked for the regime. But at the end of his life Albrecht bitterly regretted having succumbed and unlike his father he had made a final break with Nazism. His poem *The Father*, telling an Eastern legend similar to that of Pandora's Box, signified that there had been an irrevocable parting of the ways between father and son:

> A noble tale from the Orient
> Relates of evil spirits captive
> In the sea's dark night
> Sealed there by divine decree
> Until in a happy millennium
> A fisherman gains the key
> To unseal the captives
> Unless he throws his catch back into the sea.
> For my father the fates have spoken
> He once had it in his power
> To cast the demon back into the dark
> My father broke the seal
> But failed to see the evil
> He let the demon escape into the world.

Karl Haushofer had deep feelings of guilt which he admitted in private to a Roman Catholic priest, as is evident from the comments of the Reverend Edmund Walsh. Apparently Karl Haushofer understood that Albrecht had chosen to stay in Germany in 1933 and after Munich, to a large extent because his mother, to whom Albrecht was very close, had decided to remain. The most poignant of all of Albrecht's poems is *The Mother*, he might almost have foreseen what was to come.

> I see you in a candle's light
> Waiting in the dark portal
> You feel the cool mountain air;
> You shiver, Mother, and yet you stay
> You watch me pass into the night
> Wondering about my future;
> You smile, and yet you cry
> Filled with hopeless pain

227

I see you in your shining love
I see your white hair trembling
In the vast dark cool
And slowly you lower your face
While the candle still shines through
You shiver, Mother, go inside.

Major General Professor Karl Haushofer bitterly disillusioned. In the 'Sonnets of Moabit', Albrecht Haushofer wrote that his father failed to see the evil and let the demon escape into the world (Hulton-Deutsch)

Throughout his life Karl Haushofer had been an admirer of the ancient stoics and on 11 March 1946 he carried his admiration to its logical conclusion. On that Monday Karl and Martha Haushofer set out for their last walk through the woods. They stopped about half a mile from their house in a hollow by the stream under a willow tree. There they took poison. Martha was also hanged from the tree; the General was not strong enough to follow suit as the poison took effect. There they were found on the next day by Heinz. The Reverend Edmund Walsh visited the place shortly after and wrote:

> The lantern, with the extinguished candle which had lighted them through the darkness, lay beside them. Traversing their route step by step a few days after the double suicide – it was on the Ides of March – and attempting to reconstruct the scene as it was played out on that windy night on one of the loneliest hillsides in Bavaria, I could only liken it to some final act of a Greek tragedy. As if to seal his name and lifework to oblivion he left instructions to his son that no marker, memorial or other form of identification should ever be placed on or near his grave.

This was not the end of the story: in Britain most of the participants had survived. Indeed Ivone Kirkpatrick, who had identified Hess, developed a cordial relationship with Konrad Adenauer, the new Chancellor of Germany. But David Douglas-Hamilton, who had introduced Albrecht Haushofer to his brother Clydesdale, did not survive the war. He had commanded 603 (City of Edinburgh) Spitfire Squadron in Malta, and on 10 May

In Britain, Group Captain the Duke of Hamilton and Group Captain David McIntyre (left) receiving the freedom of Ayr from the Provost for services to aviation in 1944 (The Herald)

229

1942, the anniversary of Hess's flight, had led his squadron in a pitched battle for the supremacy of Malta, which turned out to be one of the most decisive victories over the Luftwaffe and almost certainly the turning point of the Second World War. It led to Hitler abandoning his invasion plans for Malta. Subsequently David had transferred to a Mosquito photo-reconnaissance squadron as a squadron leader and been killed on an operation on 2 August 1944, after being shot up over France by anti-aircraft fire, a few days before the American invasion of southern France.

His brother Malcolm, also an outstanding pilot, had been highly decorated with the Greek Air Force Cross, the Military Order of the British Empire and the Distinguised Flying Cross, after commanding another Mosquito photo-reconnaissance squadron. He went back to Germany and called on Prince Ernst August, the grandson of the Kaiser, with whom he and David had met before the war, knowing that they were to fight on opposite sides, and with whom they had argued late into the night as to how Germany should settle its differences with other nations. He knocked on the door of Schloss Blankenburg and, after a long time, a candle was seen coming down a distant corridor. The door opened and Ernst August said, 'Malcolm, I can hardly believe it'. He had survived the Gestapo interrogations in Moabit Prison.[1]

The war was at an end but most of Ernst August's lands were lost to him, for they were in East Germany and the Russian zone of occupation. Ernst August soon claimed British citizenship as a descendant of Queen Victoria, and in spite of opposition from the British Law Officers, won his case in the House of Lords.

David's third brother was Geordie, who became a group captain in East Africa. He had narrowly escaped death when the Wellington he was flying across the Bay of Biscay on 9 September 1943 had had its windscreen shot away during an attack by five Ju88 long-range fighters. The Luftwaffe records revealed that four of the Ju88s had failed to return to their base at Montpelier in France.[2] Geordie thought that one of his sergeant air gunners had shot down one and that the others ran out of fuel on the return flight.

Before long, Geordie became First Lord of the Admiralty, the First Sea Lord being Mountbatten. He had been with his brother, the Duke of Hamilton then the Marquis of Clydesdale at the Olympic Games and was certain that the latter never met Hess before the war.

As for Hamilton, he was preoccupied with Scottish matters and he treated the Hess episode as a four-day wonder. When Frau Hess wrote to him after the war asking for photographs of her husband's flight he did not reply and passed the letter on to the Foreign Office. He had not known Hess or his family before the war and in his view such requests were to be directed elsewhere.[3]

Twice in his life he had received massive publicity: when he had been the first man to fly over Mount Everest, and when Hess, whom he had never met and did not know, asked to see him. The two events had been linked, and Wolf Rüdiger Hess confirmed to the author in the House of Commons that Hess had asked to see Hamilton because the latter had been the first man to fly over Mount Everest.

Towards the end of his life Hamilton and his wife agreed to be painted by the great Austrian artist Oskar Kokoschka, whose paintings Hitler had denounced as degenerate. When Kokoschka arrived at Hamilton's house he saw a painting of Hawker Harts of 602 (City of Glasgow) Squadron diving through the air. Just as the leaders of the Luftwaffe had been impressed, so was Kokoschka, but in a very different way. The expression on his face was one of pain and anguish. He said to the author, 'I do hope they did not bomb my beautiful Vienna'. The author was able to reassure him that, while the squadron had shot down some eighty aircraft in the Battle of Britain, when equipped with Spitfires, it had not bombed Vienna.[4]

The Duke and Duchess of Hamilton *by the great Austrian artist, Oskar Kokoschka, whose painting Hitler had denounced as degenerate (Scottish National Gallery of Modern Art)*

When Hamilton spoke about Hitler's Germany, he regretted that the German resistance to Hitler had not succeeded in killing him at the time of Stauffenberg's bomb plot of 20 July 1944, or earlier for that matter. The conspirators paid heavily for that failure. More than 4,000 people involved or associated with the German Resistance to Hitler were killed, including Albrecht Haushofer – some of them hanged on piano wires. Hitler had been determined to kill those Germans capable of forming an alternative government to his own, as well as those who stood in his way. In addition, more than half of all German fatalities in the Second World War, not to mention countless other deaths of combatants and civilians alike, occurred between 20 July 1944 and the end of the war.

But in one sense the German Resistance to Hitler had not totally failed. Major General Henning von Tresckow, Albrecht's colleague in the Wednesday Society, had written:

> I believe Hitler to be the arch-enemy, not only of Germany but of the entire world . . .
> Just as God once promised Abraham that he would spare Sodom if only ten just men could be found in the city, I have reason to hope that, for our sake, he will not destroy Germany. No-one among us can complain about his death, for whoever joined our ranks put on the poisoned shirt of Nessus. A man's moral worth is established only at the point where he is prepared to give his life for his convictions.[5]

The *Sonnets of Moabit* of Albrecht Haushofer remained as a testimony of the thinking of those Germans who had held positions of responsibility and wished to be dissociated from the catastrophe brought about by the Third Reich.

What Churchill said to Hamilton in the lobby of the House of Commons in 1939 proved to be true. The war lasted as long as Hitler, almost to the day.

Aviation remained the theme of Hamilton's life. He became chairman of the Scottish Aviation Company at Prestwick, with David McIntyre (the other pilot who flew over Mount Everest with him), becoming chief executive. Prestwick became Britain's second international airport in 1946 and, after a number of mergers, Scottish Aviation became the Scottish Division of British Aerospace, employing some 2,000 people.

Hamilton was aware that advances in aviation took place at the cost of human life. In 1964 he went to search for his brother Malcolm who had disappeared with his son Niall in a light aircraft during a huge storm around Mount Cameroon, and some years later the wreckage was discovered.

In 1966 he was asked by the Prime Minister, Harold Wilson, to chair a Government Commission into the training of civil airline pilots. Its recommendations were implemented, and he became president of the British Airline Pilots Association, whose members were the most highly paid trade unionists in Britain.

An aviation industry in Scotland was the legacy which he and David McIntyre left their country. Even if they had not done that and had not lived to see the fulfilment of their dream, they would still be remembered. For Britain has not lost its ardour for adventure, and there will always be admiration for young men of courage who are willing to risk their lives and face the perils of the unknown.

Ivone Kirkpatrick returned to Germany as High Commissioner and was regarded by the younger generation of Germans as one of the architects of a modern, democratic Germany. He struck up a good working relationship with President Heuss of Germany as well as with Adenauer. When Kirkpatrick returned to Britain, he took up the appointment as head of the British Foreign Office from 1953–1957 where he worked closely with the British Prime Minister, Anthony Eden, with whom he had worked when Eden was Foreign Secretary.

But in Germany there remained Rudolf Hess.

After the war Hess was brought to Nuremberg to be tried as a Nazi war criminal, and while he was there some of the doctors began to have serious doubts as to whether he was fit to plead. In the view of some of the Allied psychiatrists, Hess appeared to be suffering from amnesia.

As Hess later admitted his amnesia was a pretence – he had hoped to be repatriated, by faking mental disorders, and had tried hard but without success. He had, however, succeeded in deceiving some of the British psychiatrists and was proud of this fact. His game included feigning mental blackouts and then being unable to recall who or where he was. When he grew fed up with having such an 'attack' he would choose to remember his own name and would gaze around in astonishment. He was well aware of the fact that he had the ability to fool psychiatrists, and he realised when he arrived at Nuremberg that it could be a useful defence to suggest that he was suffering from amnesia. With this in mind he refused to take the witness stand. Instead he indulged in play-acting and insisted on reading an average of two books a day while the trials were in progress.

He even refused to recognise Goering, Ribbentrop, Papen, Bohle of the Ausland Organisations and Karl Haushofer. The doctors at Nuremberg were puzzled and, while they all agreed that Hess was 'medico-legally' sane, many of them thought that his amnesia was genuine or partly genuine and might interfere with his ability to conduct his defence and to understand the details of the past.

Only one man told Hess to his face that he was a fraud – the American commandant, Colonel Burton C. Andrus, who was in charge of the prison. Colonel Andrus told Hess that he was feigning and that this was 'not a very manly thing to do'. 'Hess, you owe it to

Sir Ivone Kirkpatrick with President Heuss of West Germany (Deutsch Press Agency, Frankfurt)

yourself, your family and to the German nation to tell the truth. I think you should go into court and make a clean breast of this and tell them you have been faking amnesia.' Hess thanked him, obviously uncomfortable that an appeal had been made to his sense of honour.

On the next day, part of the second afternoon session was taken up with a discussion as to whether Hess was fit to plead, when suddenly Hess rose in court and surprised everyone, not least his own counsel, by making a declaration:

> In order to forestall the possibility of my being pronounced incapable of pleading in spite of my willingness to take part in further proceedings, and in order to receive sentence alongside my comrades, I would like to make the following declaration before the Tribunal. . . .
>
> Henceforth my memory will again respond to the outside world. The reasons why I simulated loss of memory were tactical. The fact is that it is only my ability to concentrate that is somewhat reduced. However, my capacity to follow the trial, to defend myself, to put questions to witnesses or even to answer questions, is not affected thereby.
>
> I emphasise that I bear the full responsibility for everything that I have done or signed as signatory or co-signatory.

The court then declared Hess fit to plead, and when the psychiatrists Douglas Kelley and G. M. Gilbert saw Hess in his cell afterwards he was 'quite like an actor after his first night'. His memory was perfect and with alacrity he answered questions about his youth, his role in the Party, his flight to Britain and his imprisonment. Hess later said that if it had not been for his acting ability he would have been sentenced

*Hess with Goering, to his left, and Ribbentrop, on his right, at the Nuremberg war trials in 1945
(Hulton-Deutsch)*

to death. There was certainly no question of his regretting anything that the Nazis had done.

When he was asked whether he thought differently of Hitler, having heard the evidence about the millions of human beings murdered in the concentration camps, Hess said, 'I suppose every genius has a demon in him – you can't blame him – it is just in him'. His view of Hitler had not changed and he still worshipped him as his leader. In his final statement from the dock, Hess gave the court the impression that if he was given the opportunity he would do everything all over again:

> I was permitted to work for many years of my life under the greatest son whom my country has brought forth in its thousand-year history. Even if I could, I would not want to erase this period from my existence. I am happy to know that I have done my duty to my people, my duty as a German, as a National Socialist, as a loyal follower of my Fuehrer. I do not regret anything.
>
> If I were to begin all over again, I would act just as I have acted, even if I knew that in the end I should meet a fiery death at the stake.

The court found Hess guilty of making preparations for war and conspiring against the peace. The presiding judge found it proven that Hess had been a willing participant in German aggression against Austria, Czechoslovakia and Poland. He also found it significant that his flight to Britain took place some ten days after the date on which Hitler decided that 22 June 1941 would be the date for attacking the Soviet Union. There had been no suggestion that Hess was not completely sane when the acts charged against him were committed and his sentence was one of imprisonment for life. With others Hess was transferred to Spandau Prison in Berlin.

The Russian judge was not satisfied with the disposal of Hess's case and he dissented on the grounds that Hess was guilty of crimes against humanity in the eastern occupied territories, and that the only justified sentence could be death, a view to which the Russian Government has adhered to this day.

As the Russian Government saw it, Russia lost between twenty and twenty-five million of its countrymen at the hands of the Nazi aggressors, and if Hess had succeeded in getting Britain out of the war in 1941 a great many more Russians might have died and the final outcome of the war might have been in doubt. So when he was sentenced to imprisonment for life as a war criminal, the Russian Government determined that that sentence would mean precisely what it said. On Friday 30 September 1966 Hess became the last prisoner in Spandau. The Nazi Youth leader Baldur von Schirach and the Nazi Minister for Armaments and War Production, Albert Speer, were released, and in silence Hess watched them depart.

During the years of his imprisonment he had kept himself occupied by working in the garden, and by writing letters to his wife which were published in three volumes. His letters were articulate, literate and erudite, showing a knowledge of history, linguistics,

Spandau Prison with Russian guards outside (UPI)

Rudolf Hess as a young Nazi (Hulton-Deutsch)

engineering, painting, music, folklore, geography, astronomy and languages. They also revealed a great interest in his son.

These letters, published in book form, have sold better in Germany than any of the works on the German resistance to Hitler, partly because his letters portrayed a human interest story, and partly because many Germans had a sneaking regard for the Nazi leader who tried to save the Third Reich from entanglement in ever-expanding war on more than one front. Besides, there was a widespread feeling in Germany that Hess was being used by the Russians as a pawn in East-West relations, and that they would not release him without major concessions in other fields from the British, Americans and French stationed in West Berlin.

For the last years of Hess's life the governments of Britain, the U.S.A. and France would have preferred to free Hess, but they were not willing to make an international issue

236

*Rudolf Hess as an old man in Spandau Prison fifty years later (*The Times*)*

over his release with the Russians. Their outlook probably had a certain amount in common with the opinion expressed by Winston Churchill:

> Reflecting upon the whole of this story, I am glad not to be responsible for the way in which Hess has been and is being treated. Whatever may be the moral guilt of a German who stood near to Hitler, Hess had, in my view, atoned for this by his completely devoted and fanatic deed of lunatic benevolence. He came to us of his own free will, and, though without authority, had something of the quality of an envoy. He was a medical and not a criminal case, and should be so regarded.

On the previous page Churchill had written, 'But he was more than a medical case', and it may be that, if he had known the extent of Hess's direct participation and involvement in all of Hitler's actions up to May 1941, he might have been less magnanimous. Nonetheless the point remains that Churchill undoubtedly would not have wished Hess to have been sent to prison for life.

Churchill was not alone in this opinion. Hess's release was strongly supported after 1970 by Airey Neave, then the most highly decorated M.P. in the House of Commons, who had served the Indictment on Hess at Nuremberg. The case for his release rested on three grounds.

First, all the evidence suggested that by 1970 he was not a danger to anybody, and that if released he would rapidly fade into the background.

Secondly, it had not served any useful purpose to keep him in Spandau guarded by a large number of soldiers at considerable cost, imposing a dull and denigrating duty on the soldiers concerned.

Thirdly, it had no symbolic value to keep him in Spandau, but has served to create sympathy for him, especially in Germany.

It seemed that even execution would have been more humane than to spend more than 37 years in prison, without any eventual hope of release. Indeed, whatever the arguments for executing Hess at Nuremberg in 1946 may have been, which the Soviet judge supported, there appeared to be no case at all for keeping him in prison after 1970, under the detention of many soldiers.

As long ago as May 1976 Cyril Townsend, Conservative MP for Bexley, Bexley Heath, and Ken Weetch, Labour MP for Ipswich, the chairman and secretary of an All Party Committee in the House of Commons to secure Hess's release, led a deputation to the Soviet Embassy. They were received by two officials who rejected all human considerations, but who were momentarily affected by the force of Ken Weetch's arguments when he said that if they kept Hess imprisoned until death, they might be making a martyr out of him.

The All Party Committee in Parliament came to the considered view that Hess, having sustained a mild stroke in December 1978, should have been looked after in the British Military Hospital in West Berlin.

Nonetheless, the Soviet Union remained determined to retain a foothold in West Berlin and to keep a military presence in Spandau. Besides, they knew that Hess remembered the details of the Nazi-Soviet Pact, formed by Ribbentrop and Molotov in 1939, all of which meant that the Russians would want Hess to stay in Spandau Prison.

Many in the West shared Churchill's view that Hess should be freed, and by 1970 few could see any point in his continued imprisonment.

On 17 August 1987 Rudolf Hess was found dead in Spandau Prison in the early afternoon. Attempts were made to resuscitate him and he was driven to the British Military Hospital. He was pronounced dead at 16.10 hours. On the next day the U.S. director of Spandau Prison, confirming that Hess had attempted to commit suicide, announced that there would be an investigation into the actual cause of death.

The four powers responsible for Spandau Prison, the U.S.A., Great Britain, the U.S.S.R. and France, carried out an investigation which included a full autopsy and an inquiry by the Special Investigation Branch of the Royal Military Police.

On 17 September 1987 a final statement was issued by the Four Powers on the death of Rudolf Hess:

> Investigations have confirmed that on 17 August Rudolf Hess hanged himself from a window latch in a small summer house in the prison garden, using an electrical extension cord which had for some time been kept in the summer house for his use in connection with a reading lamp. Attempts were made to revive him and he was then rushed to the British Military Hospital where, after further unsuccessful attempts to resuscitate him, he was pronounced dead at 16.10.

A note addressed to Hess's family was found in his pocket. This note was written on the reverse side of a letter from his daughter-in-law dated 20 July 1987. It began with the words 'Please would the Governors send this home. Written a few minutes before my death.' The senior document examiner from the laboratory of the British Government Chemist, Mr P. A. M. Beard, has examined the note, and concluded that he can see no reason to doubt that it was written by Rudolf Hess.

A full autopsy was performed on Hess's body on 19 August in the British Military Hospital by Dr J. Malcolm Cameron. The autopsy was conducted in presence of medical representatives of the Four Powers. The report noted a linear mark on the left side of the neck consistent with a ligature. Dr Cameron stated that in his opinion death resulted from asphyxia, caused by compression of the neck due to suspension.

The investigations confirmed that the routine followed by staff on the day of Hess's suicide was consistent with normal practice. Hess had tried to cut his wrists with a table knife in 1977. Immediately after this incident warders were placed in his room and he was watched 24 hours a day. This was discontinued after several months as impracticable, unnecessary and an inappropriate invasion of Hess's privacy.

There is no doubt of the accuracy of the statement by the Four Powers. Hess had tried to commit suicide twice during the war while in Britain and in Spandau in 1987 he succeeded in taking his own life.

After the cataclysm of Nazism and its fall Hess had become a relic of the past, which brings to mind Albrecht Haushofer's prescient sonnet *The Great Flood*:

*From 1966 to 1987 Rudolf Hess remained the solitary prisoner of Spandau Prison, guarded by Russian, French, American and British soldiers in rotation (*The Times*)*

> I travelled once the Mississippi
> When under its brown floods
> For thousand miles towards the bay
> The fields around were buried
> An empty image of former yields
> Of green crop, of golden harvest
> Where busy hands each year
> Had worked, home by home.
> All escaped who could:
> The rest were doomed to die.
> The plain was empty,
> Then the flood moved to the sea
> Sunlight courted the damp slime
> Soon the land woke to new life.

In a sense Albrecht was correct: the flood which had convulsed Germany and Europe has gone and Germany has revived. Albrecht had stood in its way and had been swept out to the ocean, where he was drowned. The flood also destroyed the world of his father and mother, who followed in its wake. Only Rudolf Hess remained, one of the pieces of debris which were cast up, and a grim reminder of an age forever gone.

NOTES

1. Account given to the author by Prinz Ernst August.
2. Letter dated 29 November 1985 from the Bundesarchiv in Koblenz.
3. Hamilton papers.
4. 602 (Bomber) Squadron converted to fighters shortly before the war.
5. Bullock, *Hitler and Stalin: Parallel Lives*, page 933.

Afterword

When I discussed the saga with the 14th Duke of Hamilton, whom Hess had asked for on arrival in Britain on 10 May 1941, he said that the key to the whole story was Albrecht Haushofer.

Albrecht had acted as a special adviser and special envoy to Hitler and Ribbentrop in the mid-1930s and had told them that if Germany launched a war of aggression into Eastern Europe, the British would fight with the full support of the United States of America. Both Hitler and Ribbentrop had disbelieved him and rejected his advice.

When Albrecht's letter of 23 September 1940 to Hamilton was discussed, the Intelligence Branch of the R.A.F. considered Albrecht to be a significant German. They were not alone in that view. S.S. Gruppenführer Heinrich Mueller, Chief of the Gestapo, gave orders for the murder of Albrecht as well as the last remnants of the German Resistance to Hitler.

Mueller believed that Albrecht would have been the man whom the leaders of the German Resistance to Hitler would have called in to handle peace negotiations once Hitler and the S.S. had been removed from power by the Army. In his view, Albrecht was the man with the ability and expertise to prepare the necessary plans for General Beck and Carl Goerdeler, *if only* the bomb of Klaus von Stauffenberg had killed Hitler.

Mueller also regarded Albrecht as a very clever Jew, with a famous German father, at a time when he was organising the mass murder of all Jews. There was a further reason why Mueller wanted Albrecht dead. Albrecht's advice to the German leadership had been entirely correct, and Ribbentrop and Hitler had been absolutely wrong. That was something Mueller did not wish to be revealed, and he arranged the systematic destruction of all Albrecht's papers and photographs at his former residence in Berlin. If Hitler and the Nazi regime were not to be allowed to rule, no other Germans capable of taking their place were to be allowed to do so either.

Albrecht regarded himself as a patriotic German of partly Jewish descent. In 1933 it would have been so easy to leave Germany and so wise. But Albrecht was tempted to stay, because his father was a very close friend of Hitler's deputy, Rudolf Hess. Besides, Albrecht had not wished to put at risk his mother, who was of half-Jewish origin. He had decided to stay. Thereafter, on becoming a German Foreign Affairs expert on Britain he had tried unsuccessfully to prevent the Second World War. In so doing he unwittingly became involved at a later stage in the most dramatic Nazi peace overture of the Second World War.

In different circumstances Albrecht might have risen to become head of the German Foreign Office. But he did not live in normal times but under a dictator who, in Churchill's

A photograph of Albrecht Haushofer with professors of the German Swiss faculty in 1940, one of the few photographs which S.S. Gruppenführer Mueller had failed to destroy (Bundesarchive, Potsdam)

words, was a 'maniac of ferocious genius'. As it was, he had to wait in Moabit Prison for the inevitable S.S. assassination squad, along with the last remnants of the German Resistance to Hitler. In those last hours he could see, through the cell window, the nature of the German tragedy which had engulfed Europe and so much of the rest of the world. Berlin was burning as a result of the war of Hitler and Ribbentrop, which he, Albrecht, had sought to prevent.

In his final poem he likened his fate to that of a rudderless boat being swept towards the Niagara Falls.

> Day and night were full of dreams
> Time has no value
> I forget to measure
> the hours, the weeks
> And lose all memory of them.
>
> Yet dreams pass back in time,
> I wake to the clanking key
> Announcing my midday bowl of soup
> And prepare for daily chores.
>
> Shaken from my dreams
> I know how one feels

242

In his last hours
Lashed to a rudderless boat;

Water beats against the boat.
The stream races
The hand is bound.

It was in such poems that Albrecht acknowledged that in the end with Nazism there were and could be no compromises to be made.

Appendix

THE SONNETS OF MOABIT BY ALBRECHT HAUSHOFER

These sonnets written by Albrecht Haushofer contain the anguished thoughts of a distressed man under S.S. guard in Moabit Prison, expecting to be killed. They are the poems of a person of patriotic sentiment who hated the excesses of war and all that it stood for, and whose peace plans for the German Resistance to Hitler never amounted to more than unfulfilled hopes.

These poems have been translated into English and put into verse by my great friend, Dr Eugene Pugatch of the United States of America, with the assistance of Mr Daniel Knutson.

Of the eighty poems written, some seven have been chosen which reveal the quality of his writing and the catastrophe of world war. The poem 'Barbarism' condemns Hitler for countless atrocities greater in their extent than even those of Genghis Khan. 'Acheron' is the name given to the river over which the dead were ferried in ancient Greece towards the underworld. In this and other poems Albrecht is asserting that while his father was not a Nazi, he was 'dazzled blind by dreams of power' and that he had allowed evil to swirl into the world.

'Arena' is particularly significant because it related to a meeting which Albrecht had with Lord Vansittart, head of the British Foreign Office during the Berlin Olympic Games in 1936 and of Vansittart's conviction that the celebrations and propaganda were merely a prelude to war.

'Rain of Bombs' describes the carpet bombing of Berlin and the hopes of a prisoner like himself to survive just one more day. 'Nemesis' symbolises just retribution when Judge Roland Freisler was killed. He had been the vindictive President of the Tribunal sentencing to death members of the German Resistance to Hitler. But on 3 February 1943 an American bombing raid hit the court killing Freisler who had relished sending so many to their deaths.

'Towards the End' laments the fact that the war will continue until those in command of the German Armed Forces recognise the defeat which is staring them in the face. Yet as long as Hitler lives madness will rule the land and 'misery beyond measure wells up over the earth'.

The poems he wrote are perhaps the most poignant testimonial to the German Resistance to Hitler, whose actions were too little and too late.

APPENDIX I

The Poems of Albrecht Haushofer

BARBARISM

During evil times in Syracuse
The choir chants of Aeschylus
Would spring the inmates
From miseries of jail-life.

Even Genghis Khan, covered in blood,
As his warriors raised pyramids of skulls,
Ordered spared, the artist and the wise.

Restraint has passed.
Who dares be Ghengis Khan today?
Who dares trade captives for songs?

Thus is past barbarism praised.
Today all skulls are equal.
In all, there are too many skulls.

ACHERON

A great poet asserted
That one must even move the Acheron
If gods cannot be cajoled for help.
My father has stubbornly echoed it.

Father was dazzled blind by dreams of power.
I knew all misery ahead of time;
Destruction, fire, hunger, wounding, death
The total horror of a devil's night.

I have often taken conscious leave
From all good things in life;
Home, work, love, wine, bread.

Now darkness rolls over me;
Life is distant . . . Acheron near
A tired eye searches after a star.

ARENA

At the end, I sat at night
With an English guest.
Outside, festive lights flickered;
Wine shimmered in our glasses.

His Lordship stopped to speak:
'I've asked myself . . .
What is missing from the feast?'
Now I know:
For the drunken masses,
Lions   Tigers   Blood

He sneered;
An ancient lore erupted
On his chiselled face;
A Caesar spoke:
   'The rest is lies
   Now they celebrate victory with flags
   Soon they'll scream for blood
   Then they will be authentic'

Vansittart finished;
I shut up too
His Lordship is right.

RAIN OF BOMBS

Out of a clear sky
One carpet of bombs after the other
Rushes deadly close to me.
Just how deadly near the path
Is reckoned by he, who fenced in,
Listens to the roar.

Quite well we know our lives
Are cheap as straw: The German noose,
The Russian slug behind the neck,
The British bomb presented as our lot.

Some miracle it would be were fate to grant us
Continued existence
Bereft of consequence
     meaning
     or goal
We know it: and yet thank the *game*
That *game* of chance
    Which could kill us with every throw
Yet spares us till now.
Who does not hope for the reward
Of one more day!

NEMESIS

Only yesterday he damned four to the noose;
Today he lies in ruins
    dead
His rope and axe service is over,
His realm of power a pile of rubble.

Judgment . . . a word with weight . . .
He rejoiced
When he tilted the scales to the evil side
When he ushered new necks for hanging.
No regrets
At sentences of death.

Judgment . . . was it by chance . . .
A thousand bombs rain down
On humans in this city?
Could one bomb have been the judge?

Judgment . . . many of the dead
Pleaded in vain for a reason;
For that reason, don't judge
We are all surveyed by a higher court.

TOWARDS THE END

Voices reach us from outside, shrill and hoarse.
The cripple carps in terror
Others stretch out their arms,
And with a hollow cry produce the dead salute of victory.

Even a fool with experience can sense the end.
Yet the war, this time again, cannot end
Till corporals and generals
Renounce the claim they are not lost.

What use if logic demonstrates, mathematically, the end?
Madness can comprehend
Only what it must feel.

Madness, madness alone, was master of this land;
Its path of glory ending in corpse-strewn fields.
Misery, beyond measure, wells up over the earth.

247

Sources and Select Bibliography

I. BRITISH GOVERNMENT DOCUMENTS

Since the publication of *Motive for a Mission: The Story Behind Rudolf Hess's Flight to Britain* in 1971 by the author, further official information became available at intervals. Under the Thirty Year Rule, Cabinet minutes, some Foreign Office records and some papers of the War Office, Ministry of Information and Air Ministry became accessible for public scrutiny at the Public Record Office at Kew.

(1) The Cabinet minutes relating to Hess can be traced on the open shelves.

(2) The most important series of documents are those of the Prime Minister's Office, PREM 3/219/1–7, which include Cabinet papers, reports, copies of Press cuttings, extracts from Hansard and a brief biography on Hess. These documents show clearly that the British Government's refusal to make a full public statement about the Hess mission made the Soviet Union very suspicious.

(3) The relevant Foreign Office files are FO371/26565 and 26566, although some references to Hess can be found in other files by studying the index. These files include the advice of senior officials as to how Parliamentary questions should be answered.

(4) The War Office file WO199/3288A is the Scottish Command Report, recording exactly what happened to the prisoner on 10 and 11 May 1941 after Hess's arrival at Eaglesham, near Glasgow.

(5) The Ministry of Information file 1/912 is an interesting file including letters from officials enquiring as to what facts should be made public, and extracts from letters intercepted by the censor referring to Hess, together with telegrams sent to him after his arrival.

(6) The Air Ministry file AIR19/564 contains letters from Government Ministers expressing concern about Group Captain the Duke of Hamilton's libel action against certain Communists, in case Hess might be called as a witness. It does not include a photocopy of the apology, contained in a statement which appeared in *The Times* on 19 February 1942, settling the action.

II. BRITISH GOVERNMENT DOCUMENTS RELEASED IN 1992

Some Foreign Office Records on Hess had been classified for seventy-five years. When this was raised in Parliament on 3 June 1992 the Foreign Secretary, Douglas Hurd, announced that the extensive papers would be released in two batches. The first batch was released on 10 June and the second on 2 July.

The papers released relate to the arrival, interrogation and incarceration of Hess between 10 May 1941 and the Nuremberg War Trials, after the conclusion of the war. In the first batch were papers giving:
1. details of the flight
2. the interrogation report
3. copies of correspondence between Hess and his family and friends
4. correspondence about his detention at Abergavenny and
5. miscellaneous papers including dental records

The references for these papers at the Public Record Office are FO 371/26565 extracts C5251, C5253, C5301, C5589, and also FO 1093 Piece Numbers 1–5.

The second batch of papers – some 1500 sheets – released on 2 July turned out to be much more interesting and they are contained in FO1093/6–20, covering the considerable number of aspects relating to Hess from 1941 to 1945. These include:
1. Papers relating to MI5. The few papers concerned are in FO1093/11–12 and they relate to the handling of Albrecht Haushofer's letter to the Duke of Hamilton dated 23 September 1940 which had been intercepted by the censor and which suggested a meeting in Lisbon. In FO1093/12 is the original letter itself written in Albrecht Haushofer's handwriting.

2. Personal effects of Hess. On arrival in Britain Hess's personal effects were collected. These included the visiting cards of Dr Albrecht Haushofer and of Major-General Professor Karl Haushofer and are to be found in FO1093/. There is an inventory of the medicines found on Hess in FO1093/10 and there are letters about the 1000 Reichsmarks in 100 mark notes from Hess's wallet which was converted into sterling in 1943 to cover the costs of books which Hess purchased in captivity.

3. Interrogation reports. These include Mr MacFarlane's account of a first view of Hess and the account of an interpreter of one of the first interrogations by the Home Guard. There is the original manuscript note in pencil by Ivone Kirkpatrick of his interview with Hess on 15 May in FO1093/11. Transcripts of the Hamilton/Kirkpatrick/Simon interviews were released in the first batch on 10 June 1992. Correspondence relating to Lord Simon's meeting with Hess on 9 June 1941 and Lord Beaverbrook's on 9 September 1941 is included together with papers relating to other interrogations.

4. Intelligence information from Hess. What Hess said was of little operational value. He did not give away the plans to attack Russia. However, at a later stage various written statements from Hess include lengthy memoranda on the desirability of Anglo–German co-operation against a Bolshevik enemy, set to become 'the world power of the future' in FO1093/12.

5. The failure to use Hess's presence for propaganda purposes. The Foreign Office took the view that the 'undiluted truth about the Hess case does not make good propaganda' and the Foreign Secretary Anthony Eden declined to make any public statement which was 'wide of the truth' in FO1093/7. A policy of leaving the Germans floundering and of saying nothing was adopted. A variety of proposals, such as making a broadcast from edited recordings of Hess's conversations, were not followed up. There was also considerable concern that Hess must be prevented from making any further announcement if he was called as a witness in a libel action which the Duke of Hamilton was instigating against the prominent Communist Mr Harry Pollitt in FO1093/9.

6. Medical reports on Hess. Many of the papers had been published in *The Case of Rudolf Hess* edited by Brigadier J.R. Rees, the senior consulting psychiatrist who frequently attended Hess. These papers relate to his health and medical treatment, as well as dealing with his suicide attempts and state of mind. While the doctors believed him to be mentally ill, suffering from paranoid psychosis, hysterical amnesia and delusions, he was not certifiably insane. Therefore he would not be repatriated.

7. The status of Hess. Minutes from Churchill, Eden and Cadogan deal with Hess's status as a prisoner of war, and papers relate to Hess's regular contacts with the Swiss Ministers in London, Switzerland acting as the protecting power.

8. Hess's correspondence. This includes copies of letters to his wife and aunt Frau Rothacker and to his family. There are also originals of his letters to Hitler dated 14 June 1941 in FO1093/8 and of his letter to the Duke of Hamilton of 19 May 1941 which was not transmitted, in FO1093/11. There are copies of letters to Lord Beaverbrook, to the Swiss Minister and to King George VI, along with papers about censorship of his letters.

9. The guarding of Hess. A great deal of time and effort went into the security arrangements for Hess whilst he was detained at Mytchett Place (Camp Z) near Aldershot, and at Maindiff Court, Abergavenny in Wales. Arising out of discovery of a plan by Polish Forces to kidnap Hess, security at Maindiff Court was very tight (FO1093/14).

10. Hess at Nuremberg. Some of the papers deal with the issue of Hess being eligible to stand trial as a war criminal. Since the medical reports revealed that he was not insane in 1941, Foreign Office officials believed he should be included amongst those to be charged as war criminals but that the matter of whether he was fit to plead should be left to the court (FO1093/18).

These documents virtually complete the release of the Hess papers. One paper was withheld from the batch opened on 10 June 1992 for reasons which have nothing to do with the substance of the Hess question and one paper was withheld from the release made on 2 July 1992 for similar reasons.

There was one War Office file, WO199/3288B, which had been classified for seventy-five years. Following it's review by the M.O.D. it has been available in the Public Records Office since January 1992. These are medical records relating to Hess after his arrival in Britain.

The file DEFE1/134 was also opened in 1992, and related to the facts concerning the interception of Albrecht Haushofer's letter in 1940 by the censor and the fact that delay in dealing with it was not the fault of the censor.

III. DOCUMENTS AND UNPUBLISHED MATERIAL

1. Hartschimmelhof papers, in the possession of Martin Haushofer, containing the letters of Albrecht Haushofer to his parents.
2. The Haushofer Documents, in the German Federal Archives in Koblenz.
3. The Haushofer Documents, in the National Archives of the USA and in the Manuscript Division of the Library of Congress, Washington.
4. The papers of the 14th Duke of Hamilton, accessible to scholars, and catalogued by the Scottish Record Office. These include letters from General Milch, Albrecht Haushofer and reports to the Prime Minister after Hess's Flight. His papers were voluminous with relatively little on Germany, but what was there was of interest. The letters from General Milch were found in files separate from his files on Hess and the invitation sent on behalf of Goering to the Lilienthal Society showed that they regarded him as a significant pioneering aviator.
5. Hansard 1918–1945 and documents on German foreign policy 1918–45.
6. The trial of the German Major War Criminals before the International Military Tribunal. Proceedings Vols. I–XXIII, Nuremberg 1947–1949. Documents in Evidence Vols. XXIV–XLII, Nuremberg 1947–1949.
7. The K.G.B. papers on Hess in Moscow include the allegation of Moravetz that the British Secret Service had lured Hess to Britain, something which just did not happen. It is not surprising that Moravetz's memoirs contain no repetition of this allegation.

The sources were given in full in *Motive for a Mission: The Story Behind Rudolf Hess's Flight to Britain* (Macmillan 1971) and again in the second edition published by Mainstream Publishing in 1979 and by Corgi in 1981.

The Truth About Rudolf Hess includes the newer sources to avoid confusion, the previous sources being well documented and well known.

IV. MEMOIRS DIARIES, ETC.

Andrus, Col. Burton C., *The Infamous of Nuremberg* (London, 1969).
Ansel, L., *Hitler Confronts England* (Durham, 1960).
Avon, Earl of, *The Eden Memoirs*, The Reckoning (London, 1965).
Bakker, G., *Duitse Geopolitiek 1919–45* (Assen, 1967).
Baynes, Norman H., *Hitler's Speeches 1922–39* (OUP, 1942).
Beneš, Dr Eduard, *Memoirs* (London, 1954).
Bernadotte, Folke, *The Fall of the Curtain* (London, 1945).
Best, Captain S. Payne, *The Venlo Incident* (London, 1950).
Bethge, Eberhard, *Dietrich Bonhoeffer, A Biography* (London, 1970).
Bird, Eugene K., *The Loneliest man in the world* (Secker & Warburg, 1974).
Boehm, Eric H., *We Survived* (California, 1966).
Boldt, Gerhard, *In the Shelter with Hitler* (Edinburgh, 1948).
Bonhoeffer, Dietrich, *Letters and Papers from Prison* (London, 1971).
Bowman, I., *Geography vs Geopolitics* (Geogr Rev, 1942).
Bullock, Alan, *Hitler: A Study in Tyranny* (London, 1962).
Bullock, Alan, *Hitler and Stalin: Parallel Lives* (London, 1991).
Burckhardt, Carl, *Meine Danziger Mission 1937–39* (Munich, 1969).
Churchill, Sir Winston S., *The Second World War*, vol. II (London, 1942), vol. III (London, 1950).
——, *War Speeches*, comp. Charles Eade (London, 1952).
Ciano, Count Galeazzo, *Ciano's Diary*, ed. Malcolm Muggeridge (Surrey, 1947).
Colville, John, *The Fringes of Power: 10 Downing Street Diaries 1939–55* (London, 1985).
Crankshaw, Edward, *The Gestapo, Instrument of Tyranny* (London, 1956).
Dahlerus, Birger, *The Last Attempt* (London, 1948).
Davidson, Eugene, *The Trial of the Germans, Nuremberg 1945–46* (New York, 1967).
Delmer, Sefton, *Black Boomerang* (London, 1962).

Dietrich, Otto, *The Hitler I Knew* (London, 1957).

Dorpalen, Andreas, *The World of General Haushofer* (New York, 1942).

Dulles, Allen, *Germany's Underground* (New York, 1947).

Fest, Joachim C., *The Face of the Third Reich* (London, 1970).

Fishman, Jack, *The Seven Men of Spandau* (London, 1954).

Fleming, Colonel Peter, *The Flying Visit* (London, 1940).

Freeman, T. W., *A Hundred Years of Geography* (Chicago, 1962).

Gilbert, G. M., *Nuremberg Diary* (London, 1948).

Gisevius, Hans Bernd, To the Bitter End (London, 1948).

Goebbels, Joseph, *The Early Goebbels Diaries 1925–26* (London, 1902).

Goebbels, *The Goebbels Diaries 1934–71*, Ed. Fred Taylor (London, 1982).

Gyorgy, A., *Geopolitics* (Berkeley, 1944).

Hamilton, I. B. M., *General Sir Ian Hamilton* (London, 1966).

Hanfstaengl, Ernst, *Hitler, The Missing Years* (London, 1957).

Harbeck, Karl Heinz, 'Die Zeitschrift für Geopolitik 1924–44', thesis, (Kiel University, 1963).

Hassell, Ulrich von, *The Von Hassell Diaries 1938–44* (London, 1948).

Haushofer, Albrecht, *Sonnets of Moabit* (Berlin, 1948).

Haushofer, Albrecht, *Sonnets of Moabit*. Translated by M. D. Hester Norton (W. W. Norton & Company, 1978).

Heiden, Konrad, *Der Fuehrer* (London, 1967).

Herbert, A. P., *Let us be Glum* (London, 1941).

Hess, Ilse, *England-Nürnberg-Spandau* (Druffel-Verlag, Leoni, 1952).

——, *Prisoner of Peace* (London, 1954).

——, *Gefangener des Friedens* (Druffel-Verlag, Leoni, 1955).

——, *Antwort Aus Zelle Sieben* (Druffel-Verlag, Leoni, 1967).

——, Rudolf, *Reden, NSDAP* (Munich, 1938).

Hesse, Fritz, *Das Spiel Um Deutschland* (Munich, 1953).

——, *Hitler and the English* (London, 1954).

Higgins, Trumbull, *Hitler and Russia* (London, 1966).

Hildebrandt, Rainer, *Wir Sind die Letzten* (Berlin, 1950).

Hitler, Adolf, *Mein Kampf* (New York, 1939).

——, *My New Order*, ed. Raoul de Roussy de Sales (New York, 1941).

——, *Hitler's Secret Conversations*, Ed. H. R. Trevor-Roper (New York, 1953).

Hoare, Sir Samuel, *See* Viscount Templewood.

Hoffmann, Heinrich, *Hitler was my Friend* (London, 1955).

Hutton, Bernard, *Hess: The Man and his Mission* (David Bruce & Watson Ltd., 1970).

Italiaander, Rolf, *Besiegeltes Leben* (Germany, 1949).

Jacobsen, Hans Adolf, *Nationalsozialistische Aussenpolitik 1933–38* (Metzner, 1968).

Jo, Yung-Hwan, 'Japanese Geopolitics and the Greater Asia Co-Prosperity Sphere', *University Microfilms* (Ann Arbor, Michigan, 1964).

Kelley, Douglas M., *Twenty-Two Cells in Nuremberg* (New York, 1947).

Kersten, Dr Felix, *Memoirs* (Essex, 1956).

Kirkpatrick, Sir Ivone, *The Inner Circle* (London, 1959).

Kohn, Hans, *The Mind of Germany* (London, 1965).

Laack, Dr Ursula Michel, *See* Michel, Dr Ursula.

Leasor, James, *Rudolf Hess, The Uninvited Envoy* (London, 1962).

Manvell, Roger and Fraenkel, Heinrich, *Hess* (MacGibbon & Kee, 1971).

Mattern, J., *Geopolitics* (Baltimore, 1942).

Mau and Krausnick, *German History 1933–45* (London, 1964).

M'Govern, James, *Martin Bormann* (London, 1968).

Michel, Dr Ursula, *Albrecht Haushofer and National Socialism*, thesis (Kiel University, 1964).

Neave, Airey, *Nuremberg* (Hodder & Stoughton, 1978).

Nicolson, Sir Harold, *Diaries and Letters 1939–45* (London, 1967).

Norton, Donald Hawley, 'Karl Haushofer and his Influence on Nazi Ideology and German Foreign Policy', *University Microfilms* (Ann Arbor, Michigan, 1965).

Paret, Peter, 'An Aftermath of the Plot against Hitler, The Lehrterstrasse Prison in Berlin 1944–45', *Bulletin* of the Institute of Historical Research, vol. 32 no. 85 (1959).

Percy of Newcastle, Lord, *Some Memories* (London, 1958).

Price, Ward, *I Know These Dictators* (London, 1937).

Prittie, Terence, *Deutsche Gegen Hitler* (Tübingen, 1965).

Rees, J. R., *The Case of Rudolf Hess* (Surrey, 1947).

Reitlinger, Gerald, *The SS-Alibi of a Nation* (London, 1956).

Riess, Curt, *Joseph Goebbels* (London, 1949).

Ritter, Gerhard, *The German Resistance* (Stuttgart, 1954).

Roberts, Stephen, *The House that Hitler Built* (London, 1937).

Ryan, Cornelius, *The Last Battle* (London, 1966).

Schellenberg, Walter, *Memoirs*, ed. Louis Hagen (London, 1956).

Schirach, Baldur von, *I Believed in Hitler* (German Edition, 1967).

Schmidt, Dr Paul, Hitler's *Interpreter* (New York, 1951).

Schuschnigg, Kurt von, *Austrian Requiem* (London, 1947).

Semmler, Rudolf, *Goebbels, the Man Next to Hitler* (London, 1947).

Sherwood, Robert E., *Roosevelt and Hopkins* (New York, 1948).

Shirer, William L., *The Rise and Fall of the Third Reich* (London, 1964).

Simon, Viscount, *Retrospect* (London, 1952).

Speer, Albert, *Inside the Third Reich* (London, 1970).

Speer, Albert, *Memoirs* (London, 1970).

Strausz-Hupe, R., *Geopolitics* (New York, 1942).

Stubbe, Walter, 'In Memoriam Albrecht Haushofer', *Vierteljahreshefte für Zeitgeschichte* (July, 1960).

Sykes, Christopher, *Troubled Loyalty* (London, 1969).

Taylor, Griffith, *Geography in the XX Century* (New York, 1951).

Templewood, Viscount, *Ambassador on a Special Mission* (London, 1946).

Thomas, Hugh, *The Murder of Rudolf Hess* (Hodder and Stoughton, 1979).

Thyssen, Fritz, *I Paid Hitler* (London, 1941).

Trevor-Roper, H. R., *The Last Days of Hitler* (London, 1947).

Trott Zu Solz, Adam von, *A Noble Combat: The Letters of Sheila Grant-Duff and Adam von Trott Zu Solz 1932–39*, Ed. von Klemperer (Oxford, 1988).

Valckenburg, S. van, *Geography in the XX Century* (New York, 1951).

Vansittart, Sir Robert, *Black Record: Germans Past and Present* (London, 1941).

Walsh, Edmund, *Total Power* (New York, 1948).

Warlimont, Walter, *Inside Hitler's HQ 1939–45* (London, 1964).

Weigert, H. W., *Generals and Geographers* (New York, 1942).

——, and others, *Compass of the World* (New York, 1944).

——, *New Compass of the World* (New York, 1949).

——, *Principles of Political Geography* (New York, 1957).

Weinberg, G. L., *Germany and the Soviet Union 1939–41* (Leiden, E. J. Brill, 1954).

——, 'Secret Hitler-Beneš Negotiations in 1936–7', *Journal of Central European Affairs* (January, 1960).

Weizsaecker, Carl von, *In Memoriam Albrecht Haushofer* (Hamburg, 1948).

——, Ernst von, *Memoirs* (London, 1951).

Welles, Sumner, *The Time for Decision* (London, 1944).

Werth, Alexander, *Russia at War 1941–45* (London, 1964).

Wheeler-Bennett, Sir John, *The Nemesis of Power* (London, 1964).

Whittlesey, D., *German Strategy of World Conquest* (New York, 1942).

Wulf, Joseph, *Martin Bormann, Hitler's Shadow* (Gutersloh, 1962).

Index

INDEX

INDEX